THE POLITICAL MORALITY OF THE LATE SCHOLASTICS

The late scholastics, writing in the Baroque and Early Modern periods, discussed a wide variety of moral questions relating to political life in times of both peace and war. Is it ever permissible to bribe voters? Can tax evasion be morally justified? What are the moral duties of artists? Is it acceptable to fight in a war one believes to be unjust? May we surrender innocents to the enemy if it is necessary to save the state? These questions are no less relevant for philosophers and politicians today than they were for late scholastic thinkers. By bringing into play the opinions and arguments of numerous authors, many of them little known or entirely forgotten, this book is the first to provide an in-depth treatment of the dynamic and controversial nature of late scholastic applied moral thinking which demonstrates its richness and diversity.

DANIEL SCHWARTZ is Senior Lecturer in the Departments of Political Science and International Relations at the Hebrew University of Jerusalem. He is the author of *Aquinas on Friendship* (2007) and the editor of *Interpreting Suárez* (Cambridge, 2011).

THE POLITICAL MORALITY OF THE LATE SCHOLASTICS

Civic Life, War and Conscience

DANIEL SCHWARTZ

Hebrew University of Jerusalem

CAMBRIDGE
UNIVERSITY PRESS

University Printing House, Cambridge CB2 8BS, United Kingdom

One Liberty Plaza, 20th Floor, New York, NY 10006, USA

477 Williamstown Road, Port Melbourne, VIC 3207, Australia

314–321, 3rd Floor, Plot 3, Splendor Forum, Jasola District Centre,
New Delhi – 110025, India

79 Anson Road, #06–04/06, Singapore 079906

Cambridge University Press is part of the University of Cambridge.

It furthers the University's mission by disseminating knowledge in the pursuit of education, learning, and research at the highest international levels of excellence.

www.cambridge.org
Information on this title: www.cambridge.org/9781108492454
DOI: 10.1017/9781108591522

© Daniel Schwartz 2019

This publication is in copyright. Subject to statutory exception and to the provisions of relevant collective licensing agreements, no reproduction of any part may take place without the written permission of Cambridge University Press.

First published 2019

Printed and bound in Great Britain by Clays Ltd, Elcograf S.p.A.

A catalogue record for this publication is available from the British Library.

ISBN 978-1-108-49245-4 Hardback

Cambridge University Press has no responsibility for the persistence or accuracy of URLs for external or third-party internet websites referred to in this publication and does not guarantee that any content on such websites is, or will remain, accurate or appropriate.

For my mother, Teresa

Contents

Acknowledgements	*page* x
List of Abbreviations	xii

	Introduction	1
I.1	The Late Scholastics	5
I.2	Moral Theology, Casuistry and Contemporary Applied Philosophy	7
I.3	Remarks on Method	9
I.4	Précis of the Chapters	11

PART I: CIVIC LIFE — 13

1 The Ethics of Electoral Bribing — 15
1.1	Introduction	15
1.2	Simony as a Moral Constraint to the Use of Money in Elections	18
1.3	The Distributive Rights of Electoral Candidates	19
1.4	Aquinas and Soto on Using Money to Redeem Electoral Vexations	21
1.5	Suárez and the Separability of Intentions	23
1.6	Suárez's Ungrounded Conclusion	26
1.7	Following the Argument Where It Leads	30
1.8	Epistemic Constraints	31
1.9	Summary and Conclusions	31

2 The Ethics of Tax Evasion — 33
2.1	Introduction	33
2.2	Purely Penal Law	35
2.3	Alfonso de Castro on Taxes	38
2.4	Navarrus and the Gravity of the Obligation to Pay Tax	40
2.5	Payment on Demand: Justice Through Custom	45
2.6	The Problem of the Ruler's Consent: Making Sense of Penalties	50
2.7	The Project in a Wider Perspective	55

3 Keeping Out the Foreign Poor: The City as a Private Person — 58
3.1	The Poor Law Reforms in Europe	58
3.2	The Debate Outside Moral Theology	60

vii

	3.3	Medina and His Reception	62
	3.4	Soto's *Deliberación* in Outline	64
	3.5	The Controversy That Wasn't	67
	3.6	Incorporating the Poor: The Limits of the Body Metaphor	71
	3.7	Unfairness in the Allocation of Moral Burdens: Soto and Castro	74
	3.8	Summary	76
4	**The Political Duty to Keep Your Secrets**		78
	4.1	Introduction	78
	4.2	Personal Opacity as a Social Need	80
	4.3	The Value of Reputation	81
	4.4	The Problem of Self-Defamation Under Torture	82
	4.5	Cajetan on Reputation and Community	84
	4.6	The Property Account of Reputation: Soto and Molina	86
	4.7	Cracks in the Property Account of Reputation: Aragón and Lugo	88
	4.8	Tomás Hurtado and Eminent Domain	92
	4.9	Hurtado: Citizenship and Reputation	94
	4.10	Cosimo Filiarchi and Primitive Inalienability	96
	4.11	Conclusion	97
5	**Scandal and Inexcusable Portraits**		100
	5.1	Introduction	100
	5.2	Scandal and Paintings	100
	5.3	Indecent Pictures: What They Do to You	104
	5.4	Decent Portraits for Indecent Ends	106
	5.5	Scandal, Over-Demandingness and Excuses	108
	5.6	Excusing Portraitists	111
	5.7	Francés de Urrutigoyti's Response	113
	5.8	Summary	117

PART II: WAR   119

6	**Conscientious Objection in War: From Duty to Right**		121
	6.1	Introduction	121
	6.2	Adrian's Challenge	123
	6.3	Vitoria on Doubt and Good Faith	125
	6.4	Tutiorist Defences of Obedience	126
	6.5	The Doubtful Soldier: Obliged *and* Excused	128
	6.6	Probabilist Defences of Obedience	132
	6.7	The Freedom to Disobey	138
	6.8	Domestic War That Is Just on Both Sides	141
	6.9	Two Conceptions of Subject Disobedience	142
7	**Patriotic Collaborationism: Demosthenes and Alexander**		144
	7.1	Genesis of the Controversy	144

Contents ix

7.2	False Leads	146
7.3	Overview of Leading Views	148
7.4	The Legal Way Out	149
7.5	Vázquez de Menchaca's Contractualism	151
7.6	Why the City Is *Not* Intentionally Killing the Innocent: Molina, Wiggers and Valencia	152
7.7	Why the Citizen Is Committing Suicide by Exiting the Besieged Republic: João de São Tomás	156
7.8	Taking Stock	158

8 War and the Boundaries of Punitive Jurisdiction 161
   8.1 Introduction 161
   8.2 The King as Judge 163
   8.3 Breaking the Stalemate 164
   8.4 Duties of Arbitration? 166
   8.5 Vázquez's Revisionist View 170
   8.6 Juan Sánchez and the Possibility of War That Is Just on Both Sides 179
   8.7 Summary 181

9 Justice After Victory 183
   9.1 Introduction 183
   9.2 Post-Victory Justice: Conceptual Issues 184
   9.3 Killing 186
   9.4 Plundering 191
   9.5 Enslaving and the Problem of the Moriscos 197
   9.6 Summary and Conclusions 206

Concluding Remarks 208

Bibliography 211
Index 228

Acknowledgements

This book was written during a year-long sabbatical spent at the University of Toronto. I am very grateful to the Department of Philosophy for its hospitality, and I am particularly grateful to its Chair, Professor Martin Pickavé, who also allowed me access to his wonderful private library. Donald C. Ainslie, then President of University College, Toronto, kindly provided me with a spacious room overlooking snowy parks. During my year in Toronto I was lucky to be part of the Legal Philosophy Reading Group convened by Professor Arthur Ripstein (meeting since 1979) who – happily for me – devoted that year's meetings to Francisco Suárez.

I am grateful to Martin Pickavé and Gregory Reichberg for having read the whole manuscript and for providing extremely useful comments and corrections, and to Arthur Ripstein for being a source of advice and encouragement throughout. Many other colleagues and friends have provided help either by commenting on individual chapters, facilitating finding hard-to-find bibliographical materials, helping with difficult passages or providing advice as to how best to structure this work. A possibly incomplete list includes Alejandra Alfieri, Martín Bernales Odino, Harald Braun, Brian Embry, Nicole Hochner, Vicenzo Lavenia, Kasper Lippert-Rasmussen, Daniel Novotný, Francisco O'Reilly, Iddo Porat, Marleen Rozemond, Asher Salah, Félix Santamaria Sierra, Jacob Schmutz, Rudolf Schüßler, Michael Sutton, Claude Stuczynski, Jörg Tellkamp and Johanna Thoma.

Chapters of this book were presented at Boston College, the Hebrew University of Jerusalem, Universidad de Montevideo, the University of Toronto, the University of Western Ontario and at a workshop organized by Rudolf Schüßler in Munich, on his forthcoming book on debates on probable opinions in the scholastic tradition. I have benefitted greatly from the comments of these audiences. As always, I have also benefitted from talking with my longstanding philosopher friends Shlomi Segall and Nir Eyal. I am indebted to Elizabeth Miles, who provided characteristically thorough and perceptive help with editing, Jenni Glaser and Yona

Gonopolsky, who provided vital help with the Latin, and Yulia Erport, who compiled the bibliographies.

Although none of the chapters of this book have been previously published, I have drawn from previously published material. Sections of Chapter 5 are drawn from my article 'Scandal and Moral Demandingness in the Late Scholastics', *British Journal of the History of Philosophy*, 23(2015) 256–76; some of the background research for Chapter 6 can be found in my 'Late-Scholastic Just War Theory' in Seth Lazar and Helen Frowe (eds.), *Oxford Handbook of Just War Theory* (Oxford: Oxford University Press, 2018), pp. 122–44; and the discussion on Vázquez contained in Chapter 8 comes from my 'Sovereign Supremacy in the Work of Gabriel Vázquez', *History of Political Thought*, 34(2013)177–94. I thank the editors and publishers of these publications for permitting me to use these materials.

Financial support for the project was generously provided by the Israeli Science Foundation (Grant no. 648/15). I am grateful to two anonymous reviewers from Cambridge University Press for their insights, corrections and encouraging comments. Special thanks go to Hilary Gaskin, the Philosophy Editor at Cambridge University Press, who showed an interest in the book from the very first moment and helped so much to make it real. Sophie Taylor, Emma Collison, Ursula Acton and Sunantha Ramamoorthy, also at Cambridge, provided advice and help throughout the production stage.

My greatest debt is to my family, to my sister, Sheila, and to my late father, Julio Schwartz, to whom I owe my love of reading, and to my mother, Teresa Porzecanski, to whom I owe whatever aptitude I have for writing. Yonatan and Alma, my children, inspire me with their endless curiosity and cheerfulness. Shalhevet Attar, my wife, is there for me not only with her empathy and support but also with insightful comments and her excellent sense of humour. I dedicate this book to them.

Abbreviations

c.	chapter
cas.	case
col.	column
const.	constitution
concl.	conclusion
cons.	consultation
contr.	controversy
coroll.	corollary
d.	distinction
dec.	decision
disp.	disputation
diss.	dissertation
diff.	difficulty
dub.	doubt
fol.	folio
lect.	lecture
lib.	book
membr.	part
n.	paragraph
pars	part
proem.	preface
prop.	proposition
res.	response, resolution
sect.	section
tit.	title
tract.	treatise
vol.	volume

Capital letters immediately after page numbers designate text sections in the original.

DRTDS	Domingo de Soto, *De ratione tegendi et detegendum secretum*
DCP	Domingo de Soto, *Deliberación en la causa de los pobres*
ST	Thomas Aquinas, *Summa Theologiae* (I, I-II, II-II, III, Suppl.)
In ST	Commentary on Aquinas' *Summa Theologiae* (I, I-II, II-II, III, Suppl.) (preceded by author)
In Sent.	Thomas Aquinas, *Scriptum super Libros Sententiarum Petri Lombardiensis* (I, II, III, IV)
II	*Iustitia et iure* (preceded by author)
Quodl.	*Quaestiones Quodlibetales*
IB	Francisco de Victoria, *Relectio de iure belli*

Introduction

Political life is morally demanding. Citizens vote candidates into office, pay taxes and go to war when summoned to do so. If your vote helps place in office a tremendously inept candidate, or you ignore the summons of the political authority to defend your country from an unjust attack, or you avoid fair taxes, you are failing the legitimate expectations that your compatriots have of you as a member of the political community. Foreigners may disapprove of your actions but barring exceptional circumstances they will not be wronged by them.

Our duties of justice towards co-members of our political community are the business of what Francisco Suárez (1548–1617), following Aristotelian tradition, denominates 'legal justice'. Contrary to what its name suggests, the essence of legal justice is not law-abidance. Rather, legal justice is about promoting the common good, which is the end of the law.[1] Legal justice privileges a viewpoint from which citizens are seen as parts of a whole to which they stand in a relation of duty.

Legal justice is the chief but not the only source of duty towards the polis. There are duties related to moral virtues other than justice. There is also, importantly, the theological virtue of charity, the duty to love others as oneself, as individuals who have a destiny in God. The late scholastics often considered some forms of altruistic patriotism as expressions of charity. Actions that may not be against legal justice may nevertheless fall short of what citizens morally owe to their polis and what they owe to other human beings from the purview of charity.

This book retrieves controversies about political morality held by late scholastic moral theologians.[2] Many of these controversies concern the limits of what the political community can morally require from its

---

[1] *ST* II-II, q. 58 a. 5c.
[2] On the birth of moral theology as a sub-discipline, see Ulrich G. Leinsle, *Introduction to Scholastic Theology* (Washington DC: Catholic University of America, 2010) pp. 280–90.

members. This controversial literature also engaged many equally important related questions such as: do you have political duties towards yourself? Who should be considered as a member of the political community? Can the rights that your political community has over you and your possessions be acquired by a different political community?

The fact that citizens share a physical space, a cultural and moral environment, and participate in a market makes it the case that some moral duties acquire special prominence in the polis. It is, therefore, appropriate to inspect not only controversies that concern political morality as such, but also those which concern the specific moral questions that can present themselves when people participate in the sort of intensified interaction that takes place within the state.

While political morality is this book's general theme, each controversy covered here engages a host of other important subjects. These include: distributive justice, the expressive dimensions of purchasing, the power of human law to morally oblige us, property, privacy and reputation, scandal and moral over-demandingness, ways of dealing with moral uncertainty, slavery and more.

The way late scholastics looked at civic life and war has a number of distinctive and attractive features. The first striking feature is its highly practical nature. Although the late scholastic theologians did not fail to examine the justifications for various political and social institutions and policies, when doing moral theology they tended to focus on the morality of individual conduct within the given institutional political order. The authors usually started from a practical problem: an agent – individual or collective – wants to perform an otherwise seemingly permissible action that appears to conflict with a particular moral prohibition. Most of the controversies gravitate around whether the desired action does in fact violate the moral prohibition. Historically, this construal of the moral problem is a result of moral theology's aim, namely educating the confessor to advise people placed in morally perplexing circumstances. The person in doubt about whether she has a duty to pay a tax that appears to be disproportionate to her income is not looking for a moral analysis of the fiscal system, but rather an examination of her own moral predicament.

A second feature, again connected to moral theology's confessional orientation, is the moral expert's adoption of the perspective of the advisee.[3] When you give advice to a person, as opposed to enunciating general moral

---

[3] I make this point in Daniel Schwartz, 'Probabilism Reconsidered: Deference to Experts, Types of Uncertainty, and Medicines', *Journal of the History of Ideas*, 75(2014)373–93.

truths, you need to place yourself in the shoes of the advisee. This explains the prominence that the question of moral doubt acquired in late scholastic ethics. Advisees are normally in doubt. Probabilism, an original philosophical contribution of late moral theologians, was meant as a device to cope with situations in which we find ourselves in doubt, for example when uncertain about the justice of a war that we are called on to fight.[4]

Because moral experts had to place themselves in the circumstances of the advisee, the late scholastic theologians were wary of needlessly imposing restrictions on the advisee's space of action. Just as the mark of a good physician is not just that she can cure but that she can cure using the least intrusive and aggressive treatments, so the mark of the good moral theologian is that he can give moral advice without unnecessarily constraining the space of morally unhindered action of the advisee. To impose unnecessary strictures is not to err on the side of safety but to do a sloppy job as a moral theologian.[5]

Adopting the perspective of the morally troubled agent, however, need not result in bending morality to accommodate the advisee's interests. But it does force you to think carefully about the price that the advisee will pay for your moral ruling; it makes you aware of your responsibility. If you consider what the advisee has to lose (to give some examples from this book: one's livelihood, one's office, having to pay heavy taxes), at the centre of your reflection you will try to avoid hasty prohibitions. So, the late scholastics often had to probe the outer limits of morality. This explains why many of the moral opinions held by some late scholastics border on the provocative. For example, the view that if you reasonably believe that you are the best candidate for an elected job, you may be allowed to pay

---

[4] On probabilism, see Thomas Deman, 'Probabilisme' in A. Vacant, E. Mangenot and E. Amann (eds.), *Dictionnaire de Théologie Catholique*, XIII (Paris: Letouzey et Ané, 1936) i, cols. 417–619; Ilkka Kantola, *Probability and Moral Uncertainty in Late Medieval and Early Modern Times* (Helsinki: Luther-Agricola, 1994); Rudolf Schüßler, 'On the Anatomy of Probabilism' in Jill Kraye and Risto Saarinen (eds.), *Moral Philosophy on the Threshold of Modernity* (Dordrecht: Springer, 2005) pp. 91–114 and his 'Casuistry and Probabilism' in Harald Braun and Erik de Bom (eds.), *Brill Companion to Spanish Scholasticism* (Leiden: Brill, forthcoming); Robert Aleksander Maryks, *Saint Cicero and the Jesuits: The Influence of the Liberal Arts on the Adoption of Moral Probabilism* (Aldershot: Ashgate, 2008); Julia Fleming, *Defending Probabilism: The Moral Theology of Juan Caramuel* (Washington, DC: Georgetown University Press, 2006); James Franklin, *The Science of Conjecture: Evidence and Probability before Pascal* (Baltimore: Johns Hopkins University Press, 2001) pp. 69–94; Francisco O'Reilly, *Duda y Opinión: La conciencia moral en Soto y Medina* (Pamplona: Publicaciones de la Universidad de Navarra, 2006); and my 'Probabilism Reconsidered: Deference to Experts, Types of Uncertainty, and Medicines', *Journal of the History of Ideas*, 75(2014)373–93.

[5] A poignant analysis of the tension between freedom and law as the 'moving force' of late scholastic moral theology can be found in Servais Pinckaers, *The Sources of Christian Ethics*, Sr. Mary Thomas Noble (trans.) (Washington DC: Catholic University of America Press, 1995) pp. 268–73.

people to desist from voting for someone else. Or the view that you may delay payment of tax until demanded to do so, or that you may paint a portrait that you believe will be used for morally dubious ends.

Confessors, both those of kings and of soldiers, had to pronounce on matters of war. Indeed, the thoroughness, comprehensiveness and depth of just war discussions by Francisco de Vitoria (1486–1546), Suárez, Luis de Molina (1536–1600) and others is well known and remains inspiring to many just war theorists. These modern theorists are divided on two main issues. The first issue is the thesis defending 'the moral equality of combatants'. Defenders of this thesis such as Michael Walzer argue that just and unjust combatants have the same rights, licenses and liabilities.[6] Revisionist theorists such as Jeff McMahan reject this.[7] The second issue is whether, for the purposes of moral analysis, war should be considered as a confrontation between individual agents or between collective agents.[8] There is some correlation between the stands taken on these two questions. Most of the modern theorists who believe in the moral equality of soldiers are collectivists and most of those who reject it are individualists. The late scholastic moral theologians were very different in this regard. While as a rule they vehemently rejected the moral equality of soldiers, at the same time they held a qualifiedly collectivist approach to war, as seen in Chapter 9.[9] Late scholastic just war theory is therefore relevant not only because it foreshadows many of the views advanced by today's just war theorists but also because it has the merit to challenge the way some of the present debates among contemporary just war theorists have been and are being structured.

Contemporary political theorists working in areas such as voting, taxation, immigration, poverty and obscenity, to mention some of the issues covered in this book, seem to be less aware than contemporary just war theorists of the late scholastic precedents of these discussions. In fact, many of the late scholastic arguments on these matters bear a remarkable resemblance to those offered today. Consider, for example, Domingo de Soto (1494/1500–1563) and Alfonso de Castro's [1495-1558] view that the scope of distributive justice extends beyond the boundaries of the polis, so that wealthy

---

[6] Michael Walzer, *Just and Unjust Wars* (New York: Basic Books, 2000[1977]) p. 37
[7] Jeff McMahan, *Killing in War* (Oxford: Oxford University Press, 2009) pp. 38–65.
[8] For an excellent analysis of types of collectivism and individualism in just war theory, see Seth Lazar, 'Method in the Morality of War', in Seth Lazar and Helen Frowe (eds.), *The Oxford Handbook of Ethics of War* (Oxford: Oxford University Press, 2018) pp. 21–40.
[9] As noted by McMahan (*Killing in War*, pp. 79–80) there are not many collectivist just war theorists that reject moral equality. One of them is Noam J. Zohar, 'Collective War and Individualistic Ethics: Against the Conscription of "Self-Defense"', *Political Theory* 21(1993)606–22.

communities have a duty of justice to allow the foreign poor in. Or Martín de Azpilcueta (Navarrus) [1493-1586] view that legal punishments should not be determined with a view to express moral censure but, rather, with a view to putting a price on conduct in the hope that the price will modify the behaviour of potential law breakers. One of the purposes of this book is to show that late scholastic moral philosophy has a contemporary appeal that extends well beyond just war theory.

The contribution of late scholastic discussion to contemporary moral philosophy is not, however, confined to identifying precursors to the discussions held by today's moral philosophers. Rather, its primary contribution is to illuminate blind spots in our ongoing discussions, to highlight those assumptions of ours that are taken for granted but shouldn't be, to confront us with views that although not popularly held now were at some point held by undoubtedly clear-sighted people. It is the mix between what to a modern philosopher seems like familiar arguments and what appears to come from a partly foreign intellectual world that makes the late scholastics both accessible and challenging.[10]

I.1 The Late Scholastics

Although the late scholastics are making something of a scholarly comeback, it remains the case that, for a variety of reasons, many otherwise philosophically literate people know relatively little about them.

Late scholasticism (also called 'neo-scholasticism', 'the second scholastic', 'baroque scholasticism' and 'early-modern scholasticism') refers to the revival of Catholic theology in the sixteenth, seventeenth and early eighteenth centuries by theologians active in Catholic Europe and the Spanish and Portuguese overseas colonies.[11]

One important job of these moral theologians was to solve morally thorny practical questions. Unlike most of today's academic philosophers, moral theologians actually guided the consciences of the people facing

---

[10] This thought is taken from Arthur Ripstein, who finds that Bertolt Brecht's remark on reading Descartes (that he had encountered 'someone who lived in a completely different world') applies to some extent to his own experience of reading the late scholastics. Arthur Ripstein, 'Distinction of Power and the Power of Distinctions: A Response to Professor Koskenniemi', *University of Toronto Law Journal*, 619(2011)38.

[11] For a good discussion of the origin and appropriateness of these various labels see Daniel D. Novotný, 'In Defense of Baroque Scholasticism', *Studia Neo-Aristotelica*, 6(2009)209–31. I use 'late scholasticism' simply because it is the most frequently used label to refer comprehensively to the authors under consideration in this book and also because it covers authors that could not possibly be regarded either historically or stylistically as baroque, such as Vitoria and Soto.

these moral dilemmas. They did so directly as confessors or counsellors of princes and dignitaries, and indirectly by writing manuals for confessors and collections of decisions on controverted cases, and by addressing these moral questions within their works of systematic moral theology. These works allowed parish confessors to help servants, soldiers and mercenaries, artists and craftsmen, husbands, wives and lovers, advocates and judges, wealthy citizens and street beggars, voters and candidates, if not to know where their moral duties lay, at least to know what was morally at stake in questions related to work, marriage, sex, business, the professional duties, civic life and war.

Those theologians classed as 'casuists' focused on the consideration of very concrete cases and their many variations, whether imaginary or presented to them at the confessional. 'Casuistry', defined by Thomas de Quincey as 'the moral philosophy of cases', famously earned the derision of philosophers such as Pascal and Kant (who himself was accused of engaging in this form of moral reasoning by critics). It was also resisted by those who felt that out of decorum some questions are best left unasked.[12] However, case-based ethics has been rehabilitated in the last few decades. One factor in this rehabilitation is the considerable impact of Albert Jonsen's and Stephen Toulmin's misleadingly titled book *The Abuse of Casuistry* on the field of bioethics.[13] More importantly, applied philosophy, which in many ways relies on the style of moral reasoning favoured by the casuists, has become a burgeoning and well-established branch of philosophy. In fact, some of the leading applied philosophers have been subjected to very similar kinds of criticism that the casuists met with.[14]

It would be a mistake, however, to draw a sharp line between casuists and moral theologians. It is true that there is considerable difference

---

[12] The *Provincial Letters* was Pascal's virulent and almost lethal attack against the casuists. On Kant's rejection and casuistry see H.-D., Kittsteiner, 'Kant and Casuistry' in Edmund Leites (ed.), *Conscience and Casuistry in Early Modern Europe* (Cambridge and Paris: Cambridge University Press and Maison des Sciences de l'Homme, 1989) pp. 185–213. Thomas de Quincey's phrase comes from his 'The Casuistry of Duelling' in James Hogg (ed.), *Uncollected Writings of Thomas De Quincey* (London: Swan Sonnenschein, 1890) vol. II, p. 91.

[13] See John D. Arras, 'Getting Down to Cases: The Revival of Casuistry in Bioethics', *Journal of Medicine and Philosophy*, 1991(16)29–51.

[14] In his book review, J. Carl Ficarrotta compares Frances M. Kamm to J. S. Bach, who 'wrote his masterpieces at the end of the baroque period, during a time when others had for the most part moved on stylistically, considering his compositional genre "old-fashioned." To take nothing away from the high art present in Kamm's casuistry (or to deny that her writing could plausibly be characterized as baroque), the part of the analogy I want to put weight on is this: maybe it is time to stop doing this.' Review of Frances M. Kamm's *The Moral Target*, *Ethics*, 124(2014)195.

between Vitoria's sober style and the ultimate casuist, the prolific Antonino Diana (1585–1663), who addressed some twenty thousand cases of conscience in his ten volume *Resolutiones Morales*.[15] It is also true that in some European universities' 'speculative' theology did not include the discussion of cases of conscience, which were relegated instead to a separate course attended by those whose vocation was more pastoral than contemplative.[16] At the same time, many of the greatest theologians of their time, such as Suárez, Vázquez and Molina, often discussed practical cases of conscience in great detail. So drawing a boundary between 'proper theologians' and 'mere casuists' (often presented as some form of baroque degenerate mutation of the former) is to a great extent artificial.

I.2 Moral Theology, Casuistry and Contemporary Applied Philosophy

As the discussions outlined in this book demonstrate, the type of moral inquiry favoured by the late scholastics resembles to some extent what modern philosophers refer to as applied philosophy. The late scholastic authors were in the business of a back-and-forth between principles and cases – an interplay from which both the principles and our beliefs about what one should do in specific circumstances emerge modified. In truth, the late scholastics were not just doing applied ethics, their applied ethics were actually applied by their advisees. Pascal reports the case of a servant at Jesuit College who stole some of the college's pewter tableware. When he was brought before the judge, the servant defended himself by saying that he had followed a doctrine found in Jesuit books of cases of conscience defending the permissibility of paying yourself wages out of the employer's property.[17]

Servais Pinckaers has argued in a critical vein that the mark of late scholastic moral theology is the study of moral cases in isolation from the study of human virtue (including theological virtues, and the effects of divine grace). In his view, these theologians, by focusing almost exclusively on obligation, lost sight of human perfection and excellence, which

---

[15] Albert R. Jonsen, and Stephen E. Toulmin, *The Abuse of Casuistry: A History of Moral Reasoning* (Berkeley and Los Angeles: University of California Press, 1988) p. 156.
[16] Leinsle, *Introduction to Scholastic Theology*, p. 289.
[17] A true case made much of by Blaise Pascal in *The Provincial Letters of Pascal* (Cambridge: Deighton, Bell and Co.; London: George Bell and Sons, 1880) letter VI, p. 156.

should stand in the centre of moral theology.[18] '[T]he essential work of moral theology was to determine the exact meaning of the [moral] law, the precise limits of what was allowed or forbidden, what was obligatory or prohibited, and what free. What might one or not do?'[19]

Paradoxically, it is precisely the tenets of late scholastic moral theology that critics like Pinckaers see as its main defects which constitute its virtues from the perspective of contemporary applied philosophers: for example, the focus on justice-related duties and the aspiration for precision in moral determinations. There is no doubt that an understanding of the classic medieval and post-medieval discussions of natural law and the uneasy relation between natural law, grace and virtue in their Aristotelian and Thomistic versions bring the discussions covered here into a richer perspective, but, crucially, these debates can be followed – and enjoyed – without recourse to this intellectual baggage.

The resemblances between modern applied philosophy and late scholastic moral theology should not be overstated, however. The late scholastic moral theologians discussed here approached their cases in a very different way from most of today's practitioners of applied philosophy. Their cases were not devised for the purpose of testing the reach and adequacy of principles (as one finds, for example, in the work of Frances Kamm). Rather, the cases they discussed were real situations presented at the confessional or possible variations of them. From the set of available confessional cases, those selected for examination were, naturally, not the easy ones, but precisely those that placed principles under strain.

Not unlike modern academics, late scholastic authors were often driven by the desire to stand out by introducing a novel view on a subject just when it seemed that all that could be said on it had been said. They were avid readers trying to keep abreast with the most recent peer publications (not easy given the volume and pace of publications at the time). Many of them courted controversy and were not afraid of voicing views irksome to the political and ecclesiastical hierarchies (which earned many of them more than a few Papal condemnations).

---

[18] One should temper Pinckaers's depiction by noting, as Michaud-Quentin notes, that confession as understood and organized by the casuists 'has been, together with the matrimonial consent, the great contribution to the affirmation of the personhood of each Christian, manifested in personal responsibility for one's own conduct'. Pierre Michaud-Quentin, *Sommes de casuistique et manuels de confesseurs au moyen âge (XIIe-XV^eS.)* (Louvain, Lille and Montreal: Nawelaerts, Giard and Librairie Dominicaine, 1962) p. 110 cited in Jonsen and Toulmin, *The Abuse of Casuistry*, p. 142.

[19] Pinckaers, *Sources*, p. 270.

The practice of this type of ethical inquiry demanded from moral theologians an intimate knowledge of their subject matter. By the end of his life, the Jesuit Tomás Sánchez (1550–1610), author of the greatest and most influential treatise on marriage, was attacked for impudently having discussed in too much detail and too explicitly the ethics of sex. He replied that,

> If the need to cure the human body makes it not only permissible but also necessary for doctors to know in great detail and discernment each part and organ of the human body and the properties of each of these, and for this sake books of anatomy are produced, all of which contain many unsightly things and filthy images, much more will it be permitted in order to save human souls, to know in detail the difference that exists between the human deeds and to make an anatomy of each of their kinds no matter how unsightly they be, in order to perform the job [of saving souls].[20]

The answers provided by the late scholastics exhibited considerable diversity, a fact that many of them relished rather than regretted.[21] We should think about the late scholastics not so much as a school with a consolidated set of doctrines but as a community of peers operating within a theological and philosophical tradition that provided them with a common conceptual language, premises, principles, and method of inquiry, and not less importantly, a shared repertoire of philosophical and theological puzzles.

I.3 Remarks on Method

This book is partly inspired by the sixteenth-century literary genre of books titled 'Famous Controversies'. Instead of addressing a topic systematically by moving from abstract foundations and principles to practical applications, the authors of these works went straight to the hot issues at the centre of ongoing debates.

To focus on controversies rather than on individual authors makes sense because late scholastic intellectual inquiry was quintessentially collective. Individual contributions to each debate were conceived by their authors as

---

[20] 'Memorial del P. Thomas Sanchez, acerca de lo que se oppone contra sus obras', in Archivum Romanum Societatis Iesu, F. G. 652, 223 g, and also in M. Ruiz Jurado, 'Para una biografía de Tomás Sánchez', *Archivo teológico granadino*, 45, 1982, p. 15–51 (46–51). Fernanda Alfieri kindly shared with me her transcription.

[21] Juan Caramuel y Lobkowitz, *In D. Benedicti Regulam Commentarius Historicus Scholasticus Moralis Iudicialis Politicus* (Bruges: Nreyghels, 1650) a. 3 sect. 1 n. 60 pp. 27–8 cited in Julia Fleming, *Defending Probabilism: The Moral Theology of Juan Caramuel* (Washington, DC: Georgetown University Press, 2006) p. 37.

providing a new layer to an ongoing effort and as inviting a response, rather than as an attempt to make a fresh start or to say the last word. These theologians were expressing *their* opinion, not those of their religious orders (when they belonged to one and when it had an opinion).

Here I have confined myself to *internal* late scholastic polemics. I will not be addressing cross-camp polemics with or against Protestants, Humanists, Jansenists and other currents of theological and philosophical thought. I have been inclusive, however, regarding the late scholastic literary genres from which arguments and opinions on the issues at hand have been taken. So I have not limited myself to works of systematic moral theology, but have also drawn from handbooks for confessors, collections of cases of conscience, legal works and responsa.

Often, from a humble start in a marginal observation of one author, a dispute crops out and bursts into a blossoming of opinions. Over time, the controversy effects a salutary depuration and opinions cluster and galvanize around a smaller number of views. At some point stagnation makes itself felt. The growth and decay of these controversies is a striking intellectual spectacle. Unlike scholars of scientific controversies, however, I am not interested in the more formal aspects of controversy, their typologies and classificatory elements. Rather, I am interested in what the late scholastics actually had to say about a number of pressing political and moral issues relating to civic life and war. The aim is not to simply parade the various views on each particular question, but to make sense of each controversy by approaching it as a dynamic, evolving thing, in which later views are attempts to improve on earlier ones.

Each controversy analysed in this book brings along with it its own different *dramatis personae*. Because it is impossible to include all the contributors to each specific debate I have favoured those most influential in setting the course of the controversy and often also some less influential views that seem original and suggestive. I cannot presume to have applied these criteria impartially; the selection of authors has been affected by my own personal interest, curiosity or sympathy towards specific authors.

Many of the starting points of the disputes addressed in this book can be traced back, if only in embryonic form, to medieval scholasticism or even Patristics. So, in the matter of starting points, I was forced to use some authorial prerogatives, without, I hope, being too arbitrary. The end of a late scholastic dispute is less difficult to ascertain. One can discern when disputes begin to dry up, which often took place in conjunction with the decline and agony of late scholasticism as a whole in the late seventeenth century.

I.4 Précis of the Chapters

Here is a succinct presentation of the chapters. **Part I** is a sampler of late scholastic examinations of some important moral aspects of political and civic life. The chapters that comprise Part I are not organically connected to each other. From those topics that were a matter of controversy among moral theologians (or, in the case of poverty, of a more interspersed polemical exchange), I have focused on those that feature in today's public and philosophical debate (voting, taxes, the poor and obscenity). I also included a chapter on privacy and personal reputation, a matter of undoubted importance in our lives, if not perhaps as prominent in public debate as the topics of the other chapters in this part.

Chapter 1 is concerned with elections, a standard method of appointment to office that was in place long before the advent of modern democracy. Could it ever be morally permissible for the best electoral candidate to offer money to electors? This was a pressing question for the late scholastics because they believed that electors have a moral duty to vote for the best candidate, and consequently that the best candidate has a correlative right to be voted for. This seemed to allow the candidate to use various means (including money offers to voters) to ensure that her right be met. On the other hand, attempting to buy votes was deemed impermissible insofar as it constituted a display of a demeaning attitude towards office by treating it as commensurate with temporal goods. Chapter 2 is about the morality of tax evasion, a rather consequential issue in Spain at the time, given the felt unbearability of fiscal pressure. Interestingly, the late scholastics developed a series of arguments that, without denying the justice of some of the most unpopular tax laws, provided moral justification to partial fiscal non-compliance. To do this, they resorted to the latest theories on the nature of the moral obligation imposed by human law and on customary law. Chapter 3 engages another question of obvious relevance today as relatively wealthy countries turn away the global poor: may political communities exclude the foreign poor? Reacting to new legislation banning outside beggars from the city and confining them to their hometowns, Soto wrote a fervent defence of the rights of poor persons, which, however, got a cold reception. The chapter interprets Soto's arguments, evaluates its failures, and tries to account for the muted and hostile reaction they evoked. Chapter 4 is about the wrongness of self-defamation. While the view that one's relationship to one's good name is one of ownership was the most popular among the late scholastics, some authors disagreed and argued that one has a duty to one's community to protect one's good name.

By self-defaming, even for a weighty reason, you wrong your community. I argue that, understood in context, this seemingly intriguing position is not without plausibility. Chapter 5 is about the limits to one's duty to refrain from acts that may lead other people to engage in morally self-harming actions (in theological jargon the duty not to commit 'scandal'). It was not only paintings thought of as having obscene content that were deemed scandalous but also apparently decent ones, such as small portraits exchanged between partners in an illicit relationship. It was agreed that portrait painters had to make a living. Could their need of a livelihood excuse them for the painting of these portraits? While this is not a question within political morality as defined above, it is a question about morality that is particularly relevant in the polis, insofar as it occupies itself with a moral restriction to market exchanges.

Part II is about the political morality of war. Chapter 6 explores the question of whether subjects may legitimately be required to put aside their doubts about the justice of the war they are called to fight. In Chapter 7, I turn to the question of the limits to what a polity can do to save itself. Is it permissible for it to surrender one of its own citizens at the enemy's request in order to save itself? Chapter 8 examines different views on the way wrongs perpetrated by one polity may bring it within the punitive jurisdiction of the victim polity. There was also the question of what a just victor can rightfully do to the subjects of a justly defeated state. The answers provided are analysed in historical context in Chapter 9.

...

In a letter to a fellow mathematician, Leibniz wrote, 'By calling attention to these traces of truth in the Ancients, or (more generally) in those that preceded us, one would extract gold from mud, a diamond from its ore, and light from darkness; and it would in fact be a sort of perennial philosophy'. Turning to the late scholastics he wrote more prosaically, 'There is hidden gold in the scholastic dung of the barbarians'.[22] He continued, 'I wish we could find an able man versed in Irish and Spanish philosophy, having the capacity to extract from them the good there is in them.'[23] This book is meant as a contribution to the collective effort to extract this gold, and to show that Leibniz greatly overestimated the amount of dung.

---

[22] The charge that the scholastics' Latin was unrefined and thus 'barbarian' was a standard one among Humanists.
[23] Possibly Leibniz had in mind Franciscan Scotists such as John Punch (Poncius) (1599/1603–1661) and Luke Wadding (1583–1644), whose ideas he sometimes considered. 'Letter to Nicolas-François Rémond de Montmort' in Gottfried Wilhelm Leibniz, Marcelo Dascal (ed.), *The Art of Controversies* (Dordrecht: Springer, 2006). The two fragments occur on pp. 446–7.

PART I

Civic Life

CHAPTER I

The Ethics of Electoral Bribing

1.1 Introduction

With the right to vote there comes a duty to use this right conscientiously. At a minimum, this means that electors must not vote for a candidate who, in the elector's opinion, will cause great harm to the community. At a maximum, it means they must vote for the candidate who, in the elector's considered view, is the best candidate (leaving open the meaning of 'best candidate'). Not many people today hold the view that voters are accountable to their community for the way they use their right (or privilege) to vote, but this was a view endorsed by all the late scholastic moral theologians. This view had far-reaching implications concerning the use of money in elections, which compelled these moral theologians to probe the permissibility of the economic manipulation of voters.

It may surprise some readers that sixteenth-century theologians were concerned with elections. However, as is well known, election by ballot as a method of appointment to office has not been restricted to democratic polities. In Europe, elections have regularly been held in ecclesiastical, secular and academic settings at least since the early Middle Ages. Within the Catholic Church, elections were and remain the method of appointment not only for bishops (including the Pope), but for many other offices and stations at lower hierarchical levels.

Many political offices, particularly in the Spanish imperial colonies, were elective. Judges (*oidores*), aldermen (*regidores*) and various kinds of magistrates (*alcaldes*), as well as the members of local political councils (the *cabildo*), were elected. In European universities, including those of Spain and its colonies, counselors (*conciliarios*), chaplains, examiners, grant recipients and chair holders were regularly elected by secret ballot.[1]

---

[1] On secular elections in medieval Europe, see Charles Gross, 'The Early History of the Ballot in England', *American Historical Review*, 3(1898)456–63 and John M. Najemy, *Corporatism and*

It is no surprise then that moral dilemmas concerning voting and the use of money and other incentives to affect electoral behaviour presented themselves long before the advent of modern electoral democracy. It fell to moral theologians to guide the conscience of voters and candidates. Discussions of the moral permissibility of using money to affect electoral conduct can be found in the works of the leading late scholastic moral theologians, such as Domingo de Soto, Francisco Suárez, Leonardus Lessius (1554–1623), Tomás Sánchez, Thomas de Vio ('Cajetan') (1468–1534), Navarrus, Gabriel Vázquez (1549–1604), Gregorio de Valencia (1550–1603) and Juan de Lugo (1583–1660), and also in the work of somewhat lesser-known moral theologians.

Their interest in electoral morality is easy to explain: most of them had first-hand knowledge of electoral politics both within their own religious orders and within their own universities (where at some points the members of religious orders saw their voting rights restricted or withdrawn) and so must have been acquainted with corrupt electoral practices, strategies and ruses.[2] It was their job to guide the conscience of morally perplexed voters, candidates and others with a stake in the election.

The historian Leo Moulin has done an as yet unsurpassed job of showing how the origins of modern electoral techniques should be traced back to medieval ecclesiastical electoral practice and theory.[3] However, the immense corpus of late scholastic discussions on electoral *morality* has gone almost entirely ignored. Here I will restrict myself to only one of

Consensus in Florentine Electoral Politics, 1280–1400 (Chapel Hill: University of North Carolina Press, 1982). On elections in the Church, see Léo Moulin, 'Les origines religieuses des techniques électorales et délibératives modernes', *Politix*, 11(1998)117–62 and his 'Policy-Making in the Religious Orders', *Government and Opposition*, 1(1965)25–54; Arthur P. Mohanan, *Consent, Coercion and Limit: The Medieval Origins of Parliamentary Democracy* (Montreal: McGill-Queen University Press, 1987); Josep M. Colomer, and Ian McClean, 'Electing Popes: Approval Balloting with Qualified Majority Rule', *Journal of Interdisciplinary History*, 29(1998)1–22; R. H. Helmholz, *The Spirit of Classical Canon Law* (Athens, GA: Georgia University Press, 2010); Ian McLean, Haidee Lorrey and Josep Colomer 'Voting in the Medieval Papacy and Religious Orders' in Vincenç Torra, Yasuo Narukawa and Yuji Yoshida (eds.), *Modeling Decisions for Artificial Intelligence* (Springer: Dordrecht, 2007) pp. 30–44; and Alfred H. Sweet, 'The Control of English Episcopal Elections in the Thirteenth Century', *Catholic Historical Review*, 12(1927)573–82. On university elections, see Alan B. Cobben, 'Medieval Student Power', *Past & Present*, 53(1971)28–66 and Ian McLean and Haidee Lorrey, *Voting in Medieval Universities and Orders,* Conference Paper (UCLA, 2001) at www.researchgate.net/publication/228419265_Voting_in_medieval_universities_and_religious_orders.

[2] Luis Enrique Rodríguez San Pedro Bezares and Juan Luis Polo Rodríguez, 'Cátedras y catedráticos: grupos de poder y promoción, siglos XVI-XVIII' in Luis Enrique Rodríguez San Pedro Bezares, *Historia de la Universidad de Salamanca* (Salamanca: Editorial Universidad de Salamanca, 2004) vol. II, p. 776.

[3] Moulin, 'Policy-Making in the Religious Orders'; and 'Les origines religieuses des techniques électorales et délibératives modernes'.

the questions discussed by the late scholastics:[4] when is it morally permissible to offer money to electors so that they will vote for the candidate who ought to be voted for? Readers should bear in mind that this is only one of the many electoral questions that occupied the late scholastics. Here is a list of other issues which they discussed: electoral reciprocity or 'logrolling' ('I vote for your candidate in these elections, you vote for mine in the next'); electoral promises ('If you vote for my candidate you will get this or that benefit after the election'); pre-election compacts based on the division of the expected political booty; vote soliciting and pandering; promises and offerings to persuade a candidate to step down; voting for the candidate who you do not consider to be the best but who you consider to be worthy enough; negative strategic voting (voting for a candidate who you do not consider to be the most worthy, or who you actually consider to be unworthy, in order to block the election of a candidate you deem even worse); deferring to the view of your electoral peers when in doubt about whom to vote for; revealing one's vote in a secret ballot before or after the election; and paying someone to abstain from voting.

Recently some political philosophers have defended the view that voters have a moral duty to vote for the best candidate, the one who best advances the common good. Voters are not morally permitted to select just any candidate, or the candidate that best advances their own egoistic ends at the expense of others.[5] The late scholastics agreed but considered an interesting flip-side implication of this view. It is that the best electoral candidate has a correlative right to be voted for. If the best candidate has a right to be voted for by the electors and the electors do not intend to vote for her, she may be entitled to persuade them to vote for her by offering money. In doing so, she would be only making sure that her right to be elected is met. However, such an offer seems to be blocked by the principle prohibiting purchasing votes.

The late scholastic effort in this area is best characterized as an attempt to carve out some moral space to allow the best electoral candidates to vindicate their rights without incurring the buying of votes (and offices).

---

[4] Here are a few example of works which concern themselves with these questions with reference to the sections concentrating most of the discussion on them. Zaccaria Pasqualigo, *Decisiones Morales* (Verona: Bartholomeus Merlus, 1641) dd. 224–64 at pp. 205–44; Pietro Maria Passerini, *Tractatus de electione canonica* (Roma: Felix Caefarettus, 1693) c. 7 pp. 73–120 (on simoniac elections); Jacobo Pignatelli, *Consultationum canonicarum tomus decimus* (Lyon: Gabriel and Samuel de Tournes, 1700) cons. 44 at pp. 75–85; Giacomo Francesco Raggi (Girago), *Dubiorum centuria de regimine regularium* (Lyon: Inheritors of Petrus Prost, Philippus Borde and Laurentius Arnauld, 1646) dubs. 1–28 at pp. 2–162; Francesco Maria Samuelli, *Disputationum controversiae de canonica electione* (Venice: Turrinus, 1644) dd. 2–4 at pp. 311–88.

[5] Jason Brennan, *The Ethics of Voting* (New Jersey: Princeton University Press, 2012), pp. 112–18.

In order to accomplish this there was a need to think carefully about what exactly constitutes an act of purchase and how to individuate that which is being purchased.

1.2 Simony as a Moral Constraint to the Use of Money in Elections

The common – until recently generally unchallenged – belief is that votes lie outside the moral limits of the market. Votes, like body organs, are not the sorts of things that may be bought and sold. The view that votes should not be traded is widely shared. Indeed philosophers like Michael Walzer and Michael Sandel treat votes as a typical, uncontroversial, case of goods that should not be allocated by the market.[6]

The late scholastics agreed, at least as regards the ecclesiastical sphere. Their reason for agreeing was simony: the express will to buy, sell or trade spiritual goods for temporal ones.[7] The sin was named after Simon Magus, a Christian convert who according to the New Testament offered money to the apostles John and Peter to grant him their healing power. Since many of the offices, jobs, stations and benefits conferred by the Church were classed as spiritual goods (although which exactly fell into this category was a matter of some dispute), buying these jobs, stations and benefits by buying votes constituted simony.

For Aquinas, 'by buying or selling a spiritual thing, a man treats God and divine things with irreverence, and consequently commits a sin of irreligion'.[8] For Suárez, the injustice of simony consists in the irreverence to God displayed by treating spiritual gifts as commensurate or comparable with money or other temporal goods. Attempting to sell spiritual goods amounts to treating them in a way that is incompatible with their dignity.[9] To appraise spiritual things as capable of standing in proportion to temporal ones is to belittle or even vilify them. To quote from a letter by Pope Hormisdas much cited in this regard: 'Who does not regard as vile that which is sold?'[10]

---

[6] Michael Walzer, *Spheres of Justice* (New York: Basic Books, 1983) p. 100; Michael Sandel, *What Money Can't Buy* (New York: Farrar, Straus, and Giroux, 2012) p. 10.
[7] Suárez, *De virtute et statu religionis* in *Opera Omnia*, C. Berton (ed.) (Paris: Lodovicus Vivès, 1859) v. 13, lib. 4 (*De Simonia*), c. 50 n. 1 at p. 911.
[8] *ST* II-II, q. 100 a. 1c. All translations from *ST* are taken from *The 'Summa Theologica' of St. Thomas Aquinas Literally Translated by Fathers of the English Dominican Province* (Westminster, MD: Christian Classics, 1980).
[9] Suárez, *De virtute*, c. 50 proem.
[10] Pope Hormisdas, 'Epistola Hermisdae Papa ad episcopos per hispaniam constitutos', in Francisco Antonio Gonzáles (ed.), *Colección de cánones y de todos los concilios de la iglesia española* (Madrid: Antonio Santa Coloma, 1850) letter 91, II at p. 1007. Also Suárez, *De virtute*, 49.7.

This account of the badness of simony falls roundly within what Jason Brennan and Peter Jaworski denominate the 'Semiotic Objection to the Market' that says that 'to engage in a market in some good or service X is a form of symbolic expression that communicates the wrong motive, or the wrong attitude toward X, or expresses an attitude that is incompatible with the intrinsic dignity of X, or would show disrespect or irreverence for some practice, custom, belief, or relationship with which X is associated'.[11] So, by paying for votes, one would be disrespecting or showing irreverence both for ecclesiastical office and for God.

1.3 The Distributive Rights of Electoral Candidates

The prohibition on vote buying seemed to deprive electoral candidates of an important means of protecting their rights. This is because the late scholastics, in agreement with Aristotle, thought that distributive justice demanded the allocation of offices according to merit.[12] The best candidate was deemed to have a right to be elected and thus a right to be voted for. When we think about national political elections, many people tend to think that voters have not only a legal but also a moral right to choose whomever they want or whomever will better advance their interests. However, when we consider professional appointments we adopt a different perspective and think (rightly or not) that members of the appointment committee should vote for the most qualified candidate or at least for a sufficiently qualified one. Doing otherwise seems not just noxious to the members and customers of the appointing institution but also wrong towards the most qualified or the sufficiently qualified candidate.[13] These moral intuitions can be transposed to some extent also to election to political office. We may say that citizens have a duty towards their community to vote for the candidate who, in their opinion, will do the most to promote the common good.

Who is the worthiest candidate? Approaching the matter of the ideal candidate, Tomás Sánchez provided a ranked order of desirable qualities, starting with moral probity, followed by knowledge relevant to the job, followed by prudence and industry. According to Sánchez, these qualities

---

[11] Jason Brennan and Peter Jaworski, 'Markets without Symbolic Limits', *Ethics*, 125(2015)1055.
[12] See Daniel Schwartz, 'Suárez on Distributive Justice' in Daniel Schwartz (ed.), *Interpreting Suarez: Critical Essays* (Cambridge: Cambridge University Press, 2011) pp. 163–84.
[13] Many contemporary philosophers deny that, even in professional as opposed to political settings, the best candidate has a right to be hired. See for example Richard Arneson, 'What is Wrongful Discrimination?', *San Diego Law Review*, 43(2006)785–6.

must be weighted together, so that a candidate who is not as morally excellent as another but who has superior knowledge and industry may be the worthiest candidate overall. He insisted that these qualities should not be assessed 'metaphysically', but rather 'practically', that is, by reference to the goal of the ministry. Accordingly, the worthiest candidate often may not be the most learned one or the one who lives most holily. At the same time, he believed there was a threshold below which questionable morals disqualified the candidate.[14]

Let me try to address a puzzlement that may assail modern readers: If you know who the best candidate is, why have an election in the first place? Medieval and late scholastics and canonists did not possess a complete theory of the moral justification of election as a method of appointment. When discussing forms of appointments to the papal prelacy, most of the fire was drawn by the question of whether a pope can designate his own successor. Some of the arguments against designated succession pointed to the superiority of election as a method of appointment.

Arguments for the superiority of election of a pope by ballot (or 'scrutiny' – one of three types of election, which also included election 'by compromise' and 'by inspiration') over succession appealed on a number of grounds. For one, there was the principle that a decision that concerns all must be made by all (the famous maxim, *quod omnes tangit*).[15] There was also the view that electoral procedures generally promise more political stability than designation does, and that elections were better than hereditary or designated succession at selecting the best candidate. In the work of Juan de Torquemada (1388–1468), which was quite influential on later authors, the epistemic virtues of elections – namely that they are better at tracking good candidates than their alternatives – are indeed the leading justification.[16]

---

[14] This is a very short summary of Tomás Sánchez's discussion 'Circa ius et iustitia distributiva' in Sánchez, Tomás, *Consiliorum Moralium in Consilia seu Opuscula Moralia* (Lyon: Laurentius Arnaud, Petrus Borde, Joannes & Petrus Arnaud, 1681) lib. 2 cap. 1 dub. 2 nn. 4–7 at pp. 96–7.

[15] Gaines Post, 'A Romano-Canonical Maxim: *Quod Omnes Tangit* in Bracton and in Early Parliaments', in Gaines Post, *Studies in Medieval Legal Thought: Public Law and the State, 1100–1322* (Princeton, NJ: Princeton University Press, 1964) pp. 163–240; Mohanan, *Consent, Coercion and Limit*, pp. 97–110; Yves Congar, 'Quod omnes tangit ab omnibus approbari debet' in his *Droit ancien et structures ecclésiales* (London: Variorum, 1982) pp. 210–59; Bernard Manin, *The Principles of Representative Government* (Cambridge: Cambridge University Press, 1991), pp. 87–8.

[16] Juan de Torquemada, *In Gratiani decretorum primam doctissimi commentarii* (Venice: Hieronymus Scoti, 1578) tom. 2 causa 8 q. 1 at pp. 338, 341.

People who defend elections as a procedure which produces a more epistemically reliable output than the individual judgments that serve as its input will say that while election participants must have a provisional view on who is the best candidate for the procedure to get going, they must then defer to the result of the process once there is one. That is, so long as one thinks about elections as an epistemic procedure, one cannot continue holding that the candidate that one voted for is the best once a different one gets chosen.

Although the late scholastics were familiar with these various rationales for using election as an appointment method, the rationales were not brought to bear on their discussions of the permissibility of affecting voters' conduct to improve the chances of electing the perceived worthiest candidate or to prevent the election of an unworthy candidate. When considering the practical dilemmas of voters and candidates, elections were presented as a given: some goods are allocated using elections; now the question is how to make sure that, given this, the election will distribute these goods justly. The reasons supporting the use of elections as appointment method did not constrain the range of acceptable measures to ensure that elections deliver just outcomes. Rather these constraints came from other sources, such as simony, distributive justice and, importantly, the need to meet the conditions of validity of the election (an invalid election cannot distribute any goods).

Perhaps the late scholastics had a disenchanted view of actual elections and thought that voters were not adequately informed and motivated about elections to be able to perform their epistemic role, or perhaps they did not take the epistemic rationale for elections too seriously. These observations might not resolve the puzzlement of modern readers about the conducting of elections when you already know who the best candidate is. However, they do point to an interesting fact (or flaw) about late scholastics' reflections on the way considerations of justice should morally guide election participants.

1.4 Aquinas and Soto on Using Money to Redeem Electoral Vexations

Attributing to the best electoral candidate a right to be voted for poses the question: what means are morally available to the best electoral candidate to protect himself against failure to meet his rights? In the moral vocabulary of the time, this question was framed as when is it morally permissible to use money to 'redeem a vexation'? Vexations could be just or unjust.

If a person makes public true, damning revelations about a candidate, this is a just vexation. Most of the debate concerned the redemption of (that is, liberation from) *unjust* electoral vexations through the offer of money.

To be clear, the question about the permissibility of redeeming vexations was strictly confined to the sphere of 'the tribunal of conscience' or *foro conscientiae*, that is of our duties (and permissions) of conscience. The offer of money to electors or other persons capable of affecting the election was of course legally prohibited – rightly so – by the statutes of the universities, the Church and the other institutions hosting elections. Yet moral theologians had to pronounce whether these uses of money were unexceptionally wrong *in the eyes of God*, regardless of positive legislation.

In his discussion of simony Aquinas considers the following view:[17]

> ... it happens sometimes that someone maliciously hinders a person from obtaining a bishopric or some like dignity. But it is lawful for a man to make good his grievance. Therefore it is lawful, seemingly, in such a case to give money for a bishopric or a like ecclesiastical dignity.

To which he answered:

> It would be simoniacal to buy off the opposition of one's rivals before acquiring the right to a bishopric or any dignity or prebend, by election, appointment or presentation, since this would be to use money as a means of obtaining a spiritual thing. But it is lawful to use money as a means of removing unjust opposition, after one has already acquired that right.

Soto applied Aquinas' insight specifically to the matter of elections. He explained that before one acquires a right to an elective office it would be simony to use money to remove the obstacles of those who oppose the elections, as it would amount to paving the way to purchasing something spiritual. However, once one has acquired a right, it then becomes licit to use money to remove unjust obstacles to the enjoyment of this right, for example, if a person tries to prevent the elected candidate from taking possession of office. So, for Soto, the crucial distinction is that between an acquired right and a not yet acquired right.[18]

The other central distinction that Soto relies on is that between persons who can only impede the election of a candidate and persons who can both impede and advance the appointment. According to him, only the former can be offered money to persuade them to desist from wrongful electoral grievance. The reason is that if I give money to someone who is both an

---

[17] *ST* II-II, q. 100 a. 2 ad 5.   [18] Soto, *II*, lib. 9 q. 6 a. 1 at p. 827.

obstacle but can be a facilitator, this act is immediately suspect of going beyond removing an obstacle and can become a positive act of paying my way to the office.[19]

So, says Soto, if before the election I imprison an elector so that he cannot reach the ballot box, it would be permissible for a candidate to offer me money so that I free the elector. By offering money the candidate is simply removing an unjust obstacle that stands in the way; he is doing nothing positive to improve his prospects of acquiring the job. No simony is involved. Here, even if the candidate has only a *ius acquirendum*, he cannot be said to be using money to advance his job ambitions.

According to Soto, however, not every way of interposing an impediment constituted a redeemable vexation. If I try to get you to vote for someone other than the best candidate by way of imprecation, adulation or other dubious forms of persuasion, it would be wrong for the best candidate to use money to remove this influence.[20]

Pedro de Aragón (1545–1592) and virtually all the authors after him (including Suárez) rejected this restriction as arbitrary. He argued that if an elector is prevented from voting or from voting for me not by means of violence but by means of bribes, it is permissible to offer the briber money so that he refrain from bribing.[21] This is also true if the briber is also one of the electors.

1.5 Suárez and the Separability of Intentions

Can money be offered to an elector so that he desists from refraining from voting for the best candidate? While Soto flatly denied this, Suárez thought that this question 'is not without difficulty'.[22]

In addressing it, Suárez had at his disposal the earlier treatment by Valencia. Valencia distinguished between two ways of removing a vexation: one way is by '*buying* something spiritual as a means of removing a vexation', the other is 'when money is only given a motive (*motivum*) to remove the vexation that is an obstacle to the obtaining of the spiritual thing'. Valencia observes that 'there is a great and clear difference between these two ways of removing that vexation'. In the second mode, 'the money is not given as a price but as a motive, to remove the injury that

---

[19] Ibid.   [20] Ibid.
[21] Aragón, *In ST II-II*, q. 100 at p. 793. In *Secundam secundae divi Thoma doctoris angelici commentaria* (Lyons: Petrus Landry, 1597).
[22] Suárez, *De virtute*, 50.18.

is a hindrance to obtaining the spiritual thing', and so giving it does not constitute simony. This is not buying but donating.[23]

Valencia concedes, of course, that in practice offering or giving money to electors must always be presumed to constitute an act of buying and so an act of simony, but this is only a justified legal presumption which may not reflect the truth of the matter *in foro conscientiae*.[24]

Consider a non-theological illustration. Suppose I badly need a liver transplant and I am the first in the queue according to the criteria in place (assume these criteria to be fair). The doctor, however, wrongfully decides to transplant the liver into somebody else. If I offer money to the doctor to get the transplant, would I be buying an organ? One plausible characterization of a situation like this is that this is a case of extortion on the part of the doctor, not of purchase. This judgment may be supported by the fact that the doctor has no ownership of the liver he can transfer to me. Therefore I cannot buy (get ownership rights to) it.

However this is *not* Valencia's view. For him, what is important to realize is that in this case the money offered is not given as an expression of the value of the liver, but simply as an attempt to sway the doctor away from his wrongful initial tendency (if the doctor asks for just 50 pounds and I pay it, this does not mean that I take the liver to be worth 50 pounds). Similarly, if the undisputedly worthiest candidate pays money to an elector to desist from refraining to vote for him (as he should) the money he offers would not be expressive of the monetary value of the job, and so no simony would be involved.

Suárez's approach is somewhat different from Valencia's. He proposes two different views which he fails to distinguish from each other. The first view is that by offering money to electors one *does* purchase something but that something is not the office or the vote. Rather one may be paying to free oneself from violence or wrongful harm or buying the cessation of the emotional motive [*affectio*] at the root of the violence or wrongful harm.[25] In the buying of this cessation, 'it is not contained virtually and intrinsically the buying of the spiritual thing to be acquired or, to put it otherwise, acquirable, nor is it necessary that the intention of the redeemer extends to that [the purchase], but only to giving something temporal for this cessation ... therefore from the very nature of things there is no purchase of a spiritual thing, and so no simony'.[26] The object being bought is not the

---

[23] Gregorio de Valencia, *Commentariorum theologicorum* (Ingolstadt: David Sartorius, 1595) d. 6 q. 16 punct. 3 at col. 2041B.
[24] Valencia, *Commentariorum*, d. 6 q. 16 punct. 3 at col. 2051C.   [25] Suárez, *De virtute*, 50.19.
[26] Ibid.

spiritual good itself and so there is no danger of irreverence or disrespect towards the spiritual good. Suárez completes the argument by saying that if the money offer paves the way to the spiritual thing this could be seen as an unintended (even if foreseeable) side effect of the attempt to remove an obstacle to the enjoyment of one's rights.[27]

The second of Suárez's views, closer to Valencia's, is that when the best candidate offers money to the electors no purchase is taking place. He considers the claim that since the vexation consists in not voting for the best candidate, it 'cannot be destroyed except by the contrary act [i.e. voting for him]': giving money to electors to redeem the vexation is tantamount to giving money with the intention to get the vote. Suárez replies that the money could be given with a different purpose in mind, namely the destruction of the elector's animadversion.[28] Here the money functions not as price given in exchange for the voter's cessation of his animosity but directly as psychological dissolvent of this animosity.[29] The obstacle to the fulfilment of the electoral candidate's right is not characterized directly as the action of failing to vote for him, but rather it is the motivational basis for this refraining. This is an *internal* obstacle standing in the way of a fair-minded consideration of the candidate's merits, and this is dissolved with the help of money.

Let me give an example. Suppose the undisputedly best candidate for a university position is African American. One of the members of the appointment committee is racist and for this reason he will not vote for the candidate. Since the candidate is by far the most qualified, he has a right to be elected and the racist voter is preventing him from enjoying this right. In order to dissolve the animosity of this elector, the candidate could resort to a number of strategies. He could ingratiate himself with the elector or present a small gift. The purpose of these strategies need not be directly to obtain the job, but rather to dissolve a negative affection that stands in the way of a fair-minded appraisal of his abilities and achievements.

Because the removal or weakening of the animosity is not conceptually or logically connected with actually providing the vote for the candidate, the intention to secure the former need not include the intention of obtaining the latter. This remains true even if it is foreseeable that, given the African American candidate is the best, once money removes the

---

[27] Ibid., 50.20.   [28] Ibid., 50.27.
[29] Valencia, *Commentariorum*, d. 6 q. 16 punct. 3 at col. 2051D; Suárez, *De virtute*, 12.2, 13, 21, 22. The idea is present before Valencia and Suárez in Navarrus (Martín de Azpilcueta), *Enchiridion sive Manuale confessariorum et poenitentium* (Rome: Victorinus Romanus, 1573) c. 23, n. 101 at p. 371 r.

animosity of the elector she will vote for him, for the favourable attitude towards him is produced by his merits, not by the money given.[30]

To sum up, Suárez's principle is that you do not purchase the vote if you merely eliminate an obstacle to the vote. The principle, as understood by Suárez, is indifferent between external obstacles (the person who imprisons the elector, deceives him, imprecates him and so on) and internal obstacles (racism, animadversion).

1.6 Suárez's Ungrounded Conclusion

Given the above one would expect Suárez to allow offering money to bad electors. Surprisingly, however, Suárez backtracks. He gives a very compressed and unsatisfactory explanation of the opinion that, in the end, it is impermissible to give money to electors. He first announces that the rule that prohibits redeeming vexation using money *before* there is an acquired right applies optimally to the case of voters.[31] He goes on to say that before the actual election, the candidate lacks a proper right over the thing (*ius proprium*) but at most he is worthy or suitable for the job. True, this can sometimes be sufficient ground for him to have a *ius ad rem*, the sort of right served by distributive justice. Yet this is not *ius proprium* or strict right but only rather a certain fittingness or proportion between the person and the job to which distributive justice obliges. Suárez suggests that if the worthiest candidate's *ius ad rem* right to the election is not met it is doubtful that wrongful harm has been done to him. But even if we admit that some wrongful harm would be done by bad voters in this case (as he elsewhere admits), it should not be prevented by using money, 'because that right that is conferred by the election [the right over the office] cannot be put on a par [*comparari*] with a sum of money'.[32]

---

[30] Suárez also runs the two views together in his discussion of paying ministers reluctant to give baptism. There, after arguing that the money is given to destroy or extinguish avarice, he says: 'in so far as it is ordained to removing an obstacle, nor is it [the money] given as price for the sacrament but in order to extinguish avarice or can be given as price for the deposition of hate, wrath or the vengeful appetite, if from there is born the reticence to give the sacrament' [*De virtute*, 12.21]. And he continues in the matter of sacrament that [22] 'to destroy the vexation is not immediately to destroy the lack or the denying of the sacrament but, rather, it is to destroy that depraved affection from which follows the denying of the sacrament'. So Suárez's argument about votes runs to some extent parallel to the argument about sacraments: to destroy the vexation of the non-vote is not to try to prevent the non-vote but to tackle the depraved affection which is its source. This allows him to evade the claim in *De virtute*, 12.2, that 'the destruction of the vexation is nothing else than the giving of the baptism'.

[31] Suárez, *De virtute*, 50.18; 50.29.   [32] Ibid.

A standard interpretation of Suárez's argument would take him to be arguing that since there is only a *ius acquirendum*, the giving of money to the elector constitutes a purchase. However, this flatly contradicts Suárez saying that when I am wrongfully deprived of a *ius acquirendum* there is also an infringement of a *ius acquisitum*.[33] After all, as he says, I have an acquired right to not be a victim of wrongful harm or violence, and a right to compete for benefices and offices – 'a right that I desire to conserve ready to use and available'.[34] If I offer money to voters I buy nothing more than 'the immunity of those rights'.

To give one of Suárez's own examples: if you falsely accuse me of Moslem descent, which under the law of the time would disqualify me for office, and I pay you to withdraw the accusation, what I am redeeming is not the right to acquire the job but rather *the right to run* for the job, and this is an acquired right. Suárez goes as far as to say that *every ius acquirendum* implies a *ius acquisitum*. So in those cases in which there is a vexation of a *ius acquirendum* there is also a vexation of a *ius acquisitum*. When I give money to the person infringing my right, what I pay for is the exercise of a right I have already acquired. In other words, distributive rights imply an acquired right to have a shot. So Suárez cannot argue that the best electoral candidate has no *ius acquisitum* and thus vexations against him should not be redeemed.[35]

1.6.1 The Electoral Candidate's Contractual Rights

There is another, unrelated, reason why Suárez cannot not say that electoral candidates have only *ad rem* distributive rights.[36] It is that elections generally presuppose a contractual framework binding candidates and electors.

---

[33] Ibid, 50.20.   [34] Ibid.

[35] Fernando Castro Palao, for example, read Suárez in this light and so argued that vexations can be redeemed also in the case of electors since the *acquirendum* right to be elected presupposes also a *ius acquisitum*: 'In the same way, you have an acquired right [*ius quaesitum*] that in this competition others may not be preferred. Thus the money does not acquire a right, but defends the right already had.' *Operis Moralis, pars tertia* (Lyon: Ioannes Antonius Hugetan and Guillielmi Barbier, 1669) tract. 15 d. 3. punct. 20 n. 4 at p . 338.

[36] Consider that in his *Disputatio de iustitia*, in *Opera Omnia*, M. André and C. Berton (eds.) (Paris: Vivès, 1886) vol. II, sect. 3 n. 14, Suárez writes: 'a debt originating in [the violation of] an earlier right is much stronger and more rigorous than that originating in a posterior one; but one owes more strongly to a person what is his [that person's] own, than that which is common, even when he has a right to it because of the dignity of his person or some other similar ground. As to the first type of debt all the theologians assert that from the infringement a duty to restitute is born, but that this is true of the second type of debt many, and possibly those who adjudge the best, deny.' And, he continues [3.15]: 'the pretender of a benefit or a chair, never had dominion or possession of it, or of some other equivalent thing given to him in lieu of the chair or benefit. He has however, if he is worthy of it, some right to this thing, because according to equity it is to him more than to others

There was a fair amount of writing on whether, if electors provide an office to a merely worthy candidate rather than the worthiest one, the worthiest candidate (as opposed to the community) has a just restitution claim against those who failed to vote for him.[37] Many authors thought that it makes a great difference that the election takes place in the context of an official competition stipulating the criteria of appointment.[38] When the appointment is by competition, says Lugo, what we have is an implicit pact or contract between the instituting body (the Church or the Republic) and the competitors, such that it gives the best candidate a *ius in rem*, a strict right to the benefit. If this is not given to him, he acquires a restitution claim.[39] Contractual obligations derive, for example, from the '*edictus*', the call for candidates that specifies the requirements for office and the terms of the competition. When such an edict is in place, says Enrique de Villalobos (†1637), the bad elector must make restitution to the unelected worthiest candidate, at least if his vote had a clear impact on the candidate ending up not being chosen.[40] Since Suárez seems to agree, he cannot say that electoral vexations violate only distributive rights.

1.6.2 *The Gravity of the Vexations*

Suárez could be understood in a different way. In this alternative interpretation, what Suárez is arguing is not that the redemption of the vexation involves the purchase of a spiritual good but, rather, that in the case of elections there is no sufficiently serious vexation in need of being redeemed to start with.

---

that it should be given as among the parts of his community he presents more proportion with this thing than the other persons.'

[37] See Juan de Lugo, *Disputationum de Iustitia et iure*, part 2 (Lyon: Philippe Borde, Laurent Arnaud and Claude Rigaud, 1652) d. 35 sec. 6 at pp. 490–491.

[38] Including to Suárez himself. See *De Incarnatione Verbi* in *Opera Omnia* (Paris: Vivès, 1860) vol. 17 d. 4 sec. 5 n. 63: '[I]t is clear that it [the election] does not oppose distributive justice in that it presupposes a pact and promise; rather such pact or promise is necessary for it. Consider a prince or somebody else who liberally offers some of his possessions as competition prizes, so that they will be given to the brave winners. Although this promise is liberal and gratuitous, after it has been made, and the competition has taken place, however, the prize to the winner is owed as a matter of distributive justice. Because even if on occasion a ruler must give something out of distributive justice without his previous promise, this is because he is not the owner of those things that he distributes, but a dispensator or distributer of common goods as required by a role assigned to him by the Republic or the Superior Prince. Hence with respect to the Superior Lord or the Republic [the distribution out of distributive justice] is always preceded by a promise, whether express or tacit.'

[39] Also Tomás Sánchez, *Opuscula sive consilia moralia*, lib. 2 c. 1 dub. 46 at pp. 165–166.

[40] Also Enrique de Villalobos, *Summa de la theología moral y canónica, primera parte* (Barcelona: Sebastián de Cormellas, 1637) tract. 8 diff. 8 n.15 at p. 93.

But this interpretation is implausible since Suárez believes that for a vexation to be redeemable it need not be of the sort that violates a strict right, but it suffices that it is iniquitous [*iniqua*] or noxious to the common good.[41] So, again, he cannot argue that the lack of a violation of a strict right entails the absence of an actionable vexation.

To sum up, Suárez can be taken either to be claiming (1) that since an electoral candidate lacks an acquired right, his giving money to electors constitutes an act of purchase, or (2) that the electors' failure to vote for the best candidate does not wrong him in a way that justifies his trying to prevent this wrong. (1) is untenable given Suárez's doctrine that rights to acquire include acquired rights, and that electoral candidates in competitive settings possess contractual *in rem* rights. (2) is untenable given that Suárez argues that redemptive action on the part of the vexed candidate does not require the violation of strict rights.

1.6.3 A Charitable Reading of Suárez

It is disappointing that after carefully deploying the conceptual apparatus necessary to analyse the question of offering money to those involved in the ministration of offices, the perfunctory argument that Suárez offers against the moral permissibility of such offerings is so weak.

A possible charitable reading of Suárez would be that in discussing the rejection of the view condemning giving money to bad voters he is not attempting to give an argument of his own but is simply noting the consensus between theologians on this matter. Indeed he begins his argument by saying that '[in elections] there is no controversy [among the authors]', and when he turns to the first case under examination, the collation and institution of offices, he starts by noting 'in this also there is a general consensus among the authors'.

When Suárez gives his own opinion and contrasts it with the opinions of others he typically uses expressions such as 'I think' (*censeo*), 'I say' (*dico, dicendum est*), or 'according to my view' (*mihi*), but none of these appear here. Suárez sometimes used less direct ways of conveying agreement. Having said this, his avoidance of expressions that convey strong belief and his uncommitted general tone in this area are certainly suggestive.

---

[41] See Castro Palao, *Operis Moralis*, tract. 15 d. 3. punct. 20 n. 6 at p. 338, who says that when one votes for the suboptimal candidate, even if there is no injustice there is an offence against charity, citing Suárez [*De virtute*, 50. 25], who says this infringement (i.e. the to failure to vote for the best candidate), while not absolutely unjust (*absolute iniusta*), it is iniquitous and very noxious to the common good.

Note, in addition, that when Suárez first discusses the redeeming of vexations of the person who can help the appointment, he writes, 'However, I believe that it is straightforward simony, *at least against positive right*', and that these laws were introduced to 'prevent many scandals and occasions of simony'.[42]

So what Suárez *is* certain of and committed to is that redeeming electors' vexations is against divine positive law. Here we could read Suárez as saying something like this: There are decisive reasons supporting the legal prohibition of offering money to electors. However, insofar as pre-positive morality is concerned, the view that such offers could be morally permissible is probable. Nevertheless, given that virtually all authors agree that this is morally prohibited, we have a good reason to defer to this other view.[43]

1.7 Following the Argument Where It Leads

Suárez's lukewarm rejection of the moral permissibility of offering money to electors prepared the ground or perhaps even propitiated others' defence of such offering.

Authors such as Basilio Ponce de León (1570–1629) and Pedro Hurtado de Mendoza (1578–1641) openly argued that it is permissible for the best candidate to offer money to electors who wrongly abstain from voting for him. Castro Palao – if less openly – agreed.[44]

In addition to the arguments found in Suárez and others, these writers relied on an argument inspired by Vázquez. This was the 'lesser wrong' argument. According to Vázquez, if a criminal is bent on perpetrating a terrible crime it would be permissible for me to signal to him the possibility of a much lesser crime if this would divert him away from the original plan. Applied to elections: even though the elector does wrong by accepting money to change his vote, this is morally less bad than the failure to vote for the best candidate, and so we could make known to the bad elector the possibility of taking the money.

Ponce de León held an even more extreme view. According to him, if a candidate to an academic chair considers himself worthy but not necessarily *worthier* than the other candidate, and one of the electors offers his

---

[42] Suárez, *De virtute*, 50.28.
[43] So Castro Palao (*Operis Moralis*, tract. 15 d. 3. punct. 20, n. 4) says that in fact Suárez is only denying the right to redeem these vexations *in foro externo*.
[44] Basilio Ponce de León, *De sacramento matrimonii tractatus* (Venice: Combi, 1645) lib. 5 c. 18 sect. 6 at p. 215. Pedro Hurtado de Mendoza, *Scholasticae et morales disputationes de tribus virtutibus theologicis* (Salamanca: Jacinto Taberniel, 1631). d. 173, subs. 2, n. 238 at p. 1546. After Vázquez, *De scandalo in Opuscula moralia* (Alcalá: Juan Gracián, 1617) c. 8 dub. n. 57 at p. 57.

vote up for sale, it would be licit to give him money. Basilio's view was unanimously rejected. However, the view that the *worthiest* candidate may give money to reluctant electors started to gain ground.

1.8 Epistemic Constraints

One strategy to block the view that the worthiest candidate may bribe electors was to rely on epistemic arguments. Some argued that as a candidate for an electoral office one is never in a position *to know* that one is the most qualified candidate. The knowledge necessary for it to be permissible to give money to electors is simply not accessible. This is partly because, as Villalobos and Castro Palao point out, a great variety of considerations can go into determining who is the best candidate, say, for an academic appointment. There is no formulaic way of aggregating the relevant information and producing a determinate judgment. The candidate himself is not well placed to appreciate the various considerations and their differential weights to appointment making and thus cannot know that he is the best.

A connected strategy was to rely on moral epistemology: one *ought not* to believe one is the best candidate.[45] Holding this belief would be an act of intellectual immodesty and contempt for the other candidates. Castro combines both strategies in his reply to Ponce:

> This [Ponce's view] can easily be answered by denying that you may deem yourself as the worthiest candidate, because that sort of judgment is too arrogant, vain and fallacious. Even if you excel others in learning, they themselves may excel you in virtue, prudence, diligence, and the art of teaching. How then do you dare judge yourself to be the most worthy? Even if the majority of the most learned men judge you to be the worthier candidate, there is no lack of other [learned men] who think the opposite. Thus, based on this judgment, which is entirely probable, the competitor is allowed to pursue the position.[46]

1.9 Summary and Conclusions

All the authors surveyed here believed that the worthiest electoral candidate has a right to the office. Therefore he could use money to prevent the violation

---

[45] Villalobos, *Summa, pars prima*, tract. 8 diff. 9 n. 6 at p. 96; Castro Palao, *Operis moralis, pars secunda* (Lyon: Guiglielmi Barbier, 1682) tract. 13 d. 2 punct. 11 sect. 5 n. 9 at p. 208.
[46] Castro Palao, *Operis moralis, pars secunda*, tract. 13 d. 2 punct. 11 sect. 5 n. 9 at p. 208.

of this right so long as this act falls short of being an outright purchase of his way to the job. When no purchase of the job (or vote) takes place, it is morally permissible for the best candidate to offer money to electors.

It was clear to all that, as a matter of legislation, such money offerings to voters should be prohibited because in actual practice most such givings, even if portrayed as attempts to prevent injustice, are simply acts of ordinary vote purchase. However, the legal prohibition is merely based on a presumption. It was much harder to show that, as a matter of pure morality, there can be no case in which one can make monetary offers to electors to avert the impending violation of your rights as the best electoral candidate. Most authors felt noticeably uneasy with this inference and sought to find ways of blocking it.

The arguments tepidly suggested by Suárez to close up this possibility clashed with other elements of his own doctrine. Other authors accepted *in principle* the moral permissibility of money offers to electors but denied the availability of the knowledge necessary (about oneself or about what makes a candidate the best candidate) to act on this permission or denounced the moral impropriety of adjudicating oneself such knowledge. An audacious minority of authors followed the argument where it led and advocated the view that morality sometimes allows such money offers and that the knowledge necessary to identify these cases may not always be unavailable.

The late scholastic discussions on redeeming vexations should make theorists who, like Sandel or Walzer, accept the semiotic objection to market transactions more discerning when denouncing a market transaction as demeaning the value of the exchanged good. Before condemning a transaction, one needs first to think carefully about how we individuate the object being traded, and what constitutes a transaction.

What the late scholastics show is not so much that giving money to electors who fail to vote for the best candidate is morally permissible, but rather that if it is not morally permissible, that need not be because there is an attempt to trade, which would involve irreverence towards the relevant goods. In so doing the late scholastics' discussion highlights the limited reach of the semiotic objection. This objection holds that trading in something demeans what is traded. However, the set of reprehensible transferences of goods are not exhausted by transferences that count as trading. In particular, the semiotic objection is unable to indict all of the uses of money in elections that people like Walzer or Sandel would like to condemn. If you think that giving money to electors who refrain from voting for whom they should vote for is always wrong, you need to equip yourself with a different argument.

CHAPTER 2

The Ethics of Tax Evasion

2.1 Introduction

Taxes was a vexed topic in sixteenth-century Spain. Fiscal pressure was considerable and decried as unbearable not only by the common folk but also by many contemporary literary figures, proponents of political reforms (in their time called 'arbitristas'), and moral theologians.[1] The monarchy was constantly creating new taxes or increasing those already in existence.[2] One of the great poets of the Spanish Golden Age, Francisco de Quevedo, wrote in verse to the king:

> Not to a hundred kings together has Spain granted
> The amounts to your reign provided
> And the hurting people are even fearing
> That a tax be placed on breathing[3]

---

[1] On the *arbitristas*, see Juan Ignacio Gutiérrez Nieto, 'El pensamiento económico, político y social de los arbitristas' in Ramon Menéndez Pidal and Jover Zamora (eds.), *El siglo de Don Quijote (1580–1680): Religión, filosofía, ciencia* (Barcelona: Espasa Calpe, 1993) pp. 331–465 (in series *Historia de España*, vol. 26).

[2] I have learned a great deal about the Castillian tax system from Ubaldo Gómez Álvarez, *Revisión histórica de la presión fiscal castellana (siglos XVI-XVIII)* vol. 1 (Oviedo: Universidad de Oviedo, Servicio de Publicaciones, 1993). Highly recommended also is Charles J. Jago, 'Taxation and Political Culture in Castile 1590–1640' in Richard L. Kagan and Geoffrey Parker (eds.), *Spain, Europe and the Atlantic World: Essays in Honour of John H. Elliott* (Cambridge: Cambridge University Press, 1995) pp. 48–72. To give a sense of the quantity and variety of taxes, here is a list of some of the secular taxes that afflicted Spanish subjects in the seventeenth century (though these varied across regions, cities and time): *'moneda forera', 'chapín de la Reyna', 'impuesto de lanzas', 'media anata', 'diezmos de la mar', 'almojarifazgo mayor de Sevilla', 'almojarifazgo de Indias', 'rentas de puertos secos', 'impuesto de la pasa de Málaga', 'alcabala', 'cuatro por ciento', 'millones'* and *'sisa'*. From Gómez Álvarez, p. 48. This excludes the tolls and the many Crown monopolies over specific goods, such as chocolate, that allowed collecting even more revenue.

[3] Francisco de Quevedo, 'Memorial a su Majestad Don Felipe IV, 1639' in Luis Astrana Marín (ed.), *Obras completas en verso* (Madrid: Aguilar, 1952) pp. 165–6 cited in Gómez Álvarez, *Revision histórica*, p. 13.

Some taxes, such as the *alcabala*, were particularly odious to much of the population. The *alcabala* was an indirect universal tax of about 10 per cent on all goods. It also taxed the purchase of goods for final consumption and so it was rightly regarded (along with the even more odious municipal tax on goods called *sisa*), to put it in modern terms, as regressive.[4]

The Spanish monarchy did not have the bureaucratic capacity to collect taxes through its personnel. This was left to private persons (*arrendadores*) who bought at auction the right to collect tax in a particular region and could subdivide and sell that right to minor tax collectors (*arrendadores menores*).

Concealment of transactions and smuggling were rife, for example, by entering and leaving towns at night or through hidden paths so as to avoid the gate tolls. It seems that confessors were not unsympathetic to the reluctance to pay taxes, particularly where the taxes in question were new. Unlike the *arbitristas*, they, and the moral theologians who guided them, did not consider it to be their job to redesign the tax system.[5] Rather their job was to provide practical advice to conflicted agents in their specific circumstances. These agents included authorities with the power to impose new taxes, tax collectors and the tax payers themselves. Here I focus on the latter.

The key to deciding whether tax avoidance could be permissible was of course to determine whether the tax was just. Aquinas's analysis of the requirements of just law suggested three separate tests: first, whether the tax is collected for a goal that is expedient to the common good of the community (which implies that the tax can be levied only for as long as this goal is actually being pursued); second, whether the tax is imposed in keeping with proportional equality (which first requires that the subject be capable of paying the tax and, second, that the amount of tax be proportionate to the wealth of the tax payer); and third, that the tax be imposed by the right authority.[6] For Diego Laínez, an 'immoderate' tax is one that is distributively unjust, for example, by being excessive to all.[7]

The late scholastics devoted much of their attention to verifying whether the various taxes at the time met these conditions. If a tax was unjust there

---

[4] See Gómez Álvarez, *Revisión histórica*, pp. 62–7.
[5] It is worth, however, mentioning the notable exception of Miguel Bartolomé Salón who produced a very detailed and knowledgeable diagnosis of what was wrong with the Valencian fiscal system, *Disputatio de tributis vectigalibus* in *Controversiae de iustitiae et iure, tomus secundus* (Venice: Baretius Baretius, 1608).
[6] *ST* I-II q. 96 a. 4 c.
[7] Diego (Jacobo) Laínez, *Quaestiones theologicae de vectigalibus* in Hartmannus Grisar (ed.), *Disputationes Tridentinae*, vol. 2 (Innsbruck: Felicianus Rauch, 1886) pp. 386–7.

were grounds for not having a moral obligation to pay in principle. Many of the taxes levied in the sixteenth century were felt to fall short of these conditions. The original purpose of many taxes had been long forgotten, or, as in the case of taxes concerned with the funding of the war against the Moor, the goals of the tax had been long accomplished. Other taxes had known and yet to be accomplished goals but imposed an unfair burden on the poor.

Do we always have a moral obligation to pay taxes that are severe but not unjust, or at least not clearly so? Concerning the unpopular *alcabala*, many theologians thought we do not have this obligation or at most that it is a weak obligation. Others thought that we do have a strong moral duty to pay but only when commanded to do so by the authorities (a demand that would come after the statutory period for 'spontaneous' payment had lapsed and one was already liable to penalties). In this chapter, I explore the underpinnings of these two views, which, as will become clear, aimed to justify a culture of partial non-compliance that seems to have been widespread among Spanish tax-payers, and to have been tolerated to some degree by the authorities.

One of the points of interest in this late scholastic controversy is that it presents us with a way of dealing with the moral puzzles we face as citizens that is not present, for example, in discussions about just war. As we will see in later chapters, in the just war context, the central question that the morally uneasy subject must ask himself is whether the war is just and under what conditions he can participate in it in good faith. Much of this question revolved around how to achieve practical moral certitude about the rightness of one's action despite remaining uncertain about the justice of the war itself.

One would expect that the discussion on paying taxes would have run a parallel course to the just war discussion given that in both cases the duty of obedience to the political authority is at stake. However, while in war the intentions of the commander seem straight-forward and binding (unless his order is patently unjust), taxes are different. Most taxes are imposed by law, not command, and so discussing the bindingness of taxes involves discussing the sort of moral obligation imposed by law and its dependence on or independence from the intention of the legislator. In short, laws bring with them a set of issues that commands do not, which provided a new layer of complexity to the question of the moral permissibility not to pay tax.

2.2 Purely Penal Law

The underpinnings of the view that we do not have a moral obligation to pay certain taxes is to be found in the 'theory of purely penal law'.

The theory of purely penal law, whose most important contributor was Alfonso de Castro, concerns the connection between law, blameworthiness [*culpa*] and penalty or punishment. It developed from Vitoria onwards but can be said to have roots in the medieval theologian Henry of Ghent (although some scholars disagree that this is what Henry was proposing).[8]

Proponents of this theory thought that not all human laws penalizing the non-performance of an act morally obliged the performance of the act. The legislator is capable of framing laws that simply say 'if you do not do x, you will have to endure y'. These laws do not command x, so that failure to do x does not constitute disobedience. In the language of the late scholastics, you do not have 'an obligation in conscience' to do x. Many defenders of pure penal laws thought that, being laws, purely penal laws do impose a moral obligation; not the obligation to do the act which is the condition of the penalty, but the obligation to suffer and not to resist the penalty if one fails to do the act.

A favourite example used by defenders of purely penal law was the statutes regulating the life of religious congregations and orders, such as the Dominican Order.[9] Many believed that these statutes were true laws, and at the same time that there was no fault in breaching them. In fact, the prologue added to the Dominican Constitutions in 1236 reads: 'We will and declare that our Constitutions do not oblige us *ad culpa* but rather *ad poenam*.'[10] Take the rule (c. 12) that a friar who, in full awareness, breaks the silence in the Refectory will get only water instead of his regular meal.[11] This is intended to deter friars from talking in the Refectory. For the sake of achieving this end, the threat of not getting a meal is sufficient. There is no need to make it the case that the friar will incur also the sin of disobedience by talking. Some standard secular examples of purely penal laws given by these authors were the law penalizing fugitive prisoners and the law penalizing cutting wood in the municipal forest. The prisoner does not have a moral obligation not to escape, but has a moral obligation to

---

[8] Henry of Ghent, *Quodlibeta magistri Henrici Goethals a Gandauo doctoris solemnis socii Sorbonici & archidiaconi Tornacensis* (Paris: Iodocus Badius, 1518) quodl. 3 q. 22 fol. lxxxiiB, section B. For an exhaustive and informative account of the authorities relied upon by Navarrus and Castro, see William Daniel, *Purely Penal Law Theory in the Spanish Theologians from Vitoria to Suárez* (Rome: Gregorian University Press, 1968) pp. 181–95.

[9] The best book on the history of the debate on whether monastic-religious statutes are laws remains Cándido Mazón, *Las leyes de los religiosos: su obligación y naturaleza jurídica* (Rome: Gregorian University, 1940).

[10] In Mazón, *Las reglas*, p. 238.

[11] *Regula Sancti Augustini et Constitutionum Ordinis Praedicatorum* (Rome: Niccolò Angelo Tinassi, 1690) c. 12 part 2 at p. 63.

endure the set penalty for this act. The person who needs to keep his family warm in winter does not have a moral duty to refrain from taking wood, but he has to be prepared to pay a price for doing so. A current example of a purely penal law is provided by the Jerusalem municipality. Restaurants that stay open during Shabbat are penalized with a fine. However, many restaurants stay open during Shabbat without being prevented from doing so by the municipality, which is content to simply collect the fine.

Scholars nest the theory of purely penal law in voluntarism.[12] The main claim of voluntarism (often contrasted to 'naturalism' or 'realism') is that the obligation to perform an act does not come directly from the goodness of the act itself (which may be a condition), but from the superior's command to perform the act. Versions of voluntarism about law have been advanced or subscribed to by Scotus, Ockham and Suárez.[13] The reason scholars consider the purely penal theory of law to be tied to voluntarism is that the latter assumes that it is in the power of the legislator to separate the penalty from the fault, by having the capacity through an exercise of will to make a morally good act obligatory or not, under the law in question.

Pure penalists need not believe that all human laws should be seen as merely imposing a price on conduct; they only need believe that it is in the power of the legislator to make such laws. Moreover, nothing prevents them from believing that *none* of the laws in the book are actually purely penal or that it is generally a bad idea to legislate purely penal laws.

The most powerful objection against purely penal laws is that it seems unjust to punish someone for a faultless omission (since by definition the purely penal law does not impose an obligation to perform the act, the failure to perform it is faultless). A second objection is that if there is no fault, it is unclear what criterion should be used in determining the severity of the punishment. Suárez and others tried to cope, with debatable levels of success, with these and other worries.[14]

The theory of purely penal law has been the subject of many studies, the most comprehensive of which remains William Daniel's.[15] Instead of

---

[12] See chapter 3 of Daniel, *The Purely Penal Law*.
[13] For example John Finnis, *Natural Law and Natural Rights* (Oxford: Oxford University Press, 2011, 2nd edn.) p. 45; Daniel, *Purely Penal Law*, pp. 88–92.
[14] These worries are extensively discussed in Francisco Suárez, *Tractatus de legibus ac Deo legislatore*, C. Baciero, A. M. Barrero, J. M. García Añovero and J. M. Soto (eds.) (Madrid: CSIC, 2010) lib. 5 c. 3, 4 at pp. 48–79.
[15] For a briefer, precise and incisive presentation, see Finnis, *Natural Law and Natural Rights*, pp. 325–37.

dwelling on purely penal law as such, I focus here on the application of the theory to the issue of taxation, to which Daniel devotes a few pages.[16]

Back to taxes. If you believe in purely penal laws, and you take it that some fiscal laws are purely penal laws, you can say that you do not have an obligation in conscience to pay the tax *even if the tax is just*, but you do have a moral obligation to pay a penalty for not paying the tax, if your tax evasion is detected. In other words, you should not feel moral remorse about failure to pay as you have done nothing wrong.

It all really depends on whether the legislator is understood to have imposed the tax in a preceptive manner ('pay the tax') or in a merely conditional or disjunctive manner ('if you do not pay the tax, you will face a fine' or 'either pay the tax or pay a fine'). Much turns on the legislator's intention, our access to it, and on the presumptions that it is reasonable to have about his inaccessible intentions.

The only author I have found to explicitly and unreservedly declare some tax laws to be purely penal is the first-generation Jesuit Diego Laínez (1512–1565) in an interesting text, written in the sixteenth century but not published until the late nineteenth century. He considered the tax laws of Venice, where he lived in the 1540s, to be purely penal.[17] Navarrus was also sometimes understood to believe that tax laws are purely penal, but, as we will see, this is inaccurate.[18] However, it seems that many people, although perhaps not theologians, did believe that fiscal laws were purely penal, at least to judge by the effort spent by authors such as Alfonso Castro to refute them.

2.3 Alfonso de Castro on Taxes

As noted above, the purely penal theory of law easily lends itself to a justification of tax avoidance. If tax laws are purely penal we do not have any moral obligation (grave or not) to pay taxes, only to pay the fine if caught.

Alfonso de Castro was the first to extensively lay out a theory of purely penal law.[19] One of the reasons Castro felt impelled to write about taxes

---

[16] Daniel, *The Purely Penal Law*, pp. 158–62.
[17] Ibid. pp. 181–95, for an exhaustive and informative account of the authorities relied upon by Navarrus.
[18] Laínez, *de vectigalibus*, p. 391.
[19] On Castro's theory of purely penal law, see Marcelino Rodríguez Molinero, *Origen español de la ciencia del derecho penal: Alfonso de Castro y su sistema penal* (Madrid: Editorial Cisneros, 1959). On Sylvester Prierias on taxes, see p. 149 in Rodríguez Molinero.

was the view, held by many – and especially merchants (who, as he reports consulted him on these issues) – that one's moral duty was restricted to facing the penalties for tax evasion. He was also responding to the perception that this was a view that was accepted by many of the learned.[20]

The taxes with which Castro was mostly concerned were the *alcabala*, the *portazgo*, or city gates tolls (the word originally referred to port taxes, but in Spain at the time they mostly referred to taxes collected at the city gates, or *puertas*), and the sea tithes (*diezmo del mar*).[21]

Castro attacked headlong those who believed that it was not a mortal sin to avoid paying taxes or to fail to make restitution for unpaid taxes. He attributed this view to the more fundamental belief that human laws do not oblige on pain of mortal fault (*culpa*).[22] He might here have had in mind a controversial text by Cajetan on the obligatoriness of human law.[23]

For Castro, there is an obligation under divine law to pay taxes, which precedes the imposition of penalties by human law.[24] He supports this with a number of scriptural sources, of which the best known is 'Render unto Caesar the things that are Caesar's and unto God the things that are God's' (Mark 12:17). Moreover, Castro assimilates taxes to wages paid for the ruler's services to the public, mainly defence provision. Thus, he considers that we also have a duty of natural law to pay them.[25]

So, for Castro, we have obligations deriving from divine and natural law to pay taxes. But, as he insists, 'a purely penal law never destroys a prior obligation *ad culpam*'.[26] Therefore even if the tax law considered in itself is penal and does not impose an *additional* obligation to pay the tax, it does not cancel the pre-existing moral obligation.

Notwithstanding this, human law can add an obligation on top of those derived from divine and natural law. Castro argues that we should not interpret the legislator's imposition of a temporal penalty as disclosing an intention to try to abolish or remove the obligation created by the human law itself.[27] Temporal penalties and obligations in conscience are not

---

[20] Alfonso de Castro, *De potestatis leges poenalis, libri duo* (Louvain: Antonius Maria Bergagne, 1557 c. 1500) lib. 1 c. 10 fol. 56v.; Rodríguez Molinero, *Origen español*, pp. 166–7.

[21] This is not to say that Castro thought all taxes are just, in particular he thought that the *sisa* was not. *De potestate legis poenalis*, lib. 1 c. 5.

[22] '*Culpa*' is notoriously difficult to translate into English: it lies somewhere between blame, guilt, blameworthiness and fault.

[23] Thomas de Vio, Cardinal Cajetan, *Peccatorum summula* (Douay: Balthazar Beller, 1627) 'clericus' n. 5 at p. 46–7 and 'ieiunium' cap. 4 n. 2 at p. 346. The text that was taken by Castro and Suárez to show Cajetan's being in favour of interpreting religious rules as purely penal laws was his commentary on *ST* II-II q. 186 a. 9 at p. 502 where he discusses the 1236 edition of the Dominican constitutions.

[24] Castro, *De potestate legis poenalis*, lib. 1 c. 10 at fol. 57r.   [25] Ibid.   [26] Ibid.

[27] Castro, *De potestate legis poenalis*, lib. 1 c. 10 fol. 59v.

mutually exclusive. By imposing the latter the legislator is not indicating his unwillingness or incapacity to impose moral obligations through his laws.

In this way Castro aims to preclude the use of his theory of purely penal law to justify the evasion of just taxes. Possibly, the weak point of his defence is that it is unclear that all tax laws can be easily seen to enjoin a pre-existing duty. Insofar as they do not, and given that the legislator's intentions are often open to interpretation, a leeway is left for the purely penal defence of tax evasion.

2.4 Navarrus and the Gravity of the Obligation to Pay Tax

Navarrus would exploit this leeway. His hostility to taxes may have had something to do, as Vincenzo Lavenia suggested, with anti-Castilian sentiment in his native Navarra (which was conquered by the Castilians in 1512) and the perception that the imposition of Castilian legislation conflicted with many ancient customs, including grazing rights.[28] Navarrus' hostility to taxes is felt also in the work of other authors, such as the Portuguese Luiz de Beja Perestrello.[29]

Some authors – both Navarrus's contemporaries and more recent ones – read Navarrus as arguing that all or at least some taxes are imposed by purely penal laws, and for this reason do not impose any obligations in conscience.[30] In this view, Navarrus takes Castro's theory of purely penal laws and straightforwardly applies it to tax laws. Navarrus was understood to have been following the even more lenient view of taxes advocated by the Italian Franciscan, Angelo Carletti di Chivasso (Angelus de Clavasio), who thought that the payment of *pedagium* (a form of toll) could be avoided without culpability.[31]

In his *Handbook for Confessors and Penitents*, Navarrus mentions taxes in passing. His discussion more generally addresses the topic of human laws.

---

[28] See Vicenzo Lavenia, 'Fraus et Cautela: Théologie morale et fiscalité au debut des temps modernes' in Serge Boarini (ed.), *La casuistique classique: Genèse, forms, devenir* (Saint-Juste-de-la-Pendue: Publications de'Université de Saint-Étienne, 2009) p. 50 (pp. 43–57). On grazing, see Navarrus, *Commentarii de Lege Poenali*, in *Martini ab Azpilcueta Doctoris Navarri, Iurisconsultum, ... Operum, tomus secundus* (Cologne: Ioannes Gymnici, 1626) q. 2 n. 38 at p. 239. On Navarrus' local patriotism see Mariano Arigita y Lasa, *El Doctor Navarro Don Martín de Azpilcueta y sus obras: Estudio histórico-crítico* (Pamplona: Imprenta Provincial, 1895) p. 39.

[29] Luiz de Beja Perestrello, *Responsionum casus conscientiae, secunda pars* (Venice: Ioannes Baptista and Ioannes Bernardus Sessam, 1597) casus 13 at p. 49.

[30] Vázquez, *Opuscula Theologica Omnia* (Alcalá: Juan Gracián, 1617) dub. 2 cap. 6 a. 3 n. 11 at p. 188.

[31] Angelo Carletti, *Summa Angelica de Casibus Conscientialibus* (Venice: Aegidius Regazola, 1578), 'pedagium', pp. 231–2.

He offers a number of connected thoughts to explain the motivation behind his view that it is preferable to legislate laws that do not oblige *sub poena mortalis*. Making the performance of the acts that the law wants us to perform obligatory on pain of mortal sin imposes too heavy a burden on the subjects. In fact, he says, to impose this burden is to 'condemn virtually everybody'.[32] The thought is that the acts prescribed by some laws will continue to be unperformed. By imposing an obligation under mortal sin to perform these acts, we are not increasing compliance but rather creating a pressure towards finding excuses for non-performance. He argues that bad people do not care about mortal sin and the resultant spiritual punishments; they only care about money and reputation.[33] So their level of compliance will not change because of the additional moral obligation. Good people, by contrast, do not need tax evasion to be a mortal sin for them to pay it. It suffices for them that failure to pay, constitutes a venial sin.[34] This view is reminiscent of Oliver Wendell Holmes's 'bad-man theory of law', expressed in the dictum, '[I]f we take the view of our friend the bad man we shall find that he does not care two straws' about either the morality or the logic of the law. For the bad man, "legal duty" signifies only "a prophecy that if he does certain things he will be subjected to disagreeable consequences by way of imprisonment or compulsory payment".'[35]

So making some acts (for instance the payment of some taxes) obligatory under mortal sin by making evasion an act of disobedience leaves compliance unaffected while unnecessarily increasing the punitive burden.[36] The republic gains nothing from these laws being obligatory on pain of mortal sin.

Navarrus's argument is in essence an argument about the suitability of a punishment to deter a subset of likely offenders. If a particular type of punishment does not have a deterrent effect on those most likely to commit the offence then it cannot be justified. Deterrent punishments must be tuned to what matters to the potential offenders at hand. Spiritual penalties only work for certain kinds of persons, and these are generally not the persons who are prone to evade tax.

Is Navarrus's explanation an application of the theory of purely penal law? No. In fact Navarrus rejects Castro's division between moral, penal,

---

[32] Navarrus, *Manual de Confessores y penitentes* (Valladolid: Francisco Fernández de Córdoba, 1570) c. 23 n. 65 at p. 465.
[33] Ibid. [34] Ibid.
[35] Oliver Wendell Holmes, 'The Path of Law', *Harvard Law Review*, 10(1897)461.
[36] Navarrus, *Manual*, c. 23 n. 65 at p. 465.

and mixed laws.³⁷ All moral laws (that is laws that order you to do something) impose a penalty and all penal laws presuppose fault, either mortal or venial. So all laws that really exist are in fact of the mixed class, they feature both *culpa* and penalty. Human laws always involve an obligation to perform an act (not just to endure the penalty), even when the law does not enjoin a pre-existing duty. For Navarrus the distinction between purely penal law and moral law only captures analytical *aspects* of law separable not in reality but only in the mind.

Navarrus's trademark view was that the intention of the legislator controls the *severity* of the obligations. The legislator has the power to make an act obligatory either by making transgression of the act a mortal sin or by making its transgression a merely venial sin. In both cases offenders have *culpa* and are liable to penalties. It is important to see that Navarrus's stance, namely that the severity of the moral obligation imposed by law is subject to the legislator's will, while not an affirmation of purely penal law, does not exclude it either. So, for instance, Suárez believes *both* in Navarrus's thesis and that purely penal laws can exist.³⁸

Vázquez disagreed with Navarrus. For him the severity of the obligation is entirely determined by the matter with which the law is concerned. The legislator can legislate or abstain from so doing, but if he does legislate, the severity of the moral obligation imposed by the law emerges 'automatically'; is it not subject to his control.³⁹

But how do we know the legislator's intention? Express imposition of temporal punishment, for Navarrus, is an indication that the legislator intends to oblige only in such manner that the transgression be a venial sin.⁴⁰ That this is the case was disputed, for example, by Diego Covarrubias y Leyva (1512–1577), who asked how it can be that the legislator who 'by adding a temporal punishment wishes to make his law stronger can intend to weaken it by removing all the obligation of the *culpa*?'⁴¹ More fundamentally, Navarrus does not reveal the mechanism whereby the intention

---

³⁷ Navarrus, *in Cap. Fraternitas*, q. 2 n. 27 p. 238.
³⁸ Suárez, *De obligationibus religiosorum*, lib. 1 c. 2 n. 8 at p. 8 in *Opera Omnia* (Paris: Vivès, 1860) vol. 16 part 1.
³⁹ Vázquez, *Commentariorum ac disputationum in primam secundae S. Thomae, tomus secundus* (Alcalá de Henares: Justo Sánchez Crespo, 1605) d. 158 c. 4 nn. 32–34 at pp. 132–3.
⁴⁰ Navarrus, *Manual*, c. 23 n. 65 at p. 465. Although often scholars, such as Rodríguez Molinero, misrepresent Navarrus's view as holding that the imposition penalty removes entirely any moral obligation to comply with the law. See *Origen español*, p. 174.
⁴¹ Diego Covarrubias y Leyva, *Regulae peccatum. De regul iur. Lib. IV Relectio* (Lyon: Sebastian Honoratus, 1560) part 2 sect. 5 at p. 137.

of the legislator can control the severity of the obligation imposed by his law.

Navarrus only approaches taxes explicitly in the commentary on the chapter *Fraternitas* of the *Decretals*, which was first published in truncated form in a collection of *Responsa* in 1590.[42] In that fragment he explicitly attacks Alfonso de Castro's view that when you owe just taxes to the prince you necessarily sin and must do restitution. This is true, Navarrus says, only as regards those taxes that are owed to the prince as wages for his work or as a stipend (to which category Navarrus adds taxes that can be interpreted as repayment for loans or for territorial concessions). These taxes cannot be left unpaid without mortal sin, but Navarrus leaves it open that other types of taxes can, at least in the absence of an express demand to pay.[43]

Navarrus advances a few preliminary observations for doubting Castro's view that *all* taxes generate a moral obligation to pay. He notes that this is too harsh; it condemns to mortal *culpa* all tax evaders. Advancing an argument that, as we will see, would become central, he argued that custom can moderate and alter any human law, for it can have force of law in itself. He reports that the custom in Spain dictates that if you hide your transaction without deception or perjury, you have no other obligation than to pay twofold or fourfold if caught by the auditor as required by the law (as was the case with the *alcabala*).[44] This custom leaves enough sustenance for the king, even if it reduces his income, and so one can make use of the custom and be excused.[45]

Laínez uses the word 'toleration' [*toleratione*] to characterize the authorities' attitude towards widespread tax evasion in Venice, where he lived from 1542–1543 – a place where, he reports, the majority of people routinely evaded some of the taxes, very few were caught and from those caught very few were punished (and the punishment did not carry with it *infamia*).[46]

Reflecting on Spain, Navarrus notes that many confessors do not consider it a mortal sin not to restitute for defrauded tax, and since these confessors are reputedly learned, the aforesaid custom is not just custom in the eyes of the people but also in the eyes of the learned. He adds that it is very difficult if not impossible to move merchants away from that custom.[47] Vázquez objected that this custom of evasion was not one that

---

[42] Navarrus, *in Cap. Fraternitas*, q. 2 n. 41 at p. 240.　[43] Ibid., at pp. 240–1.
[44] Gómez Álvarez, *Revisión histórica*, p. 183.　[45] Navarrus, *in Cap. Fraternitas*, q. 2 n. 41 at p. 240.
[46] Laínez, *de vectigalibus*, p. 391. On *infamia* as a public status see Chapter 4.
[47] Navarrus, *in Cap. Fraternitas*, q. 2 n. 45 at p. 240.

could be assumed to be tolerated by the sovereign.[48] Toleration requires knowledge and hidden economic transactions are by definition secret. You cannot tolerate what you do not know about. As we will see, arguments from customary law would become the core in Suárez's own discussion.

Navarrus's text ends at the point where he is preparing the ground for a fuller answer to the question of taxes by offering a taxonomy of types of tributes, one that would later be closely followed by Suárez. He distinguishes between royal, personal and mixed taxes. This taxonomy is intended to set the *alcabala* and the export and import tariffs morally apart from other types of taxes. Whereas most other taxes, as Navarrus conceded, are obligatory under pain of mortal sin because they are akin to wages to the king, stipend, rent or some sort of mortgage for lands, the *alcabala* and taxes on export and imports are suspect.

The payment of wages and rent for land are contractual duties between private individuals, binding under natural law. To the extent that some taxes can be modelled as wages to the rulers or mortgage for lands given by the sovereign, then one is bound to pay them on pain of mortal sin regardless of there being in place a preceptive law commanding one to do so. Suárez compares the keeping of these tax laws to 'laws about keeping contracts and meeting promises and generally about the payment of debt that is owed to a person as a matter of justice'.[49]

However, says Navarrus, the duty to pay non-royal taxes such as the *alcabala* is 'less natural' as they are 'extraordinarily' introduced. Navarrus says that the duty to pay these taxes is owed 'in such a way that the people must be ready to pay in accordance to the tacit or express consent of the prince or the republic'.[50] The thought seems to be that since these taxes do not enjoin a natural moral duty there is considerable room for political society to decide how they ought to be paid.

The fragment ends saying that for a law to oblige it must meet various conditions, one of which is that it must be accepted or received [*recepta*] by those who must obey it. One assumes that Navarrus went on to say that some of the tax laws fail this test.

In short, the general thrust of Navarrus is that there is a subset of tax laws, which includes the *alcabala*, which do not enjoin duties that would exist absent those laws. Further, while these tax laws are not purely penal, we must presume that the legislator intended to impose only a non-grave

---

[48] Vázquez, *De restitutione* in *Opuscula Moralia*, part 2 caps. 6–7 dub. 2 n. 27 et fol. at p. 192.
[49] Suárez, *De legibus*, lib. 5 c. 13 n. 4 at p. 271.
[50] Navarrus, *in Cap. Fraternitas*, q. 2 n. 49 at p. 241.

moral duty to pay these taxes. This is because he has imposed temporal penalties for non payment or, alternatively, because there is a customary law in place that says that one has a moral obligation to pay some taxes only when so demanded.

2.5 Payment on Demand: Justice through Custom

Suárez agrees with Castro that there are or can be purely penal laws: to know whether a law obliges or not we must know whether the legislator intended to oblige us (preceptive law) or not (purely penal law).

For Suárez, laws imposing taxes should be presumed to be preceptive and thus as creating an obligation in conscience to pay, and not just an obligation in conscience not to resist the penalty if caught red-handed.[51] However, this is not to say that he sees no role for purely penal laws in the ethics of taxation. Purely penal laws were key in the answer to a different question: whether there is a moral obligation to pay the tax spontaneously, or only to pay it upon demand by the tax collectors.

The somewhat puzzling thought that there may be a duty in conscience to pay on demand, but not to do so before, was not Suárez's own invention. Vitoria and Soto had already suggested that restricting moral obligation to payment on demand may be an acceptable way of moderating possibly unjust taxes.[52]

Vitoria notes that it could be the case that a tribute be licit and just if paid according to custom [*ex consuetudine*], but could be unjust if paid according to the rigour of the law. In this case, he explains, it is in keeping with custom and required by justice to pay only when the payment is requested. But, 'if the person who has not yet paid is condemned to pay according to the rigour of the law, this would be unjust and he has no obligation to pay'.[53] For Soto, our moral obligation is limited to paying on demand only when the amounts involved are small.[54]

Most authors thought that making it a matter of an obligation in conscience to pay *before* requested to do so was excessively demanding [*durissimus*]. Because the *alcabala* was initially justified as a levy to fund the war against the Moors, Domingo de Báñez (1528–1604), for one, says that, after the Moors were expelled from Granada (their last Iberian stronghold),

---

[51] Suárez, *De legibus*, lib. 5 c. 13 n. 9 at p. 276.
[52] Francisco de Vitoria, *Comentarios a la secunda secundae de Santo Tomás* (Salamanca: Biblioteca de Teólogos Españoles, 1934) q. 62 a. 3. n. 7 at pp. 152–3 (vol. 3). On Vitoria on taxes see Lavenia, pp. 48–51. Soto, *II*, lib. 3 q. 6 a. 7.
[53] Vitoria, *In ST II-II*, q. 62 a. 3n. 7 at p. 153.   [54] Soto, *II*, lib. 3. q. 6 a. 7.

the *alcabala* was seen as extremely harsh. He held that it should be abated from one tenth of the value of the sales to about one thirtieth, and paid only on demand. It was 'extremely harsh [*durissimus*] and intolerable that a person after conducting a sale should go after the tax collector and give him a tenth of the price, for which reason in Spain it is quite accepted [*receptissimus*] among cautious [*timoratos*], conscientious and very learned men that one need not pay unless requested to do so'.[55]

Even Juan Gutiérrez, who emphatically denied that one can be excused from failure to notify sales to the *alcabala* collector (or *alcabalero*), admitted that one could be excused from paying road, bridge and port taxes when no one was present at the time to collect them, because requesting otherwise is *durissimus*.[56] Covarrubias also felt that for this reason the transit tax law did not impose any penalties on such non-payers.[57]

Note that saying that an obligation is very harsh or, to put it another way, over-demanding is not the same as saying that it is unjust. In principle, an obligation can be both just and over-demanding. The over-demandingness, however, can provide an excuse not to carry out a genuinely binding duty. The concept of 'harshness' also offered authors a convenient vehicle to voice some moral concern about taxes without having to pronounce directly on the justice of the tax, which could, naturally, pit them against the king.

The late scholastics had other conceptual resources to argue that just laws may sometimes call for moderation or mitigation. They could deploy notions of equity [*aequitas, epieikeia*] or resort to the need for law to be interpreted. However, these were not the notions mobilized by Soto, Vitoria, Sánchez, or the other late scholastic authors.[58] Rather, arguments in favour of moderating taxes through payment on demand were based on the alleged existence of customs of not paying taxes until asked to do so.

Among the first defenders of the existence of this custom in Castile were Joseph Angles (†1588), Báñez and Pedro Núñez Avendaño (1606–1657).[59] They felt that if this custom could be shown to have the force of law,

---

[55] Domingo Báñez, *Decisiones de iustitia et iure* (Venice: Minima Societas, 1595) q. 57 a. 3 concl. 2 at p. 136.
[56] Juan Gutiérrez, *Tractatus de Gabellis* (Antwerp: Joannes and Peter Beller, 1618) q. 4. p. 13. n. 46 following Antonio de Córdoba *Tratado de casos de consciencia* (Toledo: Pedro López de Haro, 1584 first edn. 1561) q. 95 at p. 280b.
[57] Covarrubias, *Regulae peccatum*, part 2, section 5 at p. 152.
[58] Sánchez, *Consilia*, lib. 2 c. 4 dub. 10 n. 7 at p. 297.
[59] Pedro Núñez Avendaño, *Dictionarium Hispanum vocum antiquarum in Quadraginta responsa quibus quamplurimas leges regias explicantur* (Salamanca: Inheritors of Juan de Cánova, 1576) p. 171v.

conditioning payment on the demand to do so could be rendered legal. For them, the custom was justified because it brought tax collection into conformity with distributive justice.

The Valencian Miguel Bartolomé Salón (1539–1621) rejected this rationale but did not feel that an alternative one needed to be supplied. He believed that custom simply has the force of determining the form of payment. In places where there are no tax-collection offices, if the custom is to pay on demand, then this is what we are morally obliged to do. In places where there are designated tax-collection offices, their presence should be interpreted as a permanent demand to report transactions and pay the tax, so in these cases one is not morally allowed to wait for a personalized demand and one must pay the tax *as though* it was demanded personally from him.[60]

Salón says that Soto's definition of the *alcabala* as an overly rigorous tax in need of moderation is misleading. Either the tax is just or it is unjust. If it is unjust, one has no duty to pay it (setting aside any potential for scandal in not paying it).[61] If it is just, it must be paid according to the customs of the country. The custom therefore does not *correct* an injustice. Rather, custom simply establishes the way the tax should be paid, and it is also just.

Most authors took a different view from that of Salón on the justification of this custom. Bartolomé de Medina (1528–1580) and Diego Covarrubias argued that custom could 'moderate' the injustice of the tax.[62] Medina explains that payment on demand is not only an established custom, it is also a corrective measure; by applying the custom the excessive tax becomes just and fairly imposed.[63]

Many authors, particularly jurists, thought that this custom was little more than an invention. Some argued that in some of these alleged cases, the tax payer could defer the payment until requested only if he acknowledged beforehand the debt to the tax collector.[64] Jurists, such as Blas Navarro, Molina y Lassarte and Gutiérrez, simply denied that such custom

---

[60] Salón, *de tributis vectigalibus*, a. 2 contr. 6 n. 16 at p. 136, following the opinion of his teacher, Juan Blas Navarro, *Disputatio de vectigalibus et eorum exactione in foro conscientiae* (Valencia: Pedro Patricio Mey, 1587) c. 7 at p. 85. On Salón's extensive discussion on the justice of Castilian and Valencian taxes, see José Aliaga Girbés, *Los tributos e impuestos valencianos en el siglo XVI: Su justicia y moralidad según Fr. Miguel Bartolomé Salón, O.S.A. (1539?-1621)* (Rome: Instituto Español de Historia Eclesiástica: 1972).
[61] Salón, *de tributis vectigalibus*, a. 2 n. 16 at p. 136.
[62] Bartolomé de Medina, *Expositio in prima secundae angelici doctoris D. Thomae Aquinatis* (Salamanca: Mateo Gasti, 1582) q. 96 a. 4 p. 883; Covarrubias, *Regulae peccatum*, part 2 sect. 5 at p. 152.
[63] Medina, *Expositio in prima secundae*, q. 96 a. 4 p. 883.
[64] See Covarrubias, *Regula peccatum*, part 2 sect. 5 at p. 151.

exists in Castile. They noted that respected theologians such as Antonio Córdoba (1485–1578) conceded this fact. They also pointed out that the authoritative Covarrubias did not say that there is such a custom but only that, if and where there is, then it could be followed in good conscience.[65] They accused theologians like Báñez of historical ignorance and suggested that the custom referred to by Joseph Angles may belong to his hometown kingdom of Valencia rather than Castile.[66]

Castile's laws, for one thing, were very clear: after a transaction was completed, the vendor had three days to approach the tax collectors (or if absent from home, to make known to his wife or at least two neighbours his intention to pay the tax) and pay the *alcabala*. He could not just wait to be asked to pay. The penalty for failure to pay in time was double the amount owed as tax.[67]

But the law is one thing and its enforcement another. Modern political scientists, such as Alisha Holland, have shown that politicians sometimes deliberately decide not to enforce certain laws, even though they have the capacity to do so (a phenomenon which she calls 'forbearance').[68] In some Latin American countries, for example, the police are often discouraged by local government from enforcing laws on land squatting or public vending.

While it is easy to attribute such official leniency to pure electoral politics, one should not outright dismiss the politicians' avowals that forbearance is motivated by considerations of distributive justice. So the mere fact of the existence of a law penalizing some practice is not enough to show that the practice is not tolerated.

That some level of forbearance was present in tax collection is clear from Antonio de Córdoba, who tells us that it is not a mortal sin nor does it involve restitutive duties for custom officers not to register all the possessions of 'friends, merchants or passengers' entering the kingdom, for it is the usage not to inspect all of the belongings of those entering 'or to charge the entire tribute or toll that they owe but only what these persons declare or give, even though it is assumed or known that they carry or owe much more'.[69] So, at least in the case of transit taxes, it seems that there was, on the part of personnel, an established custom of forbearance. Córdoba

---

[65] Blas Navarro, *de vectigalibus*, c. 7 p. 83; Ignacio Lassarte y Molina, *De decimum venditiones & permutationis quae Alcavala nuncupatur* (Alcalá: Juan Gracián, 1589) c. 18 n. 41 at p. 191a, following Córdoba, *Tratado*, q. 95 at p. 277b. Covarrubias, *Regula peccatum*, part 2 sect. 5 at p. 152.
[66] Lassarte y Molina, *De decimum venditiones & permutationis*, c. 18 n. 45 at p. 191v; Gutiérrez, q. 3 n. 13 at p. 9 (on Báñez).
[67] *Quaderno de las alcavalas* (Salamanca: Juan de la Junta: 1547) ley 120, ley 129 (unpaginated).
[68] Alisha C. Holland, 'Forbearance', *American Political Science Review*, 110(2016)232–46.
[69] Córdoba, *Tratado*, q. 95, at p. 281a.

suggested that the reason was that full enforcement would have led travellers either to avoid entering the kingdom or to engage in smuggling. Partial enforcement gave enforcers the flexibility needed to find the optimal point beyond which increasing *de facto* tax pressure would result in less overall revenue by increasing levels of non-compliance. We do not know whether this sort of deliberate partial enforcement also applied to the collection of the *alcabala*. Báñez, for one, tells us that the penalty established by Law 120 of the *Quaderno de Alcabalas* was so harsh that it was 'never received in use' [*recepta in usu*], which is affirmed also by Pedro de Ledesma (1544–1616).[70] In any case, it is clear that we cannot rule out the existence of a custom of deferring payment until the making of a demand simply by looking at the laws in the book.

Let us assume that the disputed custom of payment on demand did in fact exist. Could following it make tax collection fairer? Daniel believes we have reason to doubt this. The weakness of the 'pay on demand' solution is its capriciousness: 'it is a matter of luck whether a person has to pay or escapes notice, and it may easily happen that the person most in need of relief has the worst luck.'[71] That may be true, although it may have been the case that the statistical probability of being demanded to pay tax was capable of rough estimation, so it was not entirely a matter of luck. In any case, if the tax is excessive then, so long as you can get away without getting a payment demand at least sometimes, it is certainly an improvement over the previous situation. Perhaps it would be better from the point of view of justice to pay only the just amount every time (say half of what is demanded), but it is unlikely that tax collectors would have accepted anything like that. The popular custom of payment on demand was possibly the only available instrument to moderate fiscal pressure.

A connected critical thought is this: if the tax is just, one has a moral obligation to pay unconditionally. If, by contrast, the tax is unjust, one has no moral obligation to pay. It seems quite absurd to say that if the tax is unjust or possibly unjust, one can morally withhold payment until a demand is made.

I believe that this charge is uncharitable. As Suárez suggests, there are two ways of approaching the problem: one is to take the law as fixed and ask whether the subject should obey it. He admits that if you adopt this approach, there will not be any space for restricting the obligation in

---

[70] Pedro de Ledesma, *Primera y segunda parte* (Lisbon: Pedro Crasbeek, 1690) tract. 7. p. 190.
[71] Daniel, *The Purely Penal Law*, p. 155.

conscience to paying only on demand. Either you have an unconditional obligation in conscience to pay, or you do not have an obligation to pay.

But there is a second approach. If I know how much tax would be fair to request, the law can be construed in such a way that it requires the payment of *that* amount. In this approach, the law is not treated as fixed but as exhibiting enough malleability to bring it into conformity with justice. There is no contradiction between the two approaches; it is simply that each starts from different premises.

Suárez suggests two different paths to construe the law so that it can be brought into conformity with justice. One is by way of interpretation by 'prudent men'. For Suárez, 'interpretation' is an *elucidation* of the meaning of law, which differs from *epieikeia* (consisting in *amending* the law to bring it into conformity with justice).[72] The second way is by the force of custom. In this mode, the will of the people, consented to by the prince, does not so much interpret the law as legislate it. That is, the subjects legislate through actions expressive of their will.[73]

2.6 The Problem of the Ruler's Consent: Making Sense of Penalties

Custom on its own does not make law. It must have the tacit or express consent of the legislator. But since failure to pay spontaneously (without demand) was penalized, this must have meant that the prince did not give either tacit or express consent to the custom of paying only on demand. On the contrary, he actively opposed this practice by penalizing it 'and punished those who hide themselves in order not to pay'.[74] Therefore, the moderation of tax law through customary law seems not even able to get off the ground. This was a point eloquently made by Vázquez, who deduced that it was inconceivable that the intention of the legislator was to limit the obligation in conscience to pay on demand.[75]

Those who believed that the custom of payment on demand was consented to by the king faced the challenge of explaining why there were penalties for following the custom. Tomás Sánchez argued that these penalties were devised 'in favour' of the *arrendatarios*, in order to help them be better able to exact tax.[76] Perhaps he meant to say that in the latter case, the *arrendatario* does not penalize in name of the king's law, but as a personal prerogative. Indeed the *arrendatario*'s right to exact penalties

---

[72] Suárez, *De legibus*, lib. 2. c. 16 n. 4 at p. 313.   [73] Suárez, *De legibus*, lib. 5 c. 18 n. 23 at p. 368.
[74] Ibid.   [75] Vázquez, *De restitutione*, dub. 2 n. 27 et fol. at p. 192
[76] Sánchez, *Consilia*, c. 4 dub. 10 n. 11 at p. 293.

derived from the terms of the contract of *arrendamiento* with the king by which he bought the right to tax collection. Thus, the king conceded to the *arrendatario*, who remained a private person, a privilege so that he could better do his job. This may explain some of the appeal of Sánchez's comment: the *arrendatario*'s penalties are not directly the king's penalties and so they do not directly express the king's intention to oblige to pay on demand.

Suárez thought that these penalties should be understood as purely penal coactions, the only goal of which was to 'prevent the subjects from taking too much license' and to 'compensate the prince for the decrease in tax revenue'.[77] In other words, Suárez believes that custom has the power to co-opt the legislative intention of the prince in such way as to transform the law requiring spontaneous payment into a purely penal law. So penalties for not paying before commanded to do so, instead of indicating the prince's resentment for our failing the moral obligations imposed by his law, are simply negative incentives designed to get us to pay before the obligation to do so kicks in.

2.6.1 Problems with Suárez's Solution: Construed Intentions and Voluntarism

Suárez's solution has been attacked on two main counts. The first count has to do with Suárez's voluntarism. For Suárez, whether a law is purely penal or not depends on the intentions of the legislator. On the other hand, in many places in Suárez it seems that the legislator's intention can be extrinsically imputed to him. So in fact, it does not really matter much what the legislator as a real person actually intends.

As seen, Suárez suggests two ways in which the intention behind the legislation can undergo alteration. One is by a new legislative act, when the will of the people, a real will, as expressed by custom, replaces the will of the legislator. The other is where prudent men *interpret* the law, that is elucidate what the legislator must have intended in making the law (rather than replacing the legislator's will with their own).

But this seems to make Suárez's legal voluntarism rather innocuous. In his discussion of Suárez's customary law, James B. Murphy argues that Suárez's voluntarism collapses into the opposite view, namely realism or naturalism (the view that there are moral obligations to do actions that derive directly from the natural goodness of those actions, not requiring for

---

[77] Suárez, *De legibus*, lib. 5 c. 18 n. 23 at p. 368.

their existing an act of imperative will by a superior). The problem, Murphy notes, may have to do with Suárez's transposition from the theological to the political case. It makes sense, as a way of finding out about God's actual will, to track the good and the just, for the one thing we know about God is that He necessarily wills what is good. However, this is clearly not the case as concerns the human legislator.[78]

> Suárez often concedes that we have no reliable way to interpret the will of a lawmaker, so we must presume his will to be just, reasonable, and conducive to the common good. But these presumptions reveal that the actual will of the lawmaker is often superfluous. What matters for the basic justification of law is not whether people actually do consent to a law but whether they ought to consent to it.[79]

Murphy may have a point as concerns the first of Suárez's modes of tax attenuation by way of interpretation of 'prudent men'. However, the second mode of attenuation, by way of customary tax law, does not readily lend itself to Murphy's point. Suárez does not directly ask, 'What version of tax law would be just, reasonable and conducive to the common good?', in order to proceed to deduce that this law happens to be prescribing only payment on demand. Rather, the reason he feels entitled to say that the legislator intends only to oblige us only to pay on demand is the presence of an actual will, this is the will of the people as expressed by custom. It is only if the legislator can plausibly be seen as making the people's will *his* that he can be taken to intend to oblige us to follow the custom. So the structure of Suárez's argument is in line with his legal voluntarism.

The custom of payment on demand itself is supported by a rationale. In Suárez's case, this is correcting injustice. But this rationale alone would be unable to allow us to interpret the legislator's will as intending to oblige us only to payment on demand had it not been the rationale for a custom which is, or at least is purported to be, a fact expressive of a will. If the will of the legislator were deemed superfluous, Suárez would feel warranted to ignore facts that seem expressive of the real intentions of the real legislator (such as statutory penalties). But he does not feel warranted to do so, and this is why he must recur to inventive ways to re-signify these facts as compatible with just intentions.

---

[78] James B. Murphy, *The Philosophy of Customary Law* (Oxford: Oxford University Press, 2014) p. 57.
[79] Ibid., p. 58.

2.6.2 The Problem of Penalties for Evasion

The second count on which Suárez is attacked is his belief in there being a royal consent to the custom of payment on demand. Suárez asks how it can be that we can say that the king consents to the custom of payment on demand and yet at the same time his law penalizes those following this custom? Are not such penalties clear proof that the king does not consent to the custom (in which case the custom cannot acquire the force of law)?

One possible way of escaping this charge is to lay emphasis on the fact that Suárez characterizes these penalties, which he describes as 'moderate', as applying to 'those who take excessive license': those 'who hide in order not to pay'.[80] So, as Suárez says, the purpose of the fines is for the king to get some compensation for the loss caused by the abuse of the custom of payment on demand. Joseph Angles argued that while laws only oblige to pay on demand, there is also a moral obligation not to conduct commercial transactions secretly.[81] Your duty is to be prepared to pay should you be asked to. Failure to report a transaction is not exactly the same as concealing it. Concealing it includes, for example, not keeping records of the transaction, thus making it non-auditable. So Suárez can be understood as saying that the penalties referred to do not evince the king's lack of consent to the custom as such, but only his resistance to its abuse or exploitation, for instance by those who hide themselves from the tax collectors. So, to the extent that the penalties set out by the law are enforced against custom abusers rather than against custom followers, these penalties are compatible with the king's consent to the custom.

But this interpretation does not do justice to Suárez's text. For the text makes it clear that it is the purely penal character of tax laws that does the job of establishing the desired conclusion, namely, that it is because the tax laws imposing the penalties are purely penal that these do not detract from the king's consent to the custom of payment on demand. All that Suárez thinks he needs in order to show the king can be taken to be consenting to the custom of payment on demand is that there is no preceptive law saying 'pay before being demanded to do so'. Saying this would allow Suárez to assert that the king's consent to the custom of deferring payment until the demand is made is compatible with the king's unjustly penalizing those who avail themselves to this custom, so long as these unjust penalties result from a purely penal law.

---

[80] Suárez, *De legibus*, lib. 5 c. 18 n. 23 at p. 368.
[81] Joseph Angles, *Flores Theologicarum*, in *q. de restitutione* (Antwerpen: Pedro Beller: 1585) at p. 19.

Yet Suárez's text presents an obstacle to the adoption of this interpretation. For in the closing paragraph Suárez writes, 'Nevertheless, custom has the power to free from the law's obligation in conscience and the prince cannot or should not resist it in this point, because human laws should be fitted for those who use them.'[82]

This could be taken to mean that the royal penalties deriving from purely penal laws are a form of resistance to the custom, and therefore declaring them purely penal would not remove the obstacle to the desired conclusion, namely that the king consents to the custom. The crucial words here are 'in this point' (*in hoc ei resistere*). We should take 'this' to refer to the purely penal character of the tax law.[83] So understood, what Suárez says is that custom turns the king's tax law into a purely penal law. That is, custom has the power to construe the intention of the king as being not willing to impose an obligation in conscience to pay before commanded to do so (i.e. 'to free from the law's obligation in conscience'). That the king cannot or should not resist this means that either (a) the king's intention to make this law preceptive rather than purely penal would be incapable of accomplishing this effect or (b) it would be capable of turning the purely penal law into a preceptive one but it would be wrong for the king to do so.

What the preceptive customary law does is to postpone the moral obligation to pay the tax until the payment is demanded. The law imposing the penalty for non-spontaneous payment, being purely penal, does not impose a moral obligation to pay the tax before being so demanded. So it does not conflict with the postponement of this moral obligation by the preceptive customary law. Therefore, the purely penal law does not involve a resistance to the proper effect of the preceptive customary law, which is to defer the moral obligation to pay the tax.

As noted, Suárez's view does not commit him to believe that every instance of penalization by this purely penal tax law is just. He can say that when the enforcement of this law is directed against those who merely follow the custom without abusing it, the penalties are unjust. Again, the presence of the king's consent does not depend on his just application of penalties; the king's consent is simply secured by the purely penal character of the laws imposing these penalties.

Daniel argues:

> [I]n the sphere of taxation the only relevant considerations are the needs of the state and the equity of the taxes in the individual case, and these

---

[82] Suárez, *De legibus*, lib. 5 c. 18 n. 23 at p. 368 (trans. Daniel)
[83] Daniel, *The Purely Penal Law*, p. 160.

objective considerations govern the conduct of the ruler as well as the private citizen. There will always be incidental injustices in any human situation, but where the whole system is judged to be unjust or at least excessive, the remedy is not to be found in the imposing of purely penal sanctions to discourage the citizens from 'going too far' but in the reform of the system.[84]

But was Suárez's goal to mitigate the injustice of the situation through legislative proposals? Suárez is not advising the king that a lax enforcement of tax law coupled with the imposition of deterring penalties to prevent fiscal libertinage is the formula to make things less unjust. Rather, Suárez's main advisee is the subject who needs a morally defensible strategy to cope in the circumstances. What Suárez provides is *not* a legislative proposal but a moral conceptualization of the existing, prevalent, partial non-compliance to tax law that could justify these coping strategies.

2.7 The Project in a Wider Perspective

The Spanish late scholastic moral theologians operated within an entrenched culture of partial fiscal non-compliance that came with its own popular justifications. These moral theologians shared with most other Spaniards the conviction that the present tax system was morally indefensible.[85] As Charles Jago recounts, moral theologians and priests were not only deeply involved in the politics of taxation, through their membership in consultative ad hoc bodies (*juntas*), but sometimes were in fact those spearheading coordinated tax-payer revolts.[86] The challenge for the theologians advising tax payers was to generate morally tenable strategies to help them cope with an unbearable tax burden without calling for outright civic disobedience. The room for manoeuvre was not great.

The vast majority of the moral theologians thought that an acceptable *modus vivendi* was to restrict the moral obligation to the payment of tax on

---

[84] Ibid., p. 162
[85] My reading on the late scholastics and Suárez on taxes is diametrically opposed to Nicole Reinhardt's recent analysis in her *Voices of Conscience: Royal Confessors and Political Counsel in Seventeenth-Century Spain and France* (Oxford: Oxford University Press, 2016) pp. 122–35. According to Reinhardt, Suárez and most other Spanish theologians at the time defended the duty to pay taxes against the popular reticence to do so. So that in the matter of taxes, they strengthened 'royal power against theories of consent' (p. 127). Further, she believes that while Suárez and most other theologians sided with the king, one can see in them 'a generalized nervousness ... over popular objections to paying' (p. 135). Reinhardt, however, fails to consider Suárez's discussion of payment on demand which, as I hope to have shown, makes clear the great lengths to which Suárez went in order to justify entrenched non-compliance with tax law.
[86] On the *juntas*, see Dolores Mar Sánchez González, *El deber de Consejo en el Estado Moderno. Las Juntas "Ad hoc" en España (1471–1665)* (Madrid: Polifemo, 1993). Jago, 'Taxation', pp. 50–53.

demand. It was not easy, however, to come to a solid and principled theoretical defence of the moral permissibility of deferral of payment until caught. One option was to straightforwardly apply Castro's theory of purely penal law to taxes. This, however, committed one to the implausible view that the legislator does not intend to impose on us a moral obligation to pay taxes at all. So, while all authors were aware of this option, none other than Laínez explicitly endorsed it.

Navarrus offered another option, saying that we have only a weak moral obligation to pay taxes but we do have a strong moral obligation to pay the penalty for non-payment if caught. Navarrus thought that it made practical sense for the legislator not to impose a grave moral obligation on payment and that this was furthermore indicated by the fact that he chose to impose a temporal penalty for non-payment. Many authors did not buy into Navarrus's theory that the legislator's intention can control the degree of obligation imposed by his laws or did not feel that the imposition of temporal penalties was informative about the legislator's intentions. More generally, it seems that Navarrus's option was felt to be too close to the pure penalist option and so was affected by the same problems.

Hence, the real challenge was to defend the practice of payment on demand without denying that we have a strong moral obligation to pay tax. To do this, two moves were necessary. The first move was to argue that tax law is preceptive, not merely penal, but what it prescribes is 'payment on demand'. This move allowed the dispute to shift from being about the moral obligations imposed by human law, to being about contents of that which we are morally obliged to do under tax law, that is, about what it is that the legislator wishes us to be obliged to do. The second move was to equate the intention of the legislator with that of the people, by arguing that there was a custom of payment on demand in place which expressed the will of the people. This custom was not arbitrary: it either was expedient or brought into conformity with justice a law that enforced otherwise would be unjust. If the custom could be shown to be consented to or at the very least tolerated by the king, it could be taken to be expressive of the ruler's intentions. It would then be possible to say that it is the king's intention to morally oblige us only to payment on demand.

This inventive solution was vulnerable to many objections. The factual existence of the custom in Castile could be doubted, and the king's consent to it seemed to some to be no more than a fiction. Finally, even if the argument could be made persuasively, it had a problematic tail. According to one solution, what we are morally obliged to pay on demand is the tax itself. However, under the law of the time, if one was found not to have paid within the statutory period, one had to pay double. But the inventive solution failed to morally account for the surcharge over the amount of owed tax. This forced Suárez to put the surcharge down as a matter of a purely penal law.

This controversy acquaints us with is a way of arguing about our obligation towards the state that is different from those seen in the next chapters. When these obligations are imposed by law, rather than by command, we need to look beyond the requirements of justice. The complex interplay between legislative intention and the force and content of moral obligation come to the fore. The answers to these intricate questions in the late scholastic controversy are not impartial inferences from theory, but rather are, in an oblique way, also guided by considerations of justice. The choice of the theories of the moral obligation of the law and the way of applying them to the cases were themselves governed by the aim that the outcome correspond as closely as possible with convictions about the justice of the taxes. This may seem to some a bad recipe for unbiased philosophical work, but it tells much about how the late scholastics conceived of the relation between theoretical inquiry and their commitment to distributive fairness.

CHAPTER 3

Keeping Out the Foreign Poor: The City as a Private Person

3.1 The Poor Law Reforms in Europe

A series of bad harvests throughout Europe at the beginning of the sixteenth century accelerated the migration of destitute peasants to the cities, greatly increasing the numbers of the urban poor. As the crowds of beggars and vagabonds grew, denizens of cities from Nuremberg to Zaragoza, both in Protestant and Catholic Europe, debated the introduction of new policies.

Late scholastic engagement with these new policies centred on whether 'our' poor deserve preferential treatment over the poor coming from outside the city and on how the boundaries of the community – understood as a group bound by obligations of reciprocity between is members – should be conceived for the purpose of establishing assistance owed to the poor. In earlier authors such as Soto, the leading thought is that we should not look at the problem by focusing on the good of the city, but rather by focusing on the reciprocal duties connecting social classes within a community territorially larger than the city. In later authors, starting from Valencia, the problem tends to be analysed in terms of the balancing of conflicting goods: the good of the city versus the well-being of the foreign poor. Some theologians, such as Adam Tanner (1572–1632), went as far as to say that the foreign poor are 'not our problem', they are their hometown's problem.

The city's excluding the foreign poor is, in this later view, conceived as a private person exercising its legitimate rights. That is, the city was seen to be exempted from having to take the public point of view, the point of view of the king or, to go further, of an ideal ruler of the world, and is instead allowed to concentrate on the furthering of the interests of its own citizens alone.

The best known of the new poor policies and a model for the rest were the ordinances of Ypres of 1525. These ordinances pursued three main aims.[1] The first aim was to put in place procedures to find out who among the poor were genuinely poor and who were falsely posing as poor in order to collect alms. There was a general suspicion, not only that many of the beggars were actually capable of working for a living, but that some of them were actually secretly wealthy. Other poor were deemed to be genuinely unable to work but only because they had self-mutilated to be more effective at attracting charity.

A second aim was to overhaul the provision of assistance to the poor. The general feeling was that the whole system was in disarray, run by uncoordinated and often corrupt charities, mostly belonging to the Church (at least in Catholic Europe), and was unable to cope with the magnitude of the problem. Beggars swamped the streets, spread bad odours and disease, and made a simple walk in town or attendance at Mass a displeasing if not a hazardous business.[2] The city government had to step in, ban street begging, and reorganize public charity. There was felt to be a need for a civil bureaucracy equipped with tools for the rational management of a significant social problem.

A third aim was to restrict the access of the poor from outside the city by prohibiting the poor from leaving their hometowns and placing increasing controls over their movement. The town beggars came not only from outside the city but also from outside the realm. In Spain, beggars from Northern countries who asked for charity, mostly by singing, were dismissively called *franchotes* (a derogative denomination for the French). In one of Don Quixote's adventures, Sancho Panza is approached by foreign beggars (*peregrinos*) who, uninterested in the bread and cheese he offers them, demand '*Guelte! Guelte!*' ('Money! Money!') instead; as it turns out, these German beggars in fact had plenty of food and money.[3] This third aim was not unrelated to the first aim of distinguishing between the genuine poor and those who were pretending to be poor, as it was often thought that it was easier to feign poverty outside one's hometown. In order to be able to

---

[1] For a history of the reforms and accounts of the controversy, see Linda Martz, *Poverty and Welfare in Habsburg Spain* (Cambridge: Cambridge University Press, 1983); Félix Santolaria Sierra, 'Estudio Introductorio' in *El gran debate sobre los pobres en el siglo XVI: Domingo de Soto y Juan de Robles 1545* (Barcelona: Ariel, 2003); Maria Jimenez Salas, *Historia de la Asistencia Social en España en la Edad Moderna* (Madrid: CSIC, 1958); and Ole Peter Grell, Andrew Cunningham and Jon Arrizabalaga, *Health Care and Poor Relief in Counter-Reformation Europe* (London and New York: Routledge, 1999). For a good analysis of Soto's view, see Andreas Blank, 'Domingo Soto on Justice to the Poor', *Intellectual History Review*, 25(2015)136–46, on the foreign poor, pp. 138–42.

[2] Juan Luis Vives, *Selected Works of J.L. Vives, De Subventione Pauperum sive De Humanis Necessitatibus, Libri II*, Constant Matheeussen and Charles Fantazzi (eds.) (Leiden and Boston: Brill, 2002) vol. 4.

[3] *Don Quijote de la Mancha*, part 2, ch. 54.

establish whether the poor were truly poor, it was decided that they should first be sent back to their hometowns where a reliable examination could be conducted and witnesses could be sought.[4] In this chapter, I shall focus only on the debates concerning this last aim: the exclusion of the foreign poor.

3.2 The Debate Outside Moral Theology

The main contributions to what has been called 'the great debate on poverty' are not works of moral theology but rather part polemical text and part policy proposals written in a humanist style aimed at catching the eye of the authorities. So while it is not entirely incorrect to speak of a 'great debate on the poor', to the extent that this debate existed it was not a debate by moral theologians and it was not a debate centred on the permissibility of the exclusion of the foreign poor.[5]

The most famous defence of these new reform proposals was by the humanist author Juan Luis Vives. Vives's *De subventione pauperum* (1526) was addressed to the government of Bruges, which was then part of the Spanish Empire. The winds of reform had already begun to reach Spain itself. In 1523, the Cortes (representative assemblies usually summoned by the king) of Valladolid reiterated previous requests from 1518 to deny access to the poor from outside the city, and, in 1525, the Cortes of Toledo requested an examination of each purported poor person, after which only those found to be genuinely poor would be issued with a licence to beg.[6] Poor crops in 1539 led the Spanish court, on Cardinal Juan Pardo de Tavera's initiative, to introduce reforms at the level of the realm in 1540, though it was a matter of dispute among controversialists at the time if and when the king actually sanctioned the law.

A new wave of urban reforms ensued. Those of the city of Zamora became best known in Spain because they were submitted to and granted approval by the theologians at Salamanca. Soto tells us that he granted his approval with some reservations, only to realize that the content of these laws had been misrepresented to him and in fact included 'many things that if I had known of them I would not have signed'.[7] The result was his

---

[4] Francisco de Osuna, *Quinta parte del abecedario espiritual* (Burgos: Juan de la Junta, 1542) tract. 2 c. 1 fol. 192r; Bernardo de la Nieva, *Sumario Manual de Información de la Christiana Consciencia* (Medina del Campo: Francisco del Canto, 1556) p. 215.
[5] As, for example, the title of Santolaria Sierra's book.
[6] Santolaria, 'Estudio introductorio', in *El gran debate*, p. 20.
[7] Soto, *Deliberación en la causa de los pobres* (Salamanca: Juan de la Junta, 1545). I am using the critical edition of the Latin and Spanish versions 'In causa pauperum deliberatio' in *Relecciones y opúsculos*, Sixto-Sánchez Lauro and Jaime Brufau Prats (eds.) (Salamanca: San Esteban, 2011) vol. II, 2, pp.

famous *Deliberación en la causa de los pobres*, published two months later in both Latin and Spanish, and which he had written in only twelve days. The *Deliberación* was partly based on lectures he wrote in 1539–1540 and 1543–1544 (now lost) on *eleemosyna*, or almsgiving.[8]

Soto's *Deliberación* was met with a response from the Benedictine Juan de Robles (also known as Juan de Medina) (1492–1572) in his *De la orden que en algunos pueblos de España se ha puesto en la limosna, para remedio de los verdaderos pobres*, published shortly after Soto's essay.[9] While Robles argues that in the provision of alms the native poor are to be given priority over the foreign poor, he agrees with Soto that the latter are not to be excluded. He believes that the prohibition of begging outside one's hometown would be licit only if every town took adequate care of its own poor. However, given that this is not the case, it would not be licit for the authorities to impede foreigners from being received and given alms in any place where they arrive.[10] Robles does seem to disagree with Soto in thinking that it should be possible for even the poorest regions of Spain to feed their own poor. Robles's main interest is to establish a system that helps only the genuinely poor and forces those who are only pretending to be poor into the labour market, but he has no animosity towards the foreign genuine poor who are unable to sustain themselves in their hometowns.

Other notable contributions to this debate, again in favour of the reforms and proposing practical measures, are Miguel de Giginta's *Tratado de remedio de pobres* (1579) and Cristóbal Pérez de Herrera's *Amparo de los Pobres* (1598).[11] To the list we can add Juan Bernal Díaz de Luco's *Doctrina y amonestación caritativa* (1547) and the more critical Gabriel del Toro's *Tesoro de la Misericordia* (1536).[12]

232–46. An English translation by Wim Decock and Joost Possemiers (to see the light in CLP Academic) is in preparation.

[8] As reported by Soto's colleague Mechor Cano in Beltran Heredia, *Domingo de Soto: Estudio biográfico documentado* (Salamanca: Biblioteca de Teólogos Españoles, 1960) p. 89.

[9] The 1545 first Spanish version is included and edited in Santolaria Sierra, *El gran debate*.

[10] Robles, *De la orden*, in Santolaria p. 132.

[11] There is a modern edition by Félix Santolaria Sierra of the 1579 editio princeps: Miguel Giginta, *Tratado del remedio de los pobres* (Barcelona: Ariel, 2000). Cristobal Pérez de Herrera, *Amparo de los pobres*, Michel Cavillac (ed.) (Madrid: Espasa-Calpe, 1975).

[12] The text can be found in Félix Santolaria Sierra (ed.), 'La "doctrina y amonestación charitativa"' (1547) de Juan Bernal Diaz de Luco. Transcripción y aproximación a su contexto social' in Javier Laspalas (ed.), *Historia y Teoría de la Educación. Estudios en Honor del Profesor Emilio Redondo García* (Pamplona: EUNSA, 1999) pp. 311–28. Gabriel del Toro, *Tesoro de la Misericordia Divina y Humana* (Valencia: Pedro de Huete, 1575).

Flanders was one of the hotspots of polemical literature on the poor. Flemish contributions included Git Wyts's *De continendis et alendis domi pauperibus* (1562), which was attacked by Lorenzo de Villavicencio's defence of Soto in his *Oeconomia Sacra circa Pauperum Curam* (1564), as well as Andreas Hyperius's *De publica erga pauperes beneficientia* (1570).[13] Earlier in the Flemish context there was Christianus Cellarius, *Oratio pro pauperibus, ut eis liceat mendicare* (1530) and his *Oratio contra mendicitatem pro nova pauperum subventione* (1531), as well as the unpublished (and unfindable) Arnoldus Oridryus (Van Bergeik), *De cura pauperum apud gesnerum*.[14]

3.3 Medina and His Reception

Within moral theology proper, the two most important discussions on the foreign poor were those of Alcalá theologian Juan de Medina (1490?–1546) (not to be confused with Robles, the author of *De la orden* . . .) and Soto.

Soto's attack on the new poor policies is the best known but it was predated by Juan de Medina's *Codex de eleemosyna*. It is unclear whether Soto had read Medina's work, or if they discussed the issue when they were both lecturing at Alcalá.

Medina dedicated his book to Cardinal Tavera of Toledo, the alma mater of poor law reform in Spain. Medina's first argument centres on need and merit. He argues that some foreign poor may be poorer and more virtuous than some domestic poor, so prioritizing the needs of the local poor over those of the foreign poor across the board, which he concedes may be right *ceteris paribus*, does not hold in these cases, for all things are *not* equal.[15]

Second, Medina says that if every town denied entrance to the poor, the poor would be forced into perpetual wandering 'with no respite, finally breathing their last in piety, or certainly, if they were able, they would be forced into stealing without just cause and finally end up either in the stocks or subject to lashes that they might not have otherwise deserved'.[16]

---

[13] Git Wyts, *De continendis et alendis domi pauperibus* (Antwerpen: Guilelmi Silvij, 1562). Lorenzo de Villavicencio, *Oeconomia Sacra circa pauperum curam* (Antwerp: Christophorus Plantini, 1564). Andrea Hyperius, *Forma subventionis pauperum* (Antwerpen: Martinus Cesar, 1531).

[14] Christianus Cellarius, *Oratio pro pauperibus, ut eis liceat mendicare* (Antwerp: 1530); *Oratio contra mendicitatem pro nova pauperum subventione* (Antwerp: Henricus Petrus Middelburgenis, 1531). Reported in Josias Simmler, *Bibliotheca instituta et collecta primum a Conrado Gesnero* (Zurich: Christophorus Froschoverum, 1579).

[15] Medina, *Codex de eleemosyna*, (Alcalá: Athanasio Salzedo, 1544) fol. 173v. [16] Ibid.

Third, he writes that local authorities should not simply say that the foreign poor 'have their own compatriots, who ought to support [them], so let them go home and be fed by their kinsmen'. He argues that those who say this ought to know that there are many nations – so many, in fact – that are burdened with such great debts, impositions, and taxes that 'you can scarcely find anyone among them who is wealthy, or who has family who can adequately help them as they ought'.[17]

He adds that

> there are many poor people who cannot go back to their hometowns, either because they have been expelled or because there are enemies conspiring against them, or because their goods have been appropriated, or because they have been disgraced and it is better for them to leave their birthplace than to stay there, so it is an unjust punishment to oblige them to change their country. [In addition,] many of these lands have been subject to enemy incursions, fires, or other disasters, so how can we expect these men to go back and live there?[18]

This was the argument used by Franciscus Sylvius (1581–1649) against the exclusion of the foreign poor, to be then followed by Diana and Eloy de la Bassée (1585?–1670). The point is not just that the poor are unable to go back but that in many cases they were not poor in their original homeland, but left their homelands for other reasons, which then resulted in their falling into poverty. This is important because it poses a difficulty for the main view that Soto and Medina were opposing, namely that each town should feed its own poor. Even if a town does feed its poor, people may still migrate for a variety of reasons and be forced into mendicancy as a consequence. So the arrival in town of poor migrants would not be completely eliminated by adequate poor relief at home.

Medina's views played an important role in an exchange that took place at the Jesuit College of Ingolstadt in Catholic-ruled Bavaria. In his *De tribus bonorum operum generibus* (1580), Theodor Peltanus (1552–1584) (von Pelten), the Chair of Theology, discussed the question of the foreign poor and opposed the new reforms. Peltanus's discussion was subject to criticism by Tanner, another Ingolstadt Jesuit, in *De Spe et Charitate* of 1606. But Peltanus had offered an earlier and shorter discussion on the foreign poor in his *De tertia et postrema satisfactionis parte* (1572). In this work, his list of reasons against the new poor policy is taken from Medina. In *De tribus bonorum*, however, almost all of Peltanus's objections to the new laws came from Soto. One of his objections in this work, nevertheless,

[17] Ibid. [18] Ibid.

came from Medina: that the poor could potentially face great danger if sent back to their home place. To this Tanner responded that 'to remove beggars to their own countries is not exile. But if, *per accidens*, this removal sometimes hastens the death of such people, it can be nevertheless required by the law for the public good of the city. The poor's death should be imputed to their own country, not to foreign provinces or the Emperor's lands.'[19]

3.4 Soto's *Deliberación* in Outline

Soto dedicates chapters 4 and 5 of his *Deliberación* to the question of the exclusion of the foreign poor from the city. 'Foreign' (*exteros, extrangeros*) here refers both to Spaniards coming from outside one's city, as well as people from other states.

Soto starts by pointing out, somewhat misleadingly, that the planned exclusion of the foreign poor is a new and unheard of policy. In order to further portray the new measures as exotic, one sympathetic commentator noted that the exclusion of foreign beggars is a common practice in China.[20]

Soto's first reason against exclusion – one that echoes Medina – is that expelling the poor is akin to exile and nobody can be exiled except as a punishment for a serious crime, which can hardly be imputed to the foreign beggars. This is because, according to both natural law and the law of nations (*ius gentium*), everyone has the liberty to go wherever he wants (in the Spanish version) or 'to unrestrictedly use the city streets' (in the Latin version), so long as he is not an enemy or causes harm (or, in the Latin, if he has *no culpa*). And even if expelling someone from a city and sending him home is not strictly exile, it deprives him of a right, which cannot be withdrawn except by reason of fault.

Soto's assertion of the poor's right under the *ius gentium* is strongly reminiscent of Vitoria's defence of the right to travel (*ius peregrinandi*) in his examination of possible justifications for the Spanish fighting against Native Americans.[21] Indeed, Annabel Brett has argued that 'Soto's *Deliberation* is important because it brings into a European context issues that are largely elsewhere dealt with in the context of overseas expansion and the laws of war'.[22] And that, in fact, 'Soto turned [Vitoria's argument

---

[19] Adam Tanner, *Theologiae scholasticae* (Ingolstadt: Ioannes Bayr & People and Senate of the City, 1627) vol. 3 d. 2 q. 5 dub. 3 n. 66 at p. 682.
[20] Antonio Cotonne, *Controversiae celebres* (Venice: Tomasinus and Hertz, 1661) lib. 5 cont. 6 n. 91 at p. 652.
[21] Vitoria, *Relectio de Indis*, in Pagden and Lawrence, q. 3 a. 1 n. 2 at p. 278.
[22] Annabel Brett, *Changes of State* (Princeton, NJ: Princeton University Press, 2011) p. 34.

on the right to travel] back [i.e. argued that foreigners are allowed to enter your land, rather than compatriots can enter foreigners]'.[23] It is worth noting, however, that the *ius gentium* right claimed by Soto for the poor differs from the *ius gentium* right claimed by Vitoria for the Spanish 'travellers' in the Indies.

The *ius gentium* right that Soto refers to is everyone's right to use public urban space (the *via publica*).[24] This is how he was understood, for example, by Tanner.[25] Soto's claim is not that under the *ius gentium* every person can travel across states, but that there are at least some streets and roads (those which constitute the *via publica*) which the city cannot prevent outsiders from using. Soto is asserting the *ius gentium* rights that subjects (although not only subjects) can exercise even *within* the territory of their own polity.

Jurists of the period carefully examined questions such as: which ways qualify as *via publica*? Can the city or the sovereign prohibit foreigners from using a public way? It was agreed that if anyone could prohibit someone from using a public way, it could only be the sovereign, not the city authorities. However, some jurists, notably the Neapolitan Matteo D'Afflitto (1447–1523), believed that under *ius gentium* even the ruler could not prohibit foreigners from using a public way: he saw such prohibition as uncharitable and iniquitous and, for that reason, not binding in conscience.[26]

There is a significant difference between asking whether outsiders can wander the streets of a city and asking whether they can enter the country. The former question was sometimes discussed in the context of the justice of the imposition of tolls at the city gates (*portazgos*).[27] So these two questions, that of the freedom to use the city and that of access to the

---

[23] Annabel Brett, 'Scholastic Political Thought and the Concept of the State' in Annabel Brett and James Tully (eds.), *Rethinking the Foundations of Modern Political Thought* (Cambridge: Cambridge University Press, 2006) p. 146.

[24] Soto uses 'viae civitatesque', *DCP*, line 70.

[25] Tanner, *Theologiae scholasticae*, d. 2 q. 5 dub. 3 n. 48 at p. 677.

[26] The most important work on the private and public legal aspects of urban life was Bartolomeo Cipolla's (1420–1475) *Tractatus de servitutibus tam urbanorum, quam rusticorum praediorum* (Cologne: Franciscus Metternich, 1701) see p. 285, first edn. 1473–4. The main defender of the view that the prince cannot prohibit outsiders from using the *via publica* was Mattheo D'Afflitto, *Commentaria in feudorum usus et consuetudines absolutissima* (Frankfurt: Clemens Schelchius and Peter de Zetter, 1629) first edn. 1543–7, lib. 3 p. 753 n. 1.

[27] This is indeed the context in which Vitoria considered the *ius gentium* provisions regarding the use of ways. See *Comentarios a la secunda secundae*, q. 63 a. 1 n. 23 at p. 232 where he says that according to Cajetan the fourth reason that may make toll imposition iniquitous is because '[the *portazgo*] is being demanded from non subjects, but the public way has always been free by the *ius gentium* and should not be possessed'. 'quia exiguntur [the *portazgo*] a non subditis, quia via publica semper fuit libera jure gentium et non debet obsideri'.

country, although not unconnected, were usually pursued separately. Clear evidence of this is provided by Molina. Molina is known for his objecting to Vitoria's open border argument and his defence of the right of the realm to exclude foreigners.[28] However, like Soto, he also thought that public ways are by the *ius gentium* open to all, foreigners included, and nobody can be legitimately prohibited from using them without good cause.[29]

It is only natural that, in the context of discussing the street beggars, Soto was more concerned with the right to use the streets rather than the right to travel as such. It is no wonder, therefore, that when Vitoria's claim that the *ius gentium* includes a right to travel was invoked in later debates – for instance, on the justifiability of Chinese isolationist policies – Soto is never mentioned.[30]

Opponents to Soto agreed that public ways (*vias publicas*), like other *loca publica* such as rivers, are open to all, even to foreigners, under the *ius gentium*. What they disagreed about was the danger posed by foreign beggars. As seen below, Soto's opponents considered them to be carriers of disease and sometimes also of heretical beliefs. In their view these considerations justified blocking the foreign poor's use of public spaces.

The second reason Soto gives against excluding the foreign poor is that while those giving charity do not have a duty, except in cases of extreme necessity, to give to a determinate beggar at a determinate time, the beggar retains his right to have his needs met, extreme and not extreme. No law can prevent the poor from going outside their towns without at the same

---

[28] Molina, *De Iustitia et iure* (Cologny [Switzerland]: Marci-Michaelis Bousquet, 1733) vol. 2 d. 105 n. 2. As asserted, for example, by Brett, 'Scholastic Political Thought', p. 146.
[29] Molina, *II*, lib. 3 d. 707 n. 5 at pp. 483–4.
[30] See the fascinating university thesis *China inhospitalis, seu de mutua peregrinandi et commercandi libertate inter gentes, dissertatio historico-politica* by Benedikt Hopffer and Buckhard Bardili (Tubingen: Reisius, 1678) where Chinese refusal to admit travellers is discussed in the light of the theories of *ius gentium* of Grotius, Vitoria, and Molina among others. Note how different is the view of the later scholastics, even those rejecting Soto on the foreign poor, from the view that even peaceful travellers can be denied admission advanced by Jean Bodin: ' the stranger might be driven out of the country not only in time of war (because then we dismiss the ambassadors themselves) but also in time of peace, lest the natural subject manners by the evil company of strangers be corrupted . . . as the East Indians of China forbid their subjects upon pain of death from receiving of strangers . . . Wherefore Cicero well foresaw not what harms hang (as it were) over our heads from strangers, when as he wrote: "They do evil which forbid strangers their cities, and cast them out as our ancestors Pennus [other versions of Cicero *de Officis* have Petronius] and, of late, Pappius . . . "' Jean Bodin, *The Six Books of a Common-Weale . . . out of the French and Latin Copies*, Richard Knolles (ed.) (London: G. Bishop, 1606). lib. 1 c. 6 at p. 76. A good description of Chinese policies towards travellers, based on Matteo Ricci's chronicles, could be found in Adam Contzen, *Politicorum Libri Decem* (Mainz: Ioannes Kinkius, 1621) lib. 7 c. 31 p. 543. The *Lex Papia de peregrinos* was one of a number of Roman laws that expelled foreigners living in Rome.

time compelling the town residents to provide for the town's poor, for otherwise one is forcing the poor to endure necessity. Since there is no law demanding cities to supply for the poor's non-extreme necessity (and Soto would object to such a law on other grounds), the poor remain at liberty to try to find a way to cover these necessities by begging elsewhere.

The third reason, to be developed in more detail in Section 3.5, is that free migration is a way of responding to the great disparities in natural wealth across the regions of the realm and across realms. Allowing the outside poor is a way of discharging the duties of mutual help between the various parts of the political body.

The fourth reason is that not only prosperity varies across regions and realms but also the charitable disposition of the inhabitants. Moreover, Soto notes that the longer a poor person remains in the same place, the fewer alms he will attract, or with time he might become ashamed of begging. Soto's thought here is that it is psychologically easier to beg where nobody knows you. In a passage reminiscent of Medina, Soto adds that there are many other reasons, not directly related to poverty, that may force a person, rich or poor, out of his hometown, such as health requirements or trouble with the law.

Soto's fifth reason against exclusion is the virtue of hospitality demanded by both divine and natural law, which is principally directed at and most perfectly exercised with the foreign poor. To support this, Soto invokes a number of passages from the Old and New Testaments stating that outsiders are owed the same treatment as local residents.

3.5 The Controversy That Wasn't

Soto's discussion of the foreign poor did not pass unnoticed but failed to generate a great amount of discussion among later late scholastics. Theological comments about exclusion of the foreign poor organized themselves into a number of clusters. First there is Soto's *Deliberación* and commentary on it by some contemporary theologians: Juan de Medina, Alfonso de Castro, Martín de Ledesma (†1548) and, later, Vázquez.[31] A second cluster consists of authors who seemed to support or at least excuse the new exclusionary policies. Led by Martin Becanus (1563–1624), it includes Théophile Raynaud (1587–1663), Jacopo Pignatelli

---

[31] Martín de Ledesma, *Secunda quartae* (Coimbra: Juan Álvarez, 1560) q. 15 a. 7 fols. 128b–31a; Alfonso de Castro, *De potestatis leges poenalis*, lib. 1 fols. 23r-v; Juan de Medina, *Codex de eleemosyna*; Vázquez, *De eleemosyna* in *Opuscula Moralia*, cap. 3 dub. 2 at p. 24.

(1625–1698), Juan Egidio Trullench (†1645) and Paul Laymann (1574–1635).[32] A third cluster includes later opponents of the exclusion of the foreign poor such as Pedro de Lorca (1561–1612), Sylvius, de la Bassée, and Diana.[33] Finally, there are the Ingolstadt authors, Valencia, Peltanus and Tanner, the latter two debating the proposed prohibition between themselves.[34]

Here is a short survey of what was I was able to find on Soto's views on the foreign poor. Some moral theologians writing in this period did support Soto. Vázquez agreed with Soto that to beg is a natural right which should not be constrained except for a very serious cause.[35] Pedro de Lorca reiterated some of Soto's arguments and argued that expelling the foreign poor wrongs the poor who cannot for a variety of reasons remain in their hometown.[36]

The great majority of those moral theologians who cared to pronounce on the foreign poor actually disagreed with Soto. The most extensive criticism – but only in relative terms – was produced by Valencia's disciple, Tanner. Valencia himself wrote only a few lines on the foreign poor, but his view is rather open to the permissibility of expelling them. In a work first published in Ingolstadt in 1595,[37] he says that one must take into account the good of the particular community and the circumstances of the particular poor: everything depends on the particulars of the case. Valencia possibly marks the inflexion point towards a more permissive view of the exclusion of the foreign poor in moral theology. He is also the first to think in terms of balancing conflicting interests: the well-being of the foreign poor and that of the city.

In 1606, Tanner pointed out the many perceived dangers of admitting the foreign poor – principally the spread of Protestantism and heresy,

---

[32] Martin Becanus, *de Fide, spe et charitate* (Lyon: Nicolas Gay, 1644) vol. 3 c. 21 at p. 447; Théophile Raynaud, *De virtutibus et vitiis* (Lyon: Horatius Boissat and Georgius Remeus, 1665) lib. 4 sect II c. 5 n. 116 at p. 469; Jacopo Pignatelli, *Consultationes canonicae*, cons. 64 at p. 117; Juan Egidio Trullench, *Operis moralis*, lib. 1. cap. 5 dub. 10 n. 8 at p. 167; Paul Laymann, *Theologia moralis* (Munich: Hendrik Niclaes, 1630) lib. 2 cap. 3 a. 6 n. 3 at p. 220.

[33] Pedro de Lorca, *Commentaria et disputationes in secundam secundae* (Madrid: Luis Sánchez, 1614) sect. 3. d. 37. a. 9 n. 19 at p. 822; Franciscus Sylvius, *In totam primam partem* (Douay: Gerardus Patte, 1649) q. 32 a. 9 q. 3 at p. 205; Eloy de la Bassée, *Flores totius theologiae practicae* (Lyon: Anisson, 1657) p. 27 n. 8; Diana, *Resolutionum moralium, pars quinta* (Lyon: Laurentii Durand, 1639) tract. 8 res. 36 at p. 131.

[34] Valencia, *Commentariorum theologicorum*, d. 3 q. 9 punct. 7 at col. 835; Theodor Peltanus, *De tertia et postrema satisfactionis parte* (Ingolstadt, Weinffenhorn, 1572) ch. 13, p. 84; *De tribus bonorum operum generibus* (Ingolstadt: Weiffenhorn, 1580) lib. 1 c. 9 at pp. 82–90; Tanner, *Theologiae scholasticae*, d. 11 q. 5 dub. 4 at pp. 684–5.

[35] Vázquez, *Opuscula*, cap. 3 dub. 2 n. 6 at p. 24.   [36] Lorca, *Commentaria*, ibid.

[37] Valencia, *Commentariorum*, ibid.

a very important matter in Bavaria, which was then the territorial frontline of the wars of religion. He then proceeds to refute the reasons given by Peltanus in support of the view that the foreign poor ought to be allowed into the city. First, he says that although the poor have a right under the *ius gentium* to use public places, this right ceases when they pose a moral and imminent danger to the republic. Second, as noted in Section 3.3, the effects of expulsion on the poor should be imputed to the hometown (which has failed to support them and/or did not allow them to come back) rather than to the expelling country. Third, says Tanner, every homeland is capable of supporting its own poor, at least insofar as extreme necessities are concerned. Fourth, he rejects an analogy suggested by Peltanus between the wrongful confinement of the domestic poor to their houses and the confinement of the foreign poor to their homelands. Fifth, the precept of hospitality to the foreigner binds only when it does not result in harm to the republic or the republic's own poor. Finally, he interprets the moving passage of Ambrose of Milano, in which he argues against expelling the poor, as referring only to the domestic poor.[38] Although Tanner's arguments are not devoid of interest, these rather cursory refutations are not the sort of material that opens up new avenues for reflection.

Another moral theologian who supported new laws was Martin Becanus, a Jesuit from Brabant. He asked if local authorities who exclude poor travellers (*pauperes preregrinos*) from their cities act rightly. He cites three reasons that may excuse them for doing so. First, there is often not enough to cater to the needs of both foreign and domestic poor, and the order of charity requires giving priority to the latter. Second, travellers may bring disease, bribery, corruption, soliciting, heresy, dissention and betrayals into the city. The alleged deleterious effect of outsiders on the virtues and customs of the citizens and their causing civil unrest was a common theme in Humanist defences of the exclusivist policies of Sparta and Rome (in particular of the *Lex Papia de peregrinos*, which ordered their expulsion from Rome).[39] Lastly, says Becanus, many of the

---

[38] Ambrose of Milano, *De officiis*, Ivor J. Davidson (ed. and trans.) (Oxford: Oxford University Press, 2011) lib. 3 c. 7 n. 45 at p. 382.

[39] See, for example, Fernando Pizarro, *Varones ilustres del nuevo mundo* (Madrid: Diego Díaz de las Carreras, 1639) *observación* 8 at p. 25 where he says that the foreigners brought about the demise of Rome by destroying the moderation and fortitude of Roman citizens (and so recommends not allowing foreigners in the Indies); and extensively Pedro Gonzales de Salcedo, *De lege politica* (Madrid: Jose Fernández del Buendía, 1678) lib. 2 c. 15, n. 29–46 at pp. 756–9. Paradoxically, no less a Stoic than Justus Lipsius is against the manumission of foreigners, which the *Lex Papia* intended to deal with, *Roma Illustrata* (Amsterdam: Elzeciriana, 1657) p. 249.

foreign beggars are capable of working. Being allowed to beg in the city encourages idleness; excluding them forces them to work, which is more honest. However, Becanus did not go through the trouble of disproving Soto's reasons. Most other opponents of Soto's views on the foreign poor did little more than repeat Becanus's view.

Most of the moral theologians listed devoted only a few lines to the matter of the foreign poor. It is to be noticed also that many of the leading moral theologians of their time, such as Suárez, Molina, Covarrubias and Navarrus, are missing from the list. This is all the more surprising given that many theologians, such as Suárez, would write treatises on *eleemosyna* (almsgiving), which could be seen to present the perfect occasion to discuss the new poor laws.

How should we explain the shift from rejection to endorsement of the new poor policies by late scholastic moral theologians? A partial conjectural explanation may have to do with the geographical location of the theologians who commented on these policies. As we have seen, the most vocal support for the new policies came from Catholic Germany. The poor laws of Bavaria underwent major revisions in 1551 and 1599, and included the expulsion of the foreign poor.[40] Here the Jesuits, the only functioning religious order in Bavaria and Catholic Germany, were much closer to the seat of power than they were in Spain. For example, Becanus was the confessor of Ferdinand II in Vienna, who was taught by Tanner at Ingolstadt. At the same university, Valencia taught Duke Maximilian of Bavaria, whose confessor was Adam Contzen (1575–1635), author of *Politicorum libri decem,* and whose preacher was Jeremias Drexel (1581–1638), author of the *Gazophylacium Christi eleemosyna* (all of these religious were Jesuits).[41] In addition, there was the fact, much stressed by Tanner, that allowing the foreign poor in presented a greater danger of spreading Protestantism in these border areas than in Spain where Protestantism struggled to make any significant inroads. This may account

---

[40] The texts of these ordinances can be found in Elisabeth Schepers, *Als der Bettel in Bayern abgeschafft werden sollte* (Regensburg: Friedrich Pustet, 2000). For the 1599 strictures on the foreign poor, see p. 240.

[41] On Contzen, see Robert Bireley, *Maximilian von Bayern, Adam Contzen S. J. und die Gegenreformation in Deutschland 1624–1635* (Göttingen: Vandenhoeck und Ruprecht, 1975). Jeremias Drexel, *Gazophylacium Christi eleemosyna* (Monaco: Widow of Ioannes Cnobbarus, 1651). Drexel himself did not seem to support the exclusion of foreign beggars and the restrictions to private almsgiving. On him, see Italo Michele Battafarano, 'Armenfürsorge bei Albertinus und Drexel. Ein sozialpolitisches Thema im erbaulichen Traktat zweier Schriftsteller des Münchner Hofes', *Zeitschrift für Bayerische Landesgeschichte* 47(1984)141–80.

for the fact that it is in Catholic Germany that we find the least sympathy for Soto's criticism of poor law reforms (with the exception of Peltanus).[42]

Today we may find the theological support for these new poor policies disturbing. But even more disappointing is the fact that these later theologians failed to engage authors of the stature of Medina, Soto, Ledesma and Castro. Perhaps the reason they failed to engage these theologians in a point-per-point argument is because they may have thought that Soto and his supporters were simply missing the big picture, or were using the wrong tools to analyse new phenomena. Soto conceived of the poor as unfortunate individuals who retained their status as equal under the law, rather than collectively, as seen by the later theologians, as a threatening aggregate. The later moral theologians may also have thought that the need for new legislation was evident to almost everyone around them, making it largely unnecessary to refute Soto.

At some point, Soto's argument may have come to be considered not so much as mistaken but as outdated. Sometimes philosophical views are pushed aside not because they have been refuted philosophically but because changes in social perceptions render them old-fashioned. Given the above, it makes more sense to concentrate on Soto than to chase after a controversy that wasn't.

3.6 Incorporating the Poor: The Limits of the Body Metaphor

In chapter 4 of his *Deliberación*, Soto makes ample use of the metaphor of the community as a body. His intention is to make the point that internal barriers within the social body impede the discharge of reciprocal duties of assistance by making the people to whom assistance is due physically unavailable to receive it. However, in order for this point to have any purchase, he must first show that the poor are part of this social body. So Soto's main purpose is to incorporate the non-working poor into the social body, that is, to turn the purportedly foreign poor into 'our poor' under a sufficiently capacious expansion of 'us'. For him, every poor person, in some capacity (as fellow Spaniard, as fellow Christian, as human being), is a member of a relevant social body to which the wealthy also belong.

Let us examine Soto's body argument. Soto starts by noting that all agree that within the city the rich must help the poor and that within bishoprics

---

[42] On this see Robert Bireley, *The Jesuits and the Thirty Year War* (Cambridge: Cambridge University Press, 2003) pp. 267–9 and his *Ferdinand II: Counter-Reformation Emperor, 1578–1637* (New York: Cambridge University Press, 2014) p. 16.

rich localities should help poor localities. Cities and bishoprics are political bodies. But so is the kingdom, of which cities and bishoprics are but parts or members (*membra*). This, coupled with the fact of inter-regional differences in soil fertility, seems to establish the need for inter-local assistance so that rich bishoprics can give alms to the beggars of poor bishoprics and rich localities can help poor localities by opening their gates. In doing so, rich localities are able to give what they owe to the social body.

The second step of the argument begins with Soto invoking St Paul's view that all Christians belong to a body (the 'mystical body'), which allows him to say that rich Christian republics have duties of assistance towards poor Christian republics.

To flesh out the idea of the Christian social body, Soto evokes the Greek fable of the blind man directed by a cripple whom he carries on his shoulders. This image features as an illustration of *mutuum auxilium* ('mutual help') in Alciatus's famous and constantly republished *Book of Moral Emblems*, containing illustrative engravings of a great number of moral maxims, which Soto may have seen.[43] The functional complementarity between the blind man and the crippled man allows us to consider them a unity, a functional body. Soto then applies the Greek fable to the allocation of functions within Christendom. In the Latin text, he argues that the wise should be like the eyes of the ignorant. The robust and strong in body should be like the arms and legs of the weak. However, the Spanish version differs: he writes that *those who can work* should be the arms and legs of *those who understand about political rule and the worship of God*. In both versions the rich are said to be like the stomach. As the stomach extracts nutrients and feeds them to the parts of the body, so do the rich with the poor. By making themselves unapproachable to the foreign poor, the rich fail to perform their social nutritive function. Selective internal barriers within the social body (however its boundaries are drawn) may be a means devised by the rich to deny the poor access to assistance.

In the Latin version of Soto's book (but interestingly not in the Spanish one, which, according to the San Esteban editor, was based on the Latin), an attempt is made to expand this community beyond the boundaries of Christianity by invoking the innate human social disposition towards bonds with all other human beings, even infidels. In a passage evoking the Stoic idea of a cosmopolis, Soto writes, 'But if things are related to natural law, the human species is by its own nature connected by such

---

[43] Andrea Alciatus, *Emblematum Liber* (Augsburg: Heyrich Steyner, 1531), *mutuum auxilium* (unpaginated princeps edition).

a tight bond that, unless others are our enemies, or we fear from them some damage to our faith, it is not allowed to exclude mendicant infidels from our republic'.[44] As Brett points out, the likely reason this text did not make it into the Spanish version is that it may have been thought of as too highbrow an argument for the court.[45]

This second step of the body argument presents a difficulty. Soto uses the body metaphor to introduce two relations of complementarity: one between wise rulers/priests (represented by the eyes) and the ignorant but able-bodied (represented by hands and arms); the other, between the wealthy and the non-working poor, is left unelaborated. The rich are compared to the stomach of the non-working poor. However, it is unclear how the non-working poor supplement a deficiency that affects the rich or what organ represents their function.

Analogies between functional parts of the body and classes of citizens had a long tradition in medieval political thought. For many medieval authors, the poor were considered to be like the feet and the arms: those who manufacture goods and work the land. In such usages, 'poor' clearly refers to only the able-bodied poor.[46] A similar metaphor comparing the poor with the feet is exploited by Luis Vives, who is mostly concerned with the non-working poor. However, Vives depicts them more as an internal threat than as a functional part of the body.[47]

Soto relies on body metaphor in the closing remarks of his *Deliberación*, where he refers to the dream of the prophet Daniel (Daniel 2:33) of a statue with a golden head, a silver torso, and feet made of metal (iron or copper) and clay. Once the clay was crushed with a stone, the rest of the statue – the gold, bronze and metal – fell apart and the statue disintegrated. In line with Del Toro's use of the same scriptural passage in his *Tesoro de la Misericordia Divina y Humana* (1536), Soto suggests that the poor are like feet of clay sustaining the republic by virtue of the merit befalling those who give them alms, and warns the Spanish king that the upper classes (the gold and silver head and torso) may disintegrate like the statue should the poor (the clay feet) be removed.

In drawing this analogy, Soto is availing himself of a tradition, which he knew and shared, that stresses that the poor benefit the rich by providing an example of humility and an occasion for good deeds. This is a *topos* amply found in the homilies of the Greek Father John Chrysostom and

---

[44] Soto, *DCP*, p. 241 at lines 165–89.   [45] Brett, *Changes of State*, p. 30 ftn. 76.
[46] See for example Alexio Venegas, *Primera parte de las differencias de libros que hay en el universo* (Madrid: Alonso Gómez, 1569) fol. 154v.
[47] Vives, *De Subventione*, lib. 2 n. 1 lines 5–10 at p. 88.

often quoted in late scholastic discussions on almsgiving. Chrysostom said, 'God did not ordain the giving of alms only in order that the poor might be fed, but also that blessings might be added to the givers, and even more for the sake of the latter than of the former.'[48]

It is intriguing why Soto, when attempting to draw some sort of complementarity between rich and poor, failed to make clear the contribution of the non-working poor to the rich. It seems that Soto struggled to assign the non-working poor a bodily organ which would correlate to their social or moral function. Soto had already allocated the arms and feet to 'those capable of working' (Spanish version) and 'those of robust and strong body' (Latin version).

Soto's inability to assign a metaphorical organic function to the non-working poor may seem like merely a minor dialectic flaw, but given that Soto's main purpose in the argument under discussion was to incorporate the non-working poor into the social body, it is interesting that the body metaphor turned out to be an unsuitable vehicle of incorporation.

3.7 Unfairness in the Allocation of Moral Burdens: Soto and Castro

Soto's aim in using the body metaphor was to incorporate foreign beggars into the social body, essentially making them non-foreign. According to Soto, since belonging to the social body imposes a reciprocity of obligations between its constitutive classes, all the rich have a collective *duty* as a class (*estado*) to take care of all the poor within the relevant social body.

If this is the case, then the stage is set for questions concerning the justice of the allocation of the burden of poor relief (for all of the poor) *among the rich*.

For Soto, the fact that the charitable spirit of the locals, like the fertility of the soil, varies from region to region means that indigenous poverty will also vary greatly from place from place. This heterogeneous territorial dispersal of indigenous poverty results in a heterogeneous distribution of the moral duty of assistance. This fact presented two different consequences: (1) the poor living in places with a low rich/poor ratio will get

---

[48] Soto could have used the first Latin translation of John Chrysostom, *Sermo de Eleemosyna*, Johannes Oecolampadius [Johannes Huszgen] (trans.) (Mainz: Schöffer, 1522). In the English translation by Margaret M. Sherwood from Migne, *Patrologia Graeca* 51, pp. 269–70: 'But to what extent do they seek to deceive you? They are fugitives, they say, strangers, worthless creatures, who have left their native land and are gathering in our city. Do you resent this, tell me, and do you pluck the crown of honor from your city, because all men consider it a common refuge, and prefer it to their own land?' in John Chrysostom, *Sermon on Alms*, Margaret M. Sherwood (trans.) (New York: New York School of Philanthropy, 1917).

little or no assistance, (2) the rich in these places will be under much more demanding moral duties than the rich living away from the poor. This was the subject tackled by the Franciscan Alfonso de Castro.

Castro, who was followed by Ledesma, was not interested in the question of the poor per se.[49] Rather his engagement with this question is embedded within a larger discussion on the requirements of just law and, in particular, on just taxation. As seen in the previous chapter, Castro's views on the burdens imposed by law were standardly cited by most other authors, such as Suárez, when examining the justice of taxation. However, none of them stopped to consider Castro's application of his view to the new poor laws.

Following the lead of Aquinas, Castro argued that the burden imposed by law should be proportionally distributed among the subjects. A law that promotes the common good but places most of the onus on one sector of the population is unjust. The poor ordinances legislated in different 'provinces of the Christian world not many years ago' constitute one of the two examples that he gives of laws that impose an unfair distribution of the burden.[50] The laws prohibiting the migration of the poor from city to city and obliging each city to support its own poor are unjust. There are small cities which contain many poor and large cities which contain few of them. So you could have a situation 'in which a hundred wealthy citizens of one city must support five hundred poor, whereas five hundred wealthy citizens of another city must support not even hundred poor.'[51] This involves injustice in the distribution of the burden of poor relief to the rich.

Castro believed that allowing the free movement of the poor would more evenly distribute the burden of charity. The thought is that the poor will naturally tend to disperse in such a way that each wealthy person would have roughly the same number of needy persons to support.

Castro's argument is built on the premise, defended by Soto, that the poor are part of the social body and so are everybody's problem. We should not speak in terms of the poor of Toledo or the poor of Zamora but, rather, of the poor of Spain or even the poor of Christendom. Just as a tax levied to fund a war that is for the benefit of the common good should be imposed fairly on all, so should the relief of poverty.

Castro's is not an argument about the burdens directly created by law. Rather, by controlling the location of the poor, the state is distributing the *moral* burdens that apply to its wealthier citizens. The law confining the

---

[49] Ledesma, *Secunda quartae*, 130r, 131r. [50] Castro, *De potestate*, lib. 1 fol. 23r-v. [51] Ibid.

poor to their hometown creates over-demanding and unfair *moral* burdens for some citizens. The primary victims of this unjust law, in Castro's argument, are not so much the poor as the wealthy living in poor towns. The spatial segregation of poor and rich impose excessive and distributively unfair moral burdens on the rich in poverty-ridden areas. The town poor will also suffer, but what they suffer from is not distributive injustice (the poor do not have a proper right to charity, though they have a right to beg and to try to find any legitimate means available to cover their needs).

Note that, for Castro, the need to have a fair distribution of moral obligations is even stronger than the need for a fair distribution of the fiscal burden. If the burden of a tax or levy is very unfairly distributed, it is not implausible to say that some taxpayers may not have a duty of conscience to pay that tax. However, in the case of moral duties, it is hard to say that the unfair distribution of the burden relieves moral agents of their duties. Consider this example: it may be unfair that of two equally sized and equipped public hospitals one receives twice as many patients than the other. But the doctors of the first overburdened hospital are duty-bound to provide medical assistance to the patients. The unfairness in the distribution of the sick does not relieve them of their moral duty.

3.8 Summary

Mass migration of the rural poor to the cities brought with it a wave of poor law reforms. Medina, Soto, Castro, Ledesma and others opposed these reforms. Some of their arguments were better than others. However, neither in the treatments on the virtue of almsgiving nor in treatments concerning the formal justice of laws – two contexts which invited discussion of poor law reform – do we see consistent late scholastic engagement with their views.

This not to say that there was not criticism and opposition to Medina, Soto, Castro, and Ledesma, but, as a rule, their arguments were not subject to the elaborate discussion that they deserved. I have conjectured that this lack of engagement had to do with a shift in the outlook on the poor, which caused Soto's arguments to be perceived not so much as mistaken as outdated and irrelevant. This was the shift from looking at the poor as individual persons, equal to others under the rule of law, to seeing them as an aggregate class with generalizable attributes.

The arguments of Soto and Castro that were not engaged with by their contemporaries are worth examining. Soto's main strategy was to incorporate the foreign poor into the social body by exploiting the body metaphor.

In doing this he exposed the shortcomings of the body metaphor when it comes to incorporating the non-working poor.

If, as Soto claims, the foreign poor are in fact our poor under an expansive notion of 'our', poor relief becomes a common good. This in turn presented the question of the fair distribution of the duty to relieve the poor. Castro convincingly argued that the new reforms distribute this moral burden unfairly.

Taking a step back from the argumentative contents of the debate over the poor, what emerges is that at some point between Soto and Tanner, the late scholastics began to narrow their understanding of the scope of 'public' in 'the public good'. For Soto, the 'public' was extendable to that which concerns all of the kingdom, or all Christian nations, or even all of humankind. For Tanner, the 'public' relevant to the discussion of the poor was merely the Duchy of Bavaria, and the foreign poor was 'not our problem'. Once the foreign poor are removed from the public then it makes sense to see their well-being as conflicting with the public good. The outside poor are members of a different public than that of the city, and it is this other public to which they should address their moral complaints.

CHAPTER 4

The Political Duty to Keep Your Secrets

4.1 Introduction

Very few people are morally impeccable. If our lives were entirely transparent to others it is very likely that our reputation would suffer considerably and many of our attachments and relationships to others would be harmed or even dissolve.

Soto compellingly made this point in his *Relection on the Hiding and Disclosure of Secrets*, a series of lectures given at Salamanca in the academic year 1540–1541.[1] By 'secrets' Soto does not mean primarily information conveyed to others under the explicit or tacit promise that it will not be divulged. This is only a very special class of secrets. Rather, 'secret' features here as opposed to 'public'; secret is that which is, and should remain, unknown to others.[2] Soto's seminal *Relection* was partly a reaction to Cajetan's *Commentary* on Aquinas's *Summa Theologiae* on the sin of detraction – the intentional lessening of someone's good name – in his treatise on *Justice*.[3]

Soto's engagement motivated other late scholastics to approach the subject as well. Notable among the later contributors to the discussion of secrets were Navarrus, Córdoba, Aragón, Hurtado, Lessius, Molina and Lugo.[4] The latter two wrote particularly comprehensive treatises on the

---

[1] Domingo de Soto, *De ratione tegendi et detegendum secretum* in *Relecciones y Opúsculos*, Antonio Osuna Fernández-Lago trans. Vol. 2-I (Salamanca: San Esteban, 2000). Soto reiterates his approach to detraction in *II*, lib. 5 q. 10.
[2] Soto, *DRTDS*, membr. 1. q. 1 at p. 189.   [3] Cajetan, *in ST II-II*, q. 73 a. 3 pp. 133–9.
[4] Navarrus, *Manual*, c. 18 n. 52–62 at pp. 334–43; Córdoba, *Libellus de Detractione et famae restitutione: cum annotationibus eiusdem in tractatum de Secreto magistri Soto Ordinis Praedicatorum* (Alcalá: Juan de Brocar, 1553); Aragón, *In ST II-II*, q. 62, Lugo, *II* (Lyon: Inheritors of Petrus Prost, Phillippus Borde and Laurentius Arnaud, 1646) d. 14 at pp. 351–400; Lessius, *II*, (Leuven: Ioannes Masus, 1605) lib. 2 c. 11 at pp. 107–124; Molina, II, lib. 4 tract. 4 d. 1-d. 51 at pp. 371–504; Tomás Hurtado, *Resolutiones orthodoxo-morales, scholasticae, historicae de vero, unico, proprio & Catholico Martyrio Fidei* (Cologne: Cornelius de Egmond, 1655) dub. 5 pp. 169–83.

matter of secrets, honour, and reputation; in the case of Molina, ranging to fifty-one distinctions distributed across 233 densely printed pages.

The importance given to the subject of reputation and honour by the late scholastics is not surprising when we consider the social centrality of having a good name and honour in sixteenth-century Spain as in all of Mediterranean Europe.[5]

However, the interest of the insights of these theologians on the issue of the disclosure of our private lives goes beyond their historical circumstance. Private individuals, judicial officers and the executive branch of the state collect potentially damaging information about our private lives. This information can then be transmitted to others. These others may be willing or tolerant recipients of it. Who among these information gatherers, communicators and receptors are acting permissibly or at least excusably? Among the questions that the late scholastics discussed we find: Is it ever permissible to open letters or to read letters that have been torn up and thrown away? Is it permissible to make anonymous denunciations? Is the person listening to defamatory comments complicit in the defamation? How can reputation be restituted once lost?[6] They also discussed the different kinds of secrets and ranked them according to the gravity of their disclosure (confessional secrets being on top of the list).

In this chapter, I shall focus on the fundamental issue of the wrongness of defamation. When we defame a person, do we violate her property rights over her reputation? If this is the case, a person has the right to defame herself at least when it is rational for her to do so, for instance, in the case discussed by the late scholastics, to avoid torture. While the property theory of reputation was the most popular among the late scholastics, some authors disagreed and argued that one has a duty to one's community to protect one's good name. By self-defaming, even for a weighty reason, you wrong your community. I shall try to gauge if there is any plausibility to this intriguing position.

---

[5] See Jeffrey A. Bowman, 'Infamy and Proof in Medieval Spain' in Thelma Fenster and Daniel Lord Smail (eds.), *Fama: The Politics of Talk and Reputation in Medieval Europe* (Ithaca and London: Cornell University Press, 2003), pp. 95–117; and Scott K. Taylor, *Honor and Violence in Golden Age Spain* (New Haven and London: Yale University Press, 2008). Also Francesco Migliorino, *Fama e infamia: problemi della società medievale nel pensiero giuridico nei secoli XII e XIII* (Catania: Gianotta, 1985); Julien Théry, 'Fama: l'opinion publique comme preuve judiciaire. Aperçu sur la révolution médiévale de l'inquisitoire (xiie-xive)' in Bruno Lemesle (ed.), *La prevue en justice: de l'Antiquité à nos jours* (Rennes: Presses Universitaires de Rennes, 2003) pp. 119–47; and the extremely helpful John Morgan Livingston, *Infamia in the Decretists from Rufinus to Johannes Teutonicus* (University of Wisconsin, Doctoral dissertation, 1961) (available online).

[6] In Molina, these are discussed in *II*, lib. 4 tract. 4 d. 36, d. 34, dd. 42–51.

Before I do so, I start by explaining Soto's account of the social need for secrecy or privacy and the moral characterization of the acts that destroy them.

4.2 Personal Opacity as a Social Need

In explaining why, as a matter of natural reason, it is fitting that some of our wrongful deeds be excluded from public view, and so remain secret, Soto gives four reasons.

The first reason is that 'virtues are on their own worthy of publicity and sins of being hidden'. He draws a parallel with aesthetics: 'nature itself determined that what is ugly in us be covered while, by contrast, the face is uncovered'. Therefore it is against nature to disclose the crimes [of others] except when this is necessary to correct them.[7] Note that 'crimes' is used here in the general sense of grave sins, rather than specifically as criminal offences.[8] This opacity is for Soto a condition for being socially attractive and lovable. In a remarkable passage Soto says:

> friendship, which is so necessary to all of us, would not exist if the evils in the heart of men were not hidden. Because if all the evils that you keep secret were known to all, nobody would love you, and if you knew the bad thoughts of others, you would not love them. In truth we have been very fortunate that God and nature willed that what is evil be hidden, so that, for this reason, the friendship between men could take place.[9]

The second reason not to reveal secrets is to avoid bringing infamy. Harming reputation violates the general principle of justice of not doing to others what you do not want to be done unto you.

Thirdly, without secrets we would not be able to take counsel from others, and also would deny ourselves the relief of being able to open up and unburden ourselves of our anxieties and sorrows and the many other benefits provided by friendship. In the absence of an obligation to keep secrets, the fear that our hearer will disclose our secrets will deter us from sincere and candid communication and from friendship in general.

Soto's final point is that if the secrets of others were made public it would bring disorder and eventually ruin to the republic. Soto does not

---

[7] Molina, *II*, lib. 1, d. 3.
[8] See 'Crímen' in Sebastian Covarrubias Orozco, *Tesoro de la Lengua castellana o Española* (Madrid: Luis Sánchez, 1611) p. 247v.
[9] Soto, *DRTDS*, membr. 1. q. 2 at p. 201.

explain exactly why this would happen but one can imagine a number of things that would follow from a massive revelation of secrets: private acts of violence such as vendettas and reprisals, political scandal and consequent distrust in the government and contempt for state institutions, and generally a social climate of cynicism.

Soto presents these arguments as independent of each other. In particular, the argument about not harming reputation is independent from the arguments about secrecy or confidentiality as a condition of interpersonal love and friendship and its benefits and as a condition of social and political order. The former is an argument mainly about wronging other persons rather than about not wronging society by eroding the conditions of friendship and peace.

4.3 The Value of Reputation

Reputation (*fama*) was considered to occupy an intermediate place in the ranking of goods. Its volatility and precariousness prevents it from being among the components of happiness. In Aristotle's conception, human happiness must be to the greatest possible extent insulated from contingency and fortune. At the same time, reputation was deemed more valuable than material external goods, such as money, and only marginally less valuable than one's life and body.[10]

Most late scholastics believed that, as with money, we own our reputation because it is the product of our own industry (unlike life, which is given and thus unowned by us). However, reputation is in some ways unlike other external goods. Unlike money, we cannot physically possess it, but it always resides in others' minds. More importantly, as Valencia points out, reputation is of crucial moral importance as a stimulus to virtue. If we have a good reputation we have an incentive to continue acting well. Once our good name is lost there is less to lose by acting wrongly.[11] Money does not perform this moral role.

Most authors addressed defamation under the rubric of commutative justice within their treatises *de Iustitia et Iure*. This means that when they

---

[10] In this chapter, I focus on reputation (*fama*) rather than honour (*honor*). These were held to differ in some important respects by the late scholastics. For example, in the type of actions that typically diminish them (*fama* was held to be typically harmed by detraction, whereas *honor* was held to be typically harmed by insult) and in the type of justice overseeing them: distributive justice in the case of honour or commutative justice in the case of *fama*. See discussion in James Gordley, *Foundations of Private Law: Property, Tort, Contract, Unjust Enrichment* (Oxford: Oxford University Press, 2006) p. 220.

[11] Valencia, *Commentariorum*, d. 5 q. 17, punct. 2 at cols. 1453B.

approached the subject they were mainly concerned with reputation as *dominium* (here in the sense of property). As a consequence, given the context, they were mainly interested in the sin called 'detraction', conceived of as a violation of ownership rights and in the restitutive means available when detraction occurs.

'Detraction' was understood as the sinful act of 'stealing away' all or some of your reputation. Note that, as Aquinas clearly puts it, it is considered irrelevant to the sinfulness of detraction whether the allegations against you are true or false.[12] Truth is not what is at stake, but reputation. So even if it is true, say, that an otherwise respectable politician has a secret drinking problem, making it public constitutes detraction. Common Law countries have allowed truth as a defence against charges of defamation for the last two hundred years or so. I can defend myself from charges of defamation by showing the truth of my allegation. But even in Common Law countries truth alone may not be enough. One may have to show in addition that there is some public utility in the disclosure and that the intent is not malicious. Still, some types of defamation, such as 'seditious libel', that is defamation of the monarch or other authorities, are immune to the truth defence. Denigrating the monarch or the House of Parliament, whether on the basis of true or false claims, with its consequent loss of respect for the sovereign, is deemed of deleterious political and social consequence. In many Civil Law countries, exceptions apart, the judicial process concerning accusations of defamation does not give the defendant the opportunity to defend himself by either showing the truth or the notoriety of his allegedly defamatory statements.[13]

4.4 The Problem of Self-Defamation Under Torture

One question that occupied all of the late scholastic authors who discussed the disclosure of personal secrets was that of the burden that one should be morally prepared to take upon oneself in order to avoid lessening someone's good name by making such disclosures. Often the question was posed in terms of whether it is permissible to commit defamation in order to put an end to torture. Judicial torture was part of the Romano-

---

[12] *ST II-II* q. 73 a. 1 ad 3. On Aquinas on detraction, see Gordley, *Foundations of Private Law*, p. 219.
[13] It is worth pointing out, however, that the *Siete Partidas* admits truth as defence. *Las Siete Partidas del Rey Don Alfonso el Sabio* (Madrid: Imprenta Real, 1807) Partida VII, Título VI, Ley VIII. On the 'truth-defence' in civil law systems as opposed to common law systems, see Gordley, *Foundations of Private Law*, 218.

canonical criminal procedure developed in the twelfth and thirteenth century. Its purpose was to exact confessions in cases of serious crimes when other conclusive proofs, such as reliable witnesses, were unavailable.[14]

The most effective way of putting an end to torture was to provide a detailed, reliable confession. To confess to a hitherto publicly unknown crime of yours is to defame yourself. Is doing this permissible? Modern audiences may take this question to refer only to the case of an innocent falsely self-incriminating or incriminating another innocent to put an end to pain. Remember, however, that defamation is a wrong even when what is revealed is true. For what constitutes defamation is simply the lessening of the good name of a person. Therefore, some of the late scholastics considered it also morally problematic to defame by making public true crimes committed by yourself or others.

Readers may consider it strange to discuss the moral duties of victims of torture given that this appears to be the ultimate case of duress. Two things are worth noting. First, torture comes in many different forms (the most frequent form in Spain at the time was the dreaded *potro* or rack) and levels of pain. Each individual has different degrees of resistance to physical and psychological pain and so it might be a false generalization to say that we lack any responsibility for anything we say under torture. Second, it is important to know whether self-incrimination or self-defamation is an excusable wrong or is no wrong at all, and, if it is a wrong, what its gravity is. Morally conscientious persons facing prospective torture might be ready to carry out wrongs of some gravity to stop the torture but not those that are morally inexcusable, so it would be important to them to know exactly how grave self-defamation is.

The question of self-defamation under torture led directly to the basic question of our moral relationship to our reputation. If one's reputation is one's property, just as money is, one is permitted to use it or squander it as one pleases. I am allowed to defame myself not only to avoid torture but even as a matter of whim (we are assuming here that the confession is true). By contrast, if I owe it to somebody other than myself as matter of justice to protect my good name, I should not easily defame myself. Considerable suffering and loss would be necessary to excuse the violation of a duty of justice.

---

[14] The best book on this is Piero Fiorelli, *La tortura giudiziaria nel diritto commune* (Varese: Giuffré, 1953) 2 vols.

4.5 Cajetan on Reputation and Community

This second view was that of Cardinal Cajetan. He poses the question of self-defamation under threat of torture and rejects the reply that just as a man can give away his money to avoid torture so he can give away his reputation. His view is that the wrong of destroying one's own name is analogous to the wrong of suicide.[15] Suicide violates the order of charity, which requires one to love oneself (and to love oneself more than other human beings). In accordance to the order of charity, to defame yourself is morally worse than to defame others.[16] According to Aquinas, the person who commits suicide wrongs his community by depriving it of a part of it – himself. This is why the suicidal is denied burial. Cajetan says something similar about the person who destroys not his life, but his good name. In the case of self-defamation, as in the case of suicide, the appropriate community (the Church or the State) is owed restitution by the self-defamer, for the community is the victim of a wrong against justice. The self-defamer must restore to himself his reputation.[17]

It follows, says Cajetan, that self-defamation is a moral sin *ex genere* (that is, in itself, considered apart from its effects), and so it cannot be excused as a way to avoid torture. Otherwise, other acts that are morally wrong in themselves such as fornicating or lying could also be done to avoid torture.

Cajetan makes a number of related points that would be taken up by later defenders of his view. First, he notes one key difference between damaging one's reputation and wasting one's money. To hand out money is to deprive oneself of money, whereas to defame yourself is not merely to deprive yourself of reputation, but to destroy it.[18]

Second, although life is more precious than reputation, sometimes one should go to greater lengths to protect one's reputation by not defaming oneself than to protect one's bodily health. The reason is that, in general, damage to health is a passive thing (it is something that happens to you or is allowed to happen by you), whereas to defame yourself is an active malfeasance (*malefacere*).[19]

Third, Cajetan calls attention to a canon that says that self-defamation extorted by torture does not produce judicial infamy.[20] This seems to allow self-defamation under torture. This canon is surprising, given that, as noted, torture was an integral part of the Romano-canonical criminal process. No less surprisingly, it was also a procedural principle that fear

---

[15] Cajetan, *In ST II-II* q. 73 a. 3 V at p. 135. Also in Cajetan, *Peccatorum summula*, 'detractio' n. 4 at p. 112.
[16] Ibid.   [17] Cajetan, *In ST II-II* q. 73 a. 3 V at p. 135.   [18] Ibid.   [19] Ibid.   [20] Ibid.

(or 'terror') invalidates confession. In practice, this meant that the tortured suspect had to be allowed to rest and recover from torture after his confession. He would then be requested to confirm the confession given under torture. A confirmed extorted confession would, according to most jurists, have the same validity as a spontaneous confession.[21]

Cajetan replied that even in those cases in which the confession given under fear of torture lacks judicial validity (while unconfirmed), *moral* self-defamation still occurs. The confession belongs to the class of acts termed by Aristotle of a mixed voluntary nature, such as in his famous example of throwing the cargo overboard in a storm to save the boat.[22] Insofar as the disclosure under torture is not entirely involuntary it is susceptible to moral evaluation.

Let us give a preliminary assessment of Cajetan's view. First, it is difficult to make sense of Cajetan's analogy between the wrong of destroying your life and the wrong of destroying your reputation. The former wrong might be explained by reference to the community's need of members: by killing yourself you deprive your community of a potential or actual soldier, taxpayer or wage-earner of a family the sustenance of which will now fall upon all the community. You might also be depriving your community of your virtues, individual talents and your contribution to public debate. Moreover, in harsh times, suicide may instil hopelessness and defeatism in others. In the case of the self-destruction of reputation, however, it is not as easy to identify the harm caused to the community. Suppose that a private individual discloses a past adulterous act. In what sense can I, as a member of the community, say that the destruction of his reputation has damaged me? In what sense can we say that the society's member's reputation is a common asset?

Aragón took Cajetan's point to be that by defaming oneself one brings disrepute to the entire community.[23] This seems to be correct in the case of public figures and state representatives, such as ambassadors. But, as Soto noted, it is hard to see how this could be true of self-disclosure by private individuals in any significant way.[24]

There is a more satisfactory explanation of Cajetan's parallel with suicide. In many places in medieval Europe, to be infamous disqualified you from a number of civic offices and in general from public life. Under the *Siete Partidas*, the greatly influential Castilian legal code, the infamous (*enfamados*) and those of bad reputation (of *mala fama*) could not serve as witnesses in trials, nor could they be appointed to many political, judicial

---

[21] See Fiorelli, *La tortura*, vol. 2 pp. 104–106. [22] Cajetan, *In ST II-II* q. 73 a. 3 V at p. 135.
[23] Aragón, *In ST II-II*, q. 62 n. 3 at p. 102. [24] Soto, *II*, lib. 4. q. 6 a. 3 at p. 345.

and ecclesiastical posts requiring a dignified status.[25] The condition of infamy was incurred by engaging in a certain occupations or conditions, which were well defined, such as jesters, usurers and widows contracting marriage before one year after the husband's decease. This historical fact lends a modicum of plausibility to Cajetan's point. By defaming himself and making himself ineligible, the citizen deprives the community of his potential contribution to the running and governing of the community.[26] One example that was sometimes mentioned by the late scholastics, although not exactly in this regard, was that of St Ambrose, who 'publicly had women of the street brought to his house' with the purpose of avoiding being appointed bishop.[27]

4.6 The Property Account of Reputation: Soto and Molina

Soto had a very different view of self-defamation. For him, self-defamation cannot be an act of injustice since it is impossible to do injustice to yourself. Self-defamation has no other direct victim than yourself. Since justice, as Aristotle said, always concerns our relation to another person, self-defamation as such is not injustice. Rather, it may perhaps be only a violation of one's duty of charity by which we are obliged to love ourselves and what we own. Therefore, self-defamation is not a mortal sin but at most a venial one.[28]

Soto has an easy job of producing arguments against treating self-defamation as necessarily morally wrong. I shall present them in a compressed fashion here.

For one, Soto points out that self-defamation need not violate duties of charity: it does not harm others, nor does it harm oneself in the respect relevant to charity. Charity concerns primarily spiritual and moral goods, such as virtue. It concerns external goods, such as reputation, only to the extent that these are necessary for virtue or salvation. I may destroy my reputation without thereby harming my virtue or my character. Therefore, just as spending or giving away my money is not a sin when it does no harm, say, to my dependents, so it is also not a sin to squander my reputation, as long as it does no harm to others to do so.[29]

---

[25] *Siete Partidas*, Partida VII, Título VI, Ley VII. [26] See Bowman, p. 103.
[27] Jacobus de Voragine, *Historia de Sancto Ambrosio*, in *The Golden Legend: Readings on the Saints*, William Granger Ryan (trans.) (New Jersey: Princeton University Press, 2012) p. 230. The story is from Soto', *DRTDS*, membr. 1. q. 3 at p. 231.
[28] Soto, *DRTDS*, membr. 1. q. 3 at p. 219. [29] Ibid. p. 223.

After rejecting Cajetan's view that self-defaming is an act of injustice, Soto moves on to his positive view holding that reputation, like money, and unlike life (which is owned by God and the Republic), is owned. As money, it belongs to us is because we earned it with hard work.[30] Soto offers a number of supporting proofs for this. He argues that many persons would trade a loss of reputation for money. Also, that a person is allowed not to demand restitution for harm to his good name, just as she is allowed not to demand restitution from a thief who stole her material goods. Soto also claims that one is not morally obliged to confront, resist or impugn one's detractors. Jesus Christ was publicly insulted but refrained from retorting. All of this could not be the case if we were not in fact owners of our reputation. Moreover, it is an important part of the Christian attitude to disdain worldly things such as reputation, honour and money. In fact, having one's reputation attacked may actually advance one's spiritual progress, by fostering humility and spiritual perfection. Confessors can impose public penance on individuals which the public will deduce to have resulted from grievous sins. If there was such a duty to preserve reputation, the Church would not have ever imposed these penances. Note further that no pastor ever reprimanded a person for disclosing his humble origins (in aristocratic societies, such as Spain at the time, the revelation of a person's humble origins would do considerable harm to his reputation, not to mention disclosing the fact of Jewish or Moslem ancestry). We also have the example of many saints, most notably Saint Augustine, who disclosed his sins and wrongs, vices and immoral deeds in full luxury of detail in his *Confessions*. Finally, Soto says that his view is in line with the common view, for people usually do not reprehend someone who discloses his past wrongs, unless he brags of them or takes pleasure in the revelations.[31]

Molina agrees with Soto that Cajetan is entirely wrong. Reputation is property (*dominium*) and, within limits, we can do with it as we please. Prodigality with your reputation need not be necessarily sinful, just as prodigality with money need not be sinful. Reputation, like money, should not be squandered without reason, but if you do so you are committing a venial, not a mortal sin. It is true that the Republic may benefit from your having a good reputation, just as it may benefit from your having money. But this does not show that your reputation belongs to the Republic any

---

[30] Lugo, *II*, d. 1 sect. 1 n. 15 at pp. 5–6. Aragón, *In ST II-II*, q. 62 n. 3 p. 103: 'reputation [*fama*] and honor are acquired and augmented by our own work and industry: therefore we are their owner'.
[31] Soto, *DRTDS*, membr. 1. q. 3 at p. 231.

more than it shows that your money belongs to it. This is confirmed by the fact that when someone's reputation is harmed it is not the Republic but the person whose reputation has been damaged to whom restitution ought to be made.[32] In other words, for Soto and Molina defamation is a strictly private wrong.

Molina lists various cases in which self-defamation may accidentally involve injustice, such as when by defaming myself I lose the ability to earn money to sustain my dependents. Yet in itself, considered apart from these and other circumstances, Molina does not consider self-defamation to be a mortal sin.[33]

In fact, he says, there are many cases in which giving up one's right over one's reputation is justifiable. If an innocent is going to be hanged for a secret crime that I committed, I can disclose my crime, even if I am not interrogated or even under suspicion.[34] One can also patiently endure defamatory allegations in order to protect the reputation of the true author of the alleged deeds, for example, if one believes that the protection of the reputation of that other person is vital for the well-being of the Republic.[35] Molina concludes that when the only consequence of disclosing one's crime is harm to one's honour or reputation and this is necessary to save oneself or another person from torture or even just from material loss, one is permitted to disclose these deeds.

4.7 Cracks in the Property Account of Reputation: Aragón and Lugo

The property model of reputation was put under strain by one of its defenders, Pedro de Aragón. According to Aragón, we are often regarded more highly by others than is warranted by our merits (Aragón calls this '*fama ultra merita*'). Then the question is whether we have property rights over this reputation or only over that part of our reputation which is strictly merited.

The reasoning behind Aragón's objection, as I understand it, is this: if a person has ownership over only merited reputation, it would be permissible for a different person to destroy some of it if the loss would *eo ipso* be compensated by some of her unmerited reputation. But nobody believes this to be permissible. Therefore, the objection concludes, we do not have ownership rights over our merited reputation. If we do not have ownership

---

[32] Molina, *II*, lib. 4. tract. 3 d. 37 n. 3 at p. 458. [33] Molina, *II*, lib. 4. tract. 4 d. 37 n. 6 at p. 459.
[34] Molina, *II*, lib. 4. tract. 4 d. 37 n. 7 at p. 459. [35] Ibid.

rights over our merited reputation, so much the less do we have ownership of our unmerited reputation. Moreover, if, alternatively, it were the case that persons have property rights over *both* types of reputation, it would follow that it would be wrong of me to reappraise a person and come to esteem him only for that reputation that he merits; but this is absurd.[36] Therefore, says the objection, people do not have property rights over either of these two reputations.[37]

Aragón replies to the objection that he presented for argumentative purposes by making a distinction between two kinds of unmerited reputation. First, there is the unmerited reputation that is warranted by what is visible to others. If a person secretly commits adultery but people hold him in respect, then the adulterer has property rights over his good name, because it is owed to him in light of what others know of him. However, if a person is esteemed by others in a way that is not warranted by what they see and know, he does not own this reputation. Aragón gives the example of a not very learned preacher whose parishioners, who are simple folk, take for a great doctor. This misjudgment of the evidence results from their lack of expertise. The preacher has no property rights over the reputation that he has in the eyes of his parishioners. It follows that I would not be wronging the preacher if I were to harm his reputation by making the parishioners see their mistake.[38]

Aragón's distinction between unmerited reputation based on lack of visible evidence and unmerited reputation based on misjudgment of evidence is hard to defend. Suppose a doctor hides the fact of past malpractice. You expose these hidden acts, incurring, for Aragón, a wrongful defamation. Once the patients have new knowledge of the doctor, the doctor has ownership rights to a much smaller amount of good reputation (whatever is left of it after the revelations). But, since at every point the esteem that the patients had for the doctor reflected their knowledge at the time, in Aragón's view the doctor was not wronged at any point. So, on Aragón's view, what could make my exposing the new evidence wrong? It cannot be the effect of the exposure on the public reputation of

---

[36] Aragón, *In ST II-II*, q. 62 at p. 104.
[37] Gordley (*Foundations of Private Law*, p. 221) retrieves from Lessius (*II*, lib. 2 c. 11 dub. 10 n. 67) and Lugo (*II*, disp. 14, sect. 2 n. 35) a way of capturing the nature of the wrongness perpetrated when you harm my unmerited reputation. Even if I do not own my undeserved reputation, I am in *possession* of it and therefore – following the *ius possidentis* principle – I cannot be deprived of it absent legal action.
[38] Aragón, *In ST II-II*, q. 62 at p. 104.

the doctor. Otherwise Aragón's argument would be circular: 'I have a right to be held in esteem by others in light of what they know and they are allowed to know only that which does not harm their esteem of me.' What people are allowed to know about me has to be defined in terms of a criterion other than impact on reputation, a criterion which Aragón fails to provide.

Lugo's discussion of self-defamation starts by giving the impression that the issue of whether we have ownership of our reputation has been already settled. So he simply summarizes Soto's and Molina's arguments against Cajetan's obsolete view.[39] Instead of flogging a dead horse (i.e. Cajetan), he chooses to call attention to some overlooked problems, such as whether a superior does injustice to his subjects by defaming himself in a way that morally disqualifies him from office; whether a single member of a corporation or a sodality wrongs the other members of a corporation by self-defaming in a way that indirectly harms their reputation as well; and whether an adulterous wife does injustice to her betrayed husband by making public her adultery.[40]

However, even for Lugo, Cajetan's horse was not as dead as it seemed, for, in his discussion of other-defamation, Lugo breaks away from the property model of reputation. There, Lugo discusses the degree of harm to oneself that one should be prepared to endure before revealing the secrets of a *different* person.

Lugo finds room for a distinction between two kinds of rights applying to two kinds of reputation. We have a 'universal right' to that reputation that is founded on true fact. Moral probity gives its bearer an 'intrinsic' right to be judged and pronounced by others as he really is. However we do not have this unlimited right to that reputation that is 'false or founded in an untrue goodness that is merely apparent or estimated [*existimata*]'.[41] Although Lugo does not refer to Aragón, this seems to be an extension of Aragón's view that not all reputation is owned.

Regarding this second kind of reputation, in light of the 'disturbance to the common good, peace and tranquillity' resulting from the disclosure of hidden defects, we have only a right that these defects should be kept secret when not doing so turns out to be expedient to the common good. When this happens to be the case, the secrets can be made public not only by

---

[39] Lugo, *II*, d. 14 sect. 10 n. 152–161 at pp. 390–2.
[40] Lugo, *II*, d. 14 sect. 10 nn. 161, 162 168 at pp. 392–393.   [41] Lugo, *II*, d. 14 sect. 7 n. 97 at p. 375.

a judge but also by private individuals.[42] From this Lugo derives the conclusion that a person need not undergo torture or great harm in order to protect this second kind of reputation, given that the right to it is of a weaker sort and that if one must endure torture to protect such secrets this shows that keeping the secret is no longer required by the common good.[43] In the same line, Soto agreed that in some cases we do well to defame the person whose reputation is based in pretence and falsity, but only when their enjoyment of this undeserved fame is to the detriment of society (for example, in the case of a person falsely pretending to be a trained physician).[44]

This distinction between the absolute and the limited right against defamation made its first appearance in Lugo when he discussed whether it is a wrong to reveal someone's secrets once these have already been made public.[45] It would seem, says Lugo, that if the allegations are true but have been unjustly disclosed, you cannot convey them to others. The reason is that in this case your conveyance of the allegations preserves and further propagates the infamy, constituting a cooperation in the violation of the person's right to a good name.

Lugo argues, however, that when the allegations are true, even if the first disclosure has been unjust, it is permissible to further convey this information. The right against defamation has two possible grounds: the lack of the alleged flaw (not having committed the alleged crime) or the secrecy of one's true defect or crime. The person whose true crimes have already been unjustly disclosed cannot resort to any of these two grounds. By contrast, the person who is innocent of defamatory allegations that have been made public retains one of the grounds against defamation – his innocence. In this case, even when the allegations are public, one has a duty not to spread them further. The innocent person who has been defamed has 'an absolute and universal right' to his reputation, that is, a right that, unlike that of the culpable person who has been defamed, is not contingent on social utility.

Lugo goes beyond Aragón, because for him *neither* the unmerited reputation that is warranted in light of publicly available evidence nor the unmerited reputation that results from misjudgment of this evidence belongs to the bearer of the reputation. If anyone has a right to this reputation, it is society. If, for example an individual makes true statements

---

[42] Ibid. [43] Ibid. [44] Soto, *II*, lib. 5 q. 10 at p. 488.
[45] Lugo, *II*, d. 14 sect. 5 n. 65 at p. 366. On Lugo and Lessius on undeserved reputation, see Gordley, p. 221.

about a politician's drinking problem which redounds in public turmoil or some other state of affairs contrary to the common good, it is the political community that is being wronged, not the politician himself.

In Lugo's view, a person's destruction of his merited reputation (by confessing to deeds he did not do) has the same if not more deleterious social effects as a person's destruction of his unmerited reputation (by confessing to what he did do). In the former case, because the person has property rights over her reputation, she is, despite the social harm caused by her self-defamation, permitted to make the disclosure (assuming there is no lying or perjury involved). In the latter case, because the person's reputation is not owned by him but is merely in the person's custody for a specific social purpose – that of preserving social peace – the recipient is accountable to society for its use.

There is, however, a farther-reaching implication of Lugo's view. If I do not have property rights over my unmerited reputation but someone else has, then it is not for me to squander it, contrary to Soto and Molina. It follows that Lugo actually agrees with Cajetan that one has a duty *to the community* to protect one's reputation, at least that part of one's reputation that one does not deserve, so long as doing otherwise is harmful to the common good.

4.8 Tomás Hurtado and Eminent Domain

Tomas Hurtado (†1659) was one of a handful of late scholastics who took it upon themselves to explicitly defend Cajetan's view that one does not own one's reputation. In his *Resolutiones Orthodoxo-morales* of 1655 he undertakes to help the 'admirable and solid' Cajetan against a host (*turba*) of authors who claim that reputation is something over which we have ownership (he lists nineteen of them).[46]

Hurtado makes two connected points. The first is that we have property over our reputation 'as concerns its exercise' but not as concerns its 'specification'.[47] Hurtado's use of the language of exercise and specification derives from discussions on the types of liberty that we have. We can be free to do or not do an act (freedom as to exercise) and/or be free to do *this or that* act (freedom as to specification). Hurtado is, therefore, saying that we are free to allow or disallow a harm to our reputation, but we are not free to decide the mode in which this harm will come about. False self-incrimination features as one of the modes we may

---

[46] Hurtado, *Resolutiones*, dub. 5 sect. 1 at p. 169. [47] Ibid. p. 171.

choose to lessen our good name. We are not free to select this or any other mode of defamation.

In saying that one has property rights over the *exercise* of one's reputation, Hurtado means that one is permitted to passively endure the destruction of one's name. He explains that one cannot actively select a way of destroying one's reputation. One way of actively destroying one's reputation is by mendaciously defaming oneself. In so doing, one irrationally forfeits not only the most precious of all external goods but also honest life (because, as Valencia pointed out, we relinquish an important moral incentive). Doing this is not only against the love we owe ourselves by charity but also an act of *iniuria* or wronging. This is the wronging of the Church if one falsely confesses to be a heretic and of the Republic if one falsely confesses to be a murderer. The Republic exacts satisfaction from the thief not only because of his private wrong to the direct victim but also because of his public wronging the Republic itself (so that restitution to the direct victim is not enough and punishment is required). Similarly, in the case of the defamer we have also a public wrong which entitles the Republic to administer a punishment.

The second, related point is that, just as the Republic has eminent domain over one's property (and money), so it has eminent domain over one's reputation.[48] Eminent domain is the doctrine that holds that property is really a socially expedient form of protected stewardship over goods. In cases of emergency the Republic is permitted to exercise a superior right and expropriate our property for the sake of the common good. According to Hurtado, if someone were to throw his gold and silver coins into the sea, it would be a violation of the Republic's eminent domain. The Republic can abstain from punishing him, but it has a right to punish him if it so wishes. Hurtado applies this to reputation as intimated by a suggestive passage in Lugo (whom he calls 'that most brilliant light of the Church').[49] If one throws away one's reputation, one wrongs the Republic's eminent

---

[48] Hurtado, *Resolutiones*, dub. 5 sect. 1 at p. 171, n. 2 colligitur 4 at p. 172.
[49] Lugo, *II*, d. 14 sect. 10 n. 153 at p. 390: 'For, at least regarding money, the Republic has a high domain [*dominium altum*] by which it can, in certain cases, use that money for common necessities. However, although the subject is a part of the Republic for which it is expedient to have citizens or subjects of good and unblemished reputation, the citizens have not obliged themselves in the name of justice to procure that common good. In fact, the republic's reputation is not harmed much by the infamy of some private citizen. However, when the infamy [of a citizen] is conjoined with terrible infamy for his community, then whether he sins, contrary to justice, against his own community [by incurring this infamy], or Order, will be discussed below.'

domain for one deprives it of something that might be useful in times of necessity.

It is unclear, however, how eminent domain can apply to reputation. For one thing, while the Republic can take my money, there is a sense in which it cannot take my reputation. Unlike money, reputation does not exist on its own; it cannot change hands. Reputation is always *someone*'s reputation. So the Republic's way of benefitting from one of its members' reputation cannot be by way of expropriation.

A country may well mobilize or use the reputation of its citizens for various ends. For instance, it may use their reputation of being hard-working, conscientious and responsible to get better loan terms from the IMF. So, in one sense, a citizen's reputation is an asset to the whole community and if a citizen besmirches his reputation, he inflicts some amount of damage on the community (and much more damage if he besmirches the reputation of other citizens or of the community itself).

So reputation may fall under eminent domain in a looser form, namely in the sense that my reputation can be used not only for my own benefit or that of my friends and dependents but to the benefit of my country, even against or independent of my will. Perhaps I cannot say to my country: 'You have no right to use my reputation to advance the common good, for my reputation is only mine and I decide for what purposes it should be mobilized'.

In the end, Hurtado's argument does not show (perhaps did not aim to show) that we do not have property rights over reputation. On the contrary, it assumes that we do have such property rights, but it also posits that these rights are limited by eminent domain just as all our other property rights are.

4.9 Hurtado: Citizenship and Reputation

When examining the practical implications of his view, Hurtado makes an interesting and insightful point. When a superior self-defames, thereby disqualifying himself for office, the victim of injustice is not so much himself as his subjects, who have a right to good government. Something similar happens, says Hurtado, when a person self-defames and destroys 'the basis of good estimation in the eyes of others'.[50] The idea seems to be that others have a right that I preserve myself in a state in which I can be

---

[50] Hurtado, *Resolutiones*, dub. 5 sect. 1 n. 2 colligitur 6 at p. 173.

esteemed, that it is somehow to their benefit that I do so, just as it is in their benefit that the prince preserves his good name.

If we want to pursue this parallel between the prince and the community member fully, we need to think about the job or function that a regular individual renders himself incapable of by self-defaming. At one point, Hurtado seems to say that by self-defaming you show yourself unable to conserve the esteem of you by others. Perhaps he means that when we hold someone in esteem we hope he will not disappoint us and embarrass us, not just by not acting disgracefully, but also by not disclosing any disgraceful acts he may have committed. If one vouches for someone's probity and that person then discloses a past misdemeanour, one is left in an embarrassing position and will likely be more careful in the future to publicly hold anyone in high esteem. After all, we assume that the person whose good name we vouch for, as *every* person, must have at least something to be ashamed of, so our high esteem for the person, at least if publicly professed, might be seen to carry with it an implicit expectation that the person will stay quiet about some details of his past and present. We may reasonably resent it if the person, arguing that it is his own reputation that is at stake and he can do with it as he wishes, does otherwise.

So in one sense, every community member is harmed by my self-defamation because by self-defaming I make it harder for each of the members to publicly uphold the reputation of the others.

But the idea goes deeper: the Republic and other associations and communities have a need, in order to function, to regard its members as basically decent, respectable persons worthy of esteem. Each member has a *political duty* to play along with this image, even when he is not personally as decent and respectable as he is taken to be. This seems to be no more than a re-elaboration of Cajetan's point that you must not do things that disqualify you as member of the association. If you do so, you harm the association because you make it impossible for its members to benefit from your membership. For citizens, these benefits include the civic services attached to membership, such as witness or jury duty, and the benefit that could be derived from your complying with your civic duties and occupying various public offices. But, at a more basic level, there is also the idea that the existence of the group requires that its members be able to think of each other as decent, respectable people.

4.10 Cosimo Filiarchi and Primitive Inalienability

Lugo and Hurtado's arguments against the property theory of reputation are attempts to develop Cajetan's insights. Before closing, however, it is worth presenting an argument that does not have such provenance. It comes from Cosimo Filiarchi (1520–1603), a priest from Pistoia. In his *De officio sacerdotis* of 1597, Filiarchi argues that the duty to preserve the reputation of others comes from the precept of fraternal correction.[51] Fraternal correction designates the duty to try to morally amend a person with a view to his own good in a brotherly or fatherly way.

One important feature of fraternal correction, which distinguishes it from other types of corrections, is that the 'correction' must act in such way that the sins of the corrected are kept secret. So, if the superior in a monastery learns that one of the monks failed to keep a fast, fraternal correction requires him to attempt to correct this without letting the other monks know. Relative to other corrective measures, such as those of a judicial kind, fraternal correction aims to preserve the person's reputation.

Filiarchi believes that the test to know whether we have ownership rights over reputation is to check whether, if a person renounces his reputation, one remains bound to preserve his reputation (as required by the virtue of fraternal correction) or, alternatively, one can publicly accuse him thereby destroying his reputation. If someone's renouncing his reputation relieves us from the duty not to harm his good name, then that is a sign that reputation is owned by its bearer. Because Filiarchi believes that a person's renouncing his reputation does not release us from the duty to preserve it, he believes also that reputation is not owned.

A simpler example of the structure of Filiarchi's reasoning is this. Some people believe we have ownership over our body. Those who believe so have to confront the objection: am I allowed to safely surgically remove a person's hand if the person freely renounces his right over it (assume this is not in order to donate it to someone else in need)? Many people believe one cannot do this, and this seems to provide some support of the view that we do not own our own body.

The argument is not conclusive. The fact that something is inalienable does not mean it is not property. For instance, in many countries one

---

[51] Cosimo Filiarchi, *De officio sacerdotis, tomus primus* (Venice: Apud Iuntas, 1597) c. 14 at p. 538.

cannot use promised pension income as collateral for a loan.[52] Yet this is not to say that we do not own our pension income. So perhaps reputation is property, but of the inalienable sort.

We can see, however, that one's body is different from an inalienable pension. In the case of the body, we may say that the reason you cannot remove my hand is that even if I renounce it, it remains in some primitive sense a part of my body. In other words, what makes my body and its parts mine is not an ownership relation to it. If, by contrast, I renounce a piece of land (or renounce my future pension if I am legally allowed to do so), my relationship to the land is thereby extinguished, and some other person or all can use the land as they please.

Filiarchi seems to be thinking in this way about reputation. What makes your reputation yours is not a property right. The relation is primitive; your reputation is always *your* reputation. If I harm your reputation, I am by necessity doing harm to you, even if you profess to have given up your reputation. So it is not so much that you should not renounce your reputation as that you cannot renounce it. That is, you cannot alter the way you are connected to your reputation by an act of will.

4.11 Conclusion

Soto eloquently explained the social need for preserving the secrecy of some of our acts, as well as the nature of the private wrong of defaming others. This wrong considered in itself is not directly derived from the adverse social effects of disclosure. Rather, as affirmed by such authors as Navarrus, Soto, Molina, Lessius and, to a great extent, Valencia, the wrongness of defaming a person consists in the violation of her property right to her reputation and this property right comes from her earning her good name through worthy deeds and the cultivation of a good character. This allowed them to say that there is no injustice in self-defaming (particularly by disclosing true facts, so that deception and perjury are not involved), for there is no injustice towards oneself. If reputation is property, then, within limits, it is up to oneself to decide how to use or abuse it. Moreover, self-defaming need not always be an affront to the love that we owe ourselves out of charity. This argument allowed these authors to say that, in most cases, one can self-defame to avoid or put an end to torture, or, at least, that there is no necessary wrongness in doing so.

---

[52] The example is taken from David Andolffato, 'A Theory of Inalienable Property', *Journal of Political Economy*, 110(2002)383.

Not all authors agreed. Filiarchi, an original voice, argued that due examination of the duty of fraternal correction shows that one's obligation to preserve a person's reputation is not removed by her renunciation of her reputation. In this sense, reputation is radically unlike property. The thinking seems to be that reputation as a matter of its very nature cannot be renounced.

Most critics of the property approach, however, attempted to cash out on Cajetan's view that a person who self-defames deprives the community of something that belongs to it. They felt that conceptualizing reputation as property fails to do justice to the social aspects of reputation that underpin Cajetan's view and that Soto himself so eloquently described. The cracks within the property approach show already in one of its defenders, Pedro de Aragón. He argued that if indeed we earn our reputation by our deeds, some of our reputation – that which goes beyond our merits – cannot be treated as property. As concerns an unmerited good reputation, we cannot claim that in self-defaming we are merely using our property rights. Essentially this is also Lugo's view.

Hurtado, who sought to support Cajetan, argued that the community has eminent domain over our reputation so that its destruction injures the community. However, this is indirectly to admit that we may have something like property rights over reputation after all. His more interesting point, however, is the analogy between the self-defaming ruler and the self-defaming community member. In both cases, thinks Hurtado, we deprive the community of something it has a right to. In order for the community to benefit from one's membership, one has a duty to preserve oneself as a person who, as far as the public knows, can be held in respect and to not purposefully disgrace oneself by revealing hidden misdeeds. This is Hurtado's way of bringing out Cajetan's point that the self-defamer wrongs the community just as the person who kills himself does.

Modern readers may be puzzled and unconvinced by Cajetan's approach. After all, the view that so long as there is no deception or perjury one is free to say what one wishes about oneself is persuasive, simple and generally in line with liberal or right-based outlooks.

Cajetan may be right that we should be aware of the social impact of our disclosures about ourselves and be accountable for these acts to our community. But this is not what is most interesting about Cajetan's view. 'Communitarians', to give a name to those who give more weight to the claims of community than to individual rights, would be expected in general to allow society greater access to the citizens' lives than liberals, for instance, on general paternalistic grounds. What Cajetan aimed to produce, however, is something like a communitarian defence of privacy: the community is harmed by our moral self-exposure, its need *not* to know prevails over our purported right to tell.

What Cajetan had in mind was a community in which every member makes it possible for others to hold her in respect. It is this community that requires keeping part of our lives secret from each other.

CHAPTER 5

Scandal and Inexcusable Portraits

5.1 Introduction

The images to which we are exposed often have a moral impact on us. Sometimes the effect may be uplifting, thought-provoking and edifying. Sometimes, however, the effect may make it more difficult for the viewer to live not only by the moral standards set by society but also by those they have set themselves to live by. This is often alleged to be at work in the case of obscene images. A question arises regarding the responsibility of those persons producing visual materials within such areas as art, entertainment and advertising. Should these persons abstain from producing images when they believe they may have a deleterious moral effect on others?

This question is not devoid of contemporary relevance. A commissioned cartoon that in itself seems innocent could be used by others to promote bigoted causes. A work of art realistically depicting a scene of torture so as to stir social criticism may be used by a sadistic viewer to derive pleasure. Should image-makers care about what people will use their images for?

5.2 Scandal and Paintings

We have a limited moral duty not to create occasions for other people's self-harm. Many of our otherwise morally permissible actions foreseeably lead other persons to freely act in ways that harm them. It seems that we have *some* duty to refrain from at least some of these actions – for example, when the cost to ourselves of doing so is negligible. I have some duty, for instance, at a party, not to drink my whisky next to a recovering alcoholic who is having a hard time keeping sober, or at least I have that duty if it would make no difference to me to have the whisky in the other corner of the room.

The problem of occasioning self-harm has been, for the most part, ignored by most moral philosophers. Late scholastic moral theology was very much interested in this problem, which was categorized as falling under the purview of the vice of 'scandal'.

Charity, one of the three theological virtues, commands us to love our neighbour and promote his spiritual well-being. Scandal is a specific form of violation of this command. From the Greek *skandalon* ('stumbling block'), scandal designates actions or omissions that causally contribute to the spiritual downfall of one's neighbour. Aquinas puts it thus: 'While going along the spiritual way, a man may be disposed to a spiritual downfall [*ruina*] by another's word or deed, in so far, to wit, as one man by his injunction, inducement or example moves another to sin.'[1] Scandal may be caused by an action or omission that is not wrong in itself but only insofar as it gives the neighbour 'an occasion of sin'.

For moral theology, sinful acts are harmful for the agent himself regardless of whether they also harm others. These acts are harmful both because (as Plato thought) they undermine the rule of reason over our other faculties, and also because they impair our chances of salvation. So preventing a person from sinning is to prevent her from self-harm. Suárez notes that the duty not to occasion sins does not come under justice, since, as a matter of principle, no one can willingly suffer injustice, and sinning is per definition always voluntary.[2] So these specific duties not to provide occasion for sin are duties of charity rather than of justice. Yet duties of charity impose genuine moral demands on our conduct; acts of charity are not supererogatory.

Aquinas' distinguished 'active scandal' from 'passive scandal', which refers to the mode of wrongful reaction ('the downfall') of the person thereby scandalized. This reaction may originate in the very nature of the act or omission of the scandalizer (according to the taxonomy of scandal it is called *scandalum datum*). However, sometimes the best explanation for this reaction is the scandalized person's own flawed way of approaching an act which, considering its very nature, may not warrant this reaction (*scandalum acceptum*). An act that does not constitute scandal in the active sense may occasion passive scandal because of the scandalized person's ignorance, weakness of will, or a maliciously tendentious understanding of the act

---

[1] Aquinas, *ST II-II*, q. 43 a. 1.
[2] Suárez, *De Charitate* in *Opera Omnia*, vol. 12, Carolo Berton (ed.) (Paris: Vivès, 1858) d. 10, proem. at p. 720.

(termed respectively the 'scandal of children', 'scandal of the weak-willed', and the 'scandal of the Pharisees').

When the late scholastics discussed the burdensome nature of scandal, they were primarily discussing the demandingness of refraining from acts that *in* normal circumstances foreseeably lead persons to act in a morally wrongful way, even though it is not this outcome that moves the agent to act. These acts include those which would normally scandalize by virtue of the very nature of the act and also those which would scandalize by virtue of a blameless characteristic of the scandalized, such as inculpable ignorance or weakness of will. Sometimes we must be willing to forgo some material goods, and refrain from the actions aimed at preserving or obtaining them, in order to avoid scandal.

Acts that result in a person being scandalized solely because of his own maliciousness were deemed not sinful and so do not require refraining from, nor do they stand in need of being excused or justified. One would not want to condemn or censure a painter merely because some among the likely viewers are culpably ignorant, immature, prudish or simply fuelled by animosity towards the artist in question or art in general.

Late scholastic moral theologians went into considerable detail in examining possible cases of scandal. Many of these cases concerned the sale of items suspected by the tradesman to be purchased for sinful purposes. These cases included selling or renting a house to a prostitute[3] and selling her immodest dress or cosmetics;[4] selling a round to a tavern customer who cannot hold his drink;[5] selling wine to a pub landlord knowing that he will sell it watered down or at an unjust price;[6] an inn keeper's taking an order on a day of religious fast;[7] selling images or idols to be used for idolatrous worship, lambs for Jewish ritual slaughter, playing cards or dice,[8] weapons to individuals likely to commit crimes or to an army fighting an unjust war,[9] and poison[10] or inflammatory books;[11] and lending money to

---

[3] Castro Palao, *Operis moralis, pars prima*, tract. 6 d. 6 punct. 12, n. 1 at p. 482.
[4] Pedro de Ledesma, *Segunda parte de la Summa* (Zaragoza: Lucas Sánchez, 1611) vol. 2 tract. 8 c. 32, p. 452.
[5] Ledesma, *Segunda parte*, tract. 8 c. 32 at p. 453; Castro Palao, *Operis moralis*, tract. 6 d. 6 punct. 14 n. 1 at p. 484.
[6] Martín Brezmes Diez de Prado, *Teatro Moral* (Salamanca: Gregorio Ortíz Gallardo y Aponte, 1685) prop. 51 at p. 290.
[7] Tomás Sánchez, *Opus morale in praecepta decalogi* (Madrid: Luis Sánchez y Juan Hasrey, 1613) lib. 1 c. 7 n. 33 at p. 47; Castro Palao, *Operis moralis*, tract. 6 d. 6 punct. 14 n. 2 at p. 483.
[8] Ledesma, *Segunda parte*, tract. 8 c. 32 at p. 453.   [9] Ibid.
[10] Navarrus, *Manual*, c. 23 n. 90 at p. 478.
[11] Villalobos, *Summa de la Teología Moral y Canónica, segunda parte* (Barcelona: Sebastián de Cormellas, 1636) tract. 21 dif. 16 n. 1 at p. 362.

someone who will use it for giving usurious loans.[12] Among these various occasions of scandal we find also those paintings considered to invite lustful thoughts and actions in viewers.

The question of the moral effects of painting exercised many late scholastic moral theologians in seventeenth-century Spain and Italy. They had at their disposal the post-Tridentine Counter-Reformation Catholic literature on images and their use. Protestant hostility to religious imagery forced Catholic theologians to engage in systematic reflection on the proper and improper use of images, resulting in important treatises by Cardinal Gabriele Paleotti (1522–1597), Cardinal Carlo Borromeo (1538–1584) and Johannes Molanus (Jan Vermeulen) (1533–1585).[13]

However, what triggered the debate, at least in Spain, had less to do with the Reformation than with the increasing proliferation of paintings depicting themes from pagan mythology, including many portraying naked or semi-naked gods and goddesses with marked erotic overtones such as those of Venus and Adonis or Jupiter and Diana. In addition, there was a growing feeling that the new style of depicting devotional themes, including scenes of nude or partially nude female saints which were an established part of Christian iconography, tended to present these persons in ways that might cause less than pious sentiments among the viewers.[14]

The popularity of paintings depicting nudity with erotic overtones was relatively new in Spain. Wealthy art collectors would sometimes have a *sala reservada*, in which the most audacious paintings would be kept for only a few to admire.[15] However, many paintings and sculptures suspected of indecency were exhibited in palaces, gardens, churches and other public places.

Because the lustful thoughts and actions stirred by these paintings were considered to be harmful to the viewers themselves, the creating, buying and selling of such materials presented questions about the responsibilities of those who are part of the art business, principally the artist and the

---

[12] Sánchez, *Opus morale*, lib. 1 c. 7 n. 36 at p. 48; Castro Palao, *Operis moralis*, tract. 6 d. 6 punct. 13, n. 1–3 at p. 483.

[13] Gabriele Paleotti, *Discourse on Sacred and Profane Images*, William McCuaig (trans.) (Los Angeles: Getty Research Institute, 2012); Carlo Borromeo, *Instructionum fabricae et supellectis ecclesiasticae, libri II* [1577] reprinted with Italian trans. (Vatican: Libreria Editrice Vaticana, 2000); Johannes Molanus (Jan Vermeulen), *De historia ss. Imaginum et picturarum, libri IV* (Leuven: Ioannes Bogardus, 1594).

[14] José de Jesús María, *Primera parte de las excelencias de la castidad* (Viuda de Juan Gracián, 1601) lib. 4 c. 15 at p. 800.

[15] On this, see Javier Portús Pérez, 'Indecencia, mortificación y modos de ver la pintura en el Siglo de Oro', *Espacio, tiempo y forma*, Serie VII, 8(1995)55–88.

collectors. The late scholastics, however, focused mostly on the responsibility of the artist himself. It has been suggested that this was because they presented a softer target than the collectors, who were wealthy members of the powerful nobility.[16]

It was not only indecent paintings or those depicting nudity that could give rise to lustful and therefore self-harmful thoughts and actions. A perfectly innocent painting could be used for the same purpose. So there was detailed discussion on the permissibility of non-indecent depictions of women painted at the request of lovers. Before surveying this discussion, however, it is important to say something about the harmful effects that were attributed to the sight of indecent images, since similar harms were imputed to the misuse of some of the decent ones.

5.3 Indecent Pictures: What They Do to You

'If the painters knew the harm that they do to the Republic and to themselves and the offence they make against the Heavens and the earth every time they paint a indecent figure it would not be possible for them to love so much their beloved art.'[17] This quote from José de Jesús María represents well the concern of many in Catholic Europe at the time.

Possibly the peak of the backlash against art suspected of indecency in Spain is marked by a collection of *pareceres* (expert views) from the major Theology Chair holders of Salamanca and Alcalá, as well as some others. The various responses were published by Enrique Braganza in 1632, who also commissioned them.[18] The theologians were asked: 'If a person has these [indecent] paintings on display, does he sin mortally by reason of the [moral] danger and scandal?'

One of the longest and most detailed answers in this collection comes from the Dominican João de São Tomás (1589–1644), who held the Chair of Vespers at Alcalá. In his report signed 27 November 1631, he first explains why indecent paintings are much more dangerous than equally indecent books. Visual imagery has a grip on the viewer that is much stronger and more difficult to control than that exerted by the written word. Moreover, paintings can potentially affect a much greater number of people. You do not need to be literate to appreciate a painting, and the painting is there for everyone to see at all times, unlike a book, which is

---

[16] Ibid., p. 64.   [17] Jesús María, *Primera parte*, lib. 4 c. 15 at p. 798.
[18] Francisco Braganza, *Copia de los pareceres y censuras de los revenderissimos padres y señores maestros catedráticos de las universidades de Salamanca y Alcalá, y de otras personas doctas sobre el abuso de las figuras* (Madrid: Viuda de Alonso Martín, 1632).

kept closed on a shelf. De São Tomás argues that we may excuse some classical authors, such as Ovid, Martial and Horace, whose works contain lewd and lascivious passages, on account of their elegance and literary style. But these books are in Latin, so only a learned few are exposed to them.[19]

De São Tomás notes that sight and touch are the sensations most capable of stirring the heart, forming representations at the behest of the will. Once visual representations adhere to our power to produce mental images (*imaginación*), it is most difficult to tear them away from it. These paintings bring to the eyes and internal senses things that are usually kept out of our sight by natural modesty. A portrait of a good friend perpetuates his memory. A portrait of a beloved, as substitute of direct sight, 'awakes the lover's will to its desires'. How much more stirring will be a nude.

For this reason, says de São Tomás, the sight of indecent paintings undoubtedly constitutes a *proximate* occasion of sin. Proximity (*propinquitas*) played an important role in discussions on scandal. The closer one's action is to the sin of another agent, the more difficult it is to excuse it or, in other words, the greater the burden one should be willing to take on in order not to occasion the sin. So it is not the same (to give examples from the literature) to transport prostitutes to the king's palace as to open the door to them or to recruit them (recruiting being more proximate occasion of sin than the other two actions). Beyond a certain threshold, your action's proximity to the sin of another turns you into a cooperator, that is you become a co-participant in the action. This is because, when proximity obtains, it is disingenuous for the helper to say that his intention does not extend to the sin of the person being helped. It is easier to justify acting in a way that involves scandal alone than acting in a way that involves both scandal and cooperation.

Although not all viewers of the paintings will indulge in sin, says de São Tomás, the morally weaker among them certainly will. But even the morally stronger are at risk since the senses also have a grip on them. De São Tomás made two additional connected points. First, that the sight of indecent paintings is an even greater moral danger than the sight of real people naked because the artist's depiction provides an idealization devoid of defects, emphasizing the most attractive features of the bodies, whereas when we see real people we also see their imperfections. Second, that such paintings are not excused by their high level of artistic accomplishment, for, in fact, the more accomplished the technique and outcome, the more

[19] *Copia*, pp. 18v-21r.

vivid the representation and thus the greater the painting's deleterious moral effect.

Nudes, which needed not be obscene, were accorded a different treatment. It was often thought that the true talent of a painter was best shown in depictions of the naked body.[20] So the Jesuit Luis Torres (1562–1655) considered the argument that the true purpose of these images could be to display the reach of the artist's skill, so that if they move some to sin, this would count as an accidental or secondary effect. He responds that a painter could be excused for painting such nudes only if it were necessary for him to display his skill, which is very rarely the case. By 'necessary' Torres must mean something along the lines of 'if the painter would pay a very onerous personal price for not displaying the full amount of his talent'. Others' defences of depictions of nudity argued that their purpose was none other than to show the perfection of the human body and thus to exalt its Creator.[21]

Nudity received a nuanced treatment in the *parecer* of the Augustinian Francisco Cornejo (1558–1638), Chair of Prima at Salamanca (the sunrise lecture), who observes: 'this [referring to nudity] is a matter of degree [*hay mas y menos*]; there are persons who, because of their natural complexion or simply out of evil tendency [*malicia*], get aroused [*se irritan*] just by the sight of a naked man or woman, but I will not condemn just because of this he who has these paintings, because on these grounds we would have to remove from churches and oratories paintings of Adam and Eve in Paradise, as well as saints who are depicted in the nude, such as Sebastian, Lawrence and others. We can only condemn those paintings ... that are dangerous to everyone who sets eyes on them, on which we must rely on the judgment of prudent and virtuous men.'[22]

5.4 Decent Portraits for Indecent Ends

Works of moral theology were not as concerned, however, with the question of the painting of indecent images, which was agreed by all to be morally forbidden, as with the question of the painting of decent images likely to be used for bad ends.

---

[20] Luis Torres, *Selectarum disputationum* (Lyon: Jacobus Cardon, 1634) centuria 4 d. 18 at p. 189. 'Quia tales imagines primarie siunt ad ostendendam perfectionem artis, ita non refert si ex accidenti moveant ad peccatum.' On the various allegations in favour of nudity, see Giovanni Domenico Ottonelli (1581–1640) with Pietro da Cortona (1596–1669), *Trattato della pittura e scultura, uso et abuso loro composto da un theologo, e da un pittore* (Firenze: Bonardi, 1652) c. 2 q. 4 at p. 38.
[21] Ottonelli and Cortona, *Trattato*, c. 2 q. 4 at p. 38.   [22] *Copia*, pp. 12v and 12r.

This was not a speculative question. A congregation in Bologna in 1719 discussed the case of a certain nun who excelled in painting and was asked by an English nobleman to paint and sell to him paintings depicting famous and beautiful women. Was she allowed to do this?[23] The fear was that the English nobleman would use the paintings for lewd purposes. In a similar vein, the late scholastics asked, should an artist refrain from producing a portrait of a woman if he knows that the lover who asks for the portrait will use it for lustful purposes?

Portraits were very often exchanged as a sign of interest or affection between people who were courting. It is indicative of their importance within illicit courtships that portraits were the second gift exchanged between a young suitor and the married concubine of an old man in Pistoia in 1578.[24] The late scholastics were thus discussing what was then a key stage in the courtship process. Portraits also play a central role in Alvise Pasqualigo's *Lettere Amorose*, an oft-reprinted epistolary novel of 1563, a true handbook for clandestine affairs.[25] The idea was that the portrait functioned as a substitute for the real presence of the portrayed person. This was no metaphor. If we believe Pasqualigo, lovers would touch and kiss the portrait as if it was the person itself.[26] The portrait was both a consolation for the lover's absence and a proxy means for the consummation of desire. These portraits were usually of small size so that they could be carried by the lover (and hidden from spouses) and constituted an important source of revenue for painters.[27] Importantly, these portraits were usually for the eyes of the lover only. So, unlike the larger paintings, the only effects that mattered to their moral analysis were the effects on the lover itself.

What should a painter do if asked to paint a portrait that, although not indecent in itself, is foreseeably going to be used for lustful purposes? On the one hand, the pious painter would not like to commit scandal by giving occasion to the sins of the customer. On the other hand, the painter is in need not only of the income for this particular work, but also to

---

[23] Giacomo Boncompagno and Francesco-Luigi Barelli da Nizza, *Resolutionum practicarum pro confessariis monialum, in congregationibus mensualibus habitis* (Bologna: Fernandus Pisarri, 1719) vol. 2 res. 21 at pp. 120–6.
[24] Donald Weinstein, *The Captain's Concubine: Love, Honor and Violence in Renaissance Tuscany* (Baltimore and London: Johns Hopkins University Press, 2000) p. 62.
[25] Alvise Luigi Pasqualigo, *Lettere Amorose* (Venice: Niccolo Moretti, 1587) letter 33, lib. I at p. 39.
[26] Pasqualigo, *Lettere*, letter 9 at p. 14.
[27] Juan Zavaleta, *Obras históricas, polííticas, filosóficas y morales de Juan Zavaleta* (Barcelona: Ioseph Texido, 1704), p. 22.

preserve his relationship with the patron. His and his family's livelihood may be at stake.

5.5 Scandal, Over-Demandingness and Excuses

This section introduces two important moral distinctions used by the late scholastics in their analysis of scandal. These were the distinction between indifferent and non-indifferent acts, and the distinction between enabling and inducing the sins of others. As we will see in the next section both distinctions played an important role in arguments about the excusability of painting portraits of women.[28]

Avoiding scandal may be unduly onerous for most moral agents. A passage from Augustine's letter to Publicola illustrates this well. Augustine says,

> God forbid that we should be blamed for accidents which, without our desire, happen to others through things done by us or found in our possession, which are in themselves good and lawful. In that event, we ought to have no iron implements for the house or the field, lest someone should by them lose his own life or take another's; no tree or rope on our premises, lest someone hang himself; no window in our house, lest someone throw himself down from it. But why mention more in a list which must be interminable? For what good and lawful thing is there in use among men which may not become chargeable with being an instrument of destruction?[29]

We might add paintings to the list of possible instruments of self-harm.

Moral theologians often appealed to the doctrine of 'indifferent' objects and actions to solve the problem of over-demandingness pointed out by Augustine. Some things, such as poison, seem destined by their very nature to be used for evil purposes. Other things are 'indifferent': they can be used for good or for evil. But, Suárez notes, the distinction will not be very helpful if left at this, since nothing or almost nothing is by its very nature necessarily destined to a bad use. A pagan idol, for example, could be used for decorative purposes or as a memento of antiquity, as an artistic

---

[28] For a more exhaustive discussion of these distinctions in the context of scandal, see my ' Scandal and Moral Demandingness in the Late Scholastics', *British Journal of the History of Philosophy*, 23(2015) 256–76.

[29] St Augustine, Letter 47 in *CSEL* 34:2, Alois Goldbacher (ed.) (Leipzig: G. Freytag, Vienna and Prague: F. Tempsky, 1898) pp. 129–36., trans. by J. G. Cunningham from *Nicene and Post-Nicene Fathers*, First Series, vol. 1. Philip Schaff (ed.) (Buffalo, NY: Christian Literature Publishing Co., 1887).

expression, for laughter, or even as wood for heating.[30] He therefore proposes to talk instead about natural and manmade objects that human consensus or law has prohibited (such as poison and crossbows) even though there could be conceivably permissible uses for them.[31] So, in fact, there are no natural non-indifferent objects and actions, only conventional ones.

If you are producing or selling an indifferent artefact and you *do not know* or *do not presume* that it will be used for bad ends, you may produce it or sell it. Naturally, this raised the question of whether the seller has a duty to find out about the purchaser's planned use of the merchandise. The general view was not only that no such duty exists, but that such inquiries are inappropriate. According to Suárez, Cajetan says that no private person has the duty or right to examine the conscience of another person; in public everyone is presumed good.[32] Pedro Aragón agrees: 'It is not the business of the seller to inquire on the mores of others and discern between those who buy for good purposes and those who buy for evil ones. Such curiosity is pernicious to the commonwealth.'[33] The same applied to the case of the artist or the art dealer. Giovanni Domenico Ottonelli, citing others, says that it is not the painter's duty to inquire whether the young man commissioning a painting has a virtuous or vicious intention.[34]

The real question, however, concerned those cases in which the seller *does* know or suspect that the buyer will make sinful use of an indifferent thing, as, in our current case, when a painter knows that his or her painting will be used for bad ends. Many authors, such as Molina, thought that in these cases, if the thing produced or sold is indifferent, its production or sale could be excusable in some circumstances even if it is foreknown by the producer or the seller to be used for sinful ends, whereas if the object is not indifferent, it could not.

Suárez rejected Molina's solution. For him neither indifferents (i.e. actions and things conventionally regarded as usable for good and for bad) nor non-indifferents are intrinsically bad. Actions and the production and purveyance of things become intrinsically bad and thus inexcusable only when they become instances of cooperation in sin, which depends on

---

[30] The examples are from Sánchez, *Opus morale*, lib. 1 c. 7 n. 6 at pp. 38–9.
[31] Suárez, *De fide, spe et charitate*, d. 10 n. 1 at p. 729.
[32] Suárez, *De fide, spe et charitate*, d. 10 sect. 4 n. 3 at p. 728 referring to Cajetan in *ST II-II* q. 10 a. 4 n. 4 at p. 83–84. Cajetan only asserts that there is no duty to inquire about the future use of the sold item.
[33] Aragón, *In ST II-II*, q. 77 a. 4 at p. 459.
[34] Ottonelli and Cortona, *Trattato*, c. 3 q .7 aggiunta prima p. 136.

the actual circumstances in which they take place, rather than on their being indifferent or non-indifferent.[35]

This is not to say that Suárez has no use for the indifferent/non-indifferent distinction. In the case of conventional non-indifferents (such as, according to Suárez's example, poison), we should presume as a rule that the thing or action will be misused.[36] The distinction between indifferents and non-indifferents is therefore relevant for determining on whom falls the burden of proof. It is the poison buyer who must demonstrate that he does not intend to do evil. By contrast, if a retailer refuses to sell rope (which is an indifferent) it is he who must demonstrate that the buyer has evil plans. The indifferent/non-indifferent distinction, however, does not establish the deep morality of producing and selling, but only the location of evidential burdens.

A second important moral distinction is that between merely occasioning sins and actually inducing them. Sometimes we only enable the predisposed sinner to sin. There is a difference between merely enabling someone to continue along his planned sinful path and rerouting a person from a non-sinful path of action to a sinful one. In the latter case, what we are doing is inducing a sin.

This moral distinction was already sketched by Aquinas in his treatment of the permissibility of requesting loans from usurers, which was followed by Domingo Soto, among many others.[37] The request for the loan enables the usurer to grant a usurious loan, but does not *induce* him to do so, since as a matter of his walk of life, he is always predisposed to give such loans whenever the opportunity arises. If the action that enables the sin is not one of inducement, exculpatory factors can come into play. For example, a request to obtain a loan from a usurer may be exculpated by a great need for the money. In these cases, to use Augustine's phrase, I 'use the sin of my neighbour'.[38] It was commonly agreed that the amount of loss that could excuse one for merely occasioning a sin is much lower than the amount of loss required to excuse inducing a sin.

Equipped with an understanding of the basic elements of excusable scandal, we can return to the question of portraits.

---

[35] Suárez, *de Censuris*, in *Opera Omnia*, vol. 23 d. 21 sect 2 n. 61 p. 525.
[36] Suárez, *De fide, spe et charitate*, d. 10 n. 1 at 729.
[37] *ST II-II*, q. 78 a. 5 c. Soto, *II*, lib. 8 q. 2 a. 4 at p. 760, lib. 6. q. 1 a. 5 at p. 533.
[38] See *ST II-II*, q. 78 a. 4c. and Augustine, *ad Publicolam*, n. 2 pp. 130–1.

5.6 Excusing Portraitists

That lovers and suitors would misuse decent portraits was held to be a sensible presumption given what lovers were believed to generally be like.[39] It is clear from the context that the late scholastics were discussing portraits given, exchanged or produced in the context of a desired or existing illicit relationship and not, say, of portraits exchanged between spouses. This is not to say that portraits between spouses were not capable of presenting dangers, because sexual arousal not open to procreation was deemed morally suspect also among spouses.

In his *Discorso*, Gabriele Paleotti touched on this question as one within the broader morality of portrait painting, which concerned such other questions as, Who can be portrayed? Is it permissible to make a portrait sketch of a person without her consent? It is permissible to disguise in a portrait the less fortunate features of the person portrayed? Where should portraits be hung?

On the matter under consideration, Paleotti takes a very strict view. If the painter knows that the portrait is 'sought for vicious and dishonest ends' he should refuse the commission, for otherwise he would share in the sin of the purchaser. Thus, the sin of the painter is not so much scandal (giving occasion of sin) but rather the cooperation in the lascivious sin of the young man who purchased the painting.[40]

The late scholastic controversy starts, however, with Juan Azor's (1536–1603) *Institutiones* (published in 1600), with Azor declaring that the making of these portraits is sinful, without offering any possible excuses.[41] There is some early treatment of the matter in Cosimo Filliarchi's *De officio sacerdotis*, published before Azor in 1597.[42] Interestingly, Filliarchi is more concerned with the possession of these portraits than in their production. He says that if the painting of a woman is itself decent and contains no nudity, it may still be a sin to *own* it because even this decent image can be loved without honesty; the image is constantly present to be seen, enjoyed and desired. What is worse, says Filliarchi, some people carry these small images around their neck, or carry letters, locks of hair, or other mementos

---

[39] Antonio Naldi (†1645), *Summa seu Resolutiones practicae* (Cologne: Peter Henning, 1625) *amasius*, at p. 33.
[40] Paleotti, *Discorso*, p. 308.
[41] Also Martino Bonacina, *Opera Omnia* (Lyon: Claude Landry, 1629) vol. 2, disp. 2, *de peccatis*, q. 4 punct. 2 unicus prop. 3 n. 29 at p. 168.
[42] Cosimo Filliarchi, *De officio sacerdotis*, lib. 3 c. 9 at p. 431.

to look at whenever they wish (all of which is done by the lovers of Pasqualigo's *Lettere Amorose*, mentioned above).[43]

Tomás Sánchez's briefly stated but influential view is more lenient. The painter making a painting of a concubine at the petition of her lover sins mortally by giving occasion for sin but he can be morally excused if there is a *legitimate* cause. However, Sánchez fails to tell us what constitutes a legitimate cause.[44]

Castro Palao holds a rather more stringent view. He likens the case of the portraitist to that of an artist asked to paint an idol by a non-Christian.[45] Because the act of painting is itself indifferent and could be used for both good and bad ends, it can be rendered morally permissible by a grave cause. He interprets Sánchez as saying that if the painting will foment lustful love and idolatry it must not be done without *gravissima causa* (a most weighty reason rather than merely a legitimate one). This *gravissima causa* excusing the painting cannot simply consist in the failure to secure the offered price for the painting, for otherwise painters would always be able to be excused. According to Castro Palao, the only reason that could be sufficient to excuse a painter is fear of death or serious bodily harm. In the absence of any such excuse, to produce a painting of this sort is not unlike selling a sword to a person who is bent on killing an innocent.[46]

Girolamo Ferrantino de Ancona (1576–1655), an Italian Jesuit, found this view excessively rigid.[47] His main argument was that the person commissioning the painting is already predisposed to sin; the painting does not as such induce the sinning but merely enables it. On this basis, Ferrantino believes that for the painter to be excused we need not require a grave cause, such as fear of death or bodily harm, but simply a reasonable cause (*causa rationabile*).

Indeed, he says, the case of the painter should not be treated differently than the case of asking a loan from a usurer (who, like the commissioner of the painting, is predisposed to loan money at interest). Reasonable cause, according to most authors, is sufficient to excuse the loan petitioner, and so it should be in the case of the painter.

By making the point that this case is not a case of inducement, and that therefore it makes sense to treat the painter as similarly positioned to the loan petitioner, Ferrantino is lowering the amount of loss required for the painter to excusably paint the portrait.

---

[43] Pasqualigo, *Lettere*, letter 96 at p. 102.   [44] Sánchez, *Opus morale*, lib.1 c. 7 n. 40 p. 49.
[45] Castro Palao, *Operis Moralis*, tract. 6 d. 6 punct. 12 n. 6 at p. 483.   [46] Ibid.
[47] Girolamo Ferrantino de Ancona, *Theoreticae ac practicae disputationes* (Roma: Inheritors of Corbelletti, 1653) q. 69 n. 57–61 at pp. 345–6.

This is fleshed out by one of Ferrantino's supporters, the Jesuit Vincenzo Tancredi. Tancredi (1609–1659) says that sufficient cause is provided by the painter being in need of the money to help his family live in dignity, or by the painter's fear that he will lose a friend (the patron) or will miss out on a considerable sum.[48]

Ferrantino's provocative view (published in 1653) was met with general disapproval. Diana asserted in 1639, against Azor and Martino de Bonacina (1585–1631), that painting these images could in some cases be excusable. But he took a much stricter view when he returned to the question of the moral conscience of the painter in 1655,[49] rejecting Ferrantino by citing the opposing views of recent Jesuit authors such as Alberto Alberti (1593–1676),[50] Trullench[51] and Ottonelli.[52]

Some authors produced new arguments to debate Ferrantino. Two of them are Leandro del Santísimo Sacramento (1592–1604) and Manuel de la Concepción (1627–1700). They concede to Ferrantino that, although the sin of painting the portrait is not worse than the sin involved in asking for a usurious loan, the moral danger involved in painting the portrait is much greater because in matters of lust we are continuously exposed to many occasions to incur in sin. Requesting the portrait is an expression of a stronger drive towards having a picture of the woman than that involved in asking for the loan. In a curious comment, Leandro says that it follows that just as the portrait painter would be sinning by selling a picture of the concubine, so would a physician sin if he were to sell to the married lover of a concubine for two gold coins the bandage used to dress the concubine in a surgery.[53]

5.7 Francés de Urrutigoyti's Response

A more interesting argument against Ferrantino comes from the Franciscan Tomás Francés de Urrutigoyti (†1682). He starts by allowing

---

[48] Vicenzo Tancredi, *Quaestiones morales* (Palermo: Josephus Bisagni, 1659) vol. 2 tract. 3 q. 4 at pp. 104–5.
[49] Diana, *Resolutionum moralium, pars quinta*, tract. 7 res. 5 at p. 175, compare with *Resolutionum moralium, pars undecima, Miscellanea* (Lyon: Borde, Arnauld and Rigaud, 1655) tract. 5 resol. 50 at p. 276.
[50] Alberto Alberti, *Paradoxia moralia de ornatu mulierum* (Milano: Montiae, 1650) d. 1 c. 5 sect. 10 n. 160 p. 89.
[51] Trullench, *Operis Moralis, tomus secundus* (Lyon: Anisson, 1652) lib. 6 c. 6 dub. 12 n. 13 at p. 91.
[52] Ottonelli and Cortona, *Trattato*, p. 136.
[53] Manuel de la Concepción and Leandro del Santísimo Sacramento, *Quaestionum Moralium* (Avignon: the Authors, 1692) pars 5 d. 4 q. 8 at p. 207.

as not implausible the view that it is morally permissible to portray a young woman if the painting itself is not indecent. In support of this view, it could be said that, just as a woman is within her right to embellish herself within the limits of modesty, regardless of how the sight of her might be used by male spectators, so the painter need not renounce his right to make a profit, simply because the customer is going to foreseeably make ill use of the painting. He is simply using his right to sell his art in order to make a living. If, therefore, the painter depicts the young woman in a realistic and honest way, the effect of the concupiscent thoughts of the buyer should be blamed on the buyer. If there is scandal, it is only pharisaic scandal (self-righteous, smug, hypocritical), not a genuine one.

Francés de Urrutigoyti's appeal to the idea of rights is a throwback to earlier discussions on scandal. In considering the moral permissibility of renting one's house to prostitutes, Navarrus argued that 'the general law of God does not oblige us not to use our right [*dejar de usar de nuestro derecho*], even if the neighbour will make use of it for scandal and an occasion to sin'.[54] Suárez, too, argued that the landlord cannot be asked to keep the house unrented just in order to prevent the sins of prostitutes and their customers. The landlord does not have to deprive himself of his right (*privare se suo jure*) given that he does not intend the sins of these persons nor does he prompt them (*excitat*) or provide the matter of sin (*materiam peccati*).[55]

Against the view introduced at first, Francés de Urrutigoyti proceeds to present the, for him, no less probable contrary view of Castro Palao, arguing that, by portraying the woman, the painter is fomenting forbidden libidinousness which cannot be excused except in cases of real and serious danger to him. The painter cannot be excused by appealing to the aim of showing artistic talent or because he is satisfying the curiosity of the purchaser to find out the true extent of the artist's skill.

After presenting these two conflicting views, Francés de Urrutigoyti makes his own original move. It consists in affirming that it just does not matter that the painting, considered in itself, contains no obscenity, for at the sight of it the lover's memory will call up (*reducit*) indecent or obscene images, which in turn poses the danger of a 'consented pollution' (i.e. emission) by the lover.

---

[54] Navarrus, *Capitulo veynte y ocho: de las addiciones del Manual de confessores* (Zaragoza: Widow of Bartholome de Nágera, 1570 c. 1563) p. 27.
[55] Suárez, *De fide, spe et charitate*, d. 10. sect. 4. n. 4 at p. 730.

To understand this last sentence we should note that theological discussions of the morality of *delectatio morosa*, 'the deliberate complacency in forbidden things or thoughts',[56] were often devoted to some aspect of the question about the permissibility of retrieving and rekindling memories of past sexual intercourse (including intercourse with a now dead or absent spouse) that could cause sexual arousal. In determining the permissibility of the deliberate use of memory for producing sexual arousal, it was held important whether it posed the danger of pollution. Pollution itself was not so morally problematic as the consenting to it, which consisted not merely of deriving pleasure from it but also of giving approval to it.[57]

Francés de Urrutigoyti resists considering the painting separately from its effect; the painting's moral status is determined by its interaction with the purchaser's memories. As a resource to trigger the lover's erotic memories, it is an indecent painting no matter what you actually paint. To be clear, Francés de Urrutigoyti's point is not that the judgment of whether a work of art is decent or indecent is a subjective matter. Rather the work is susceptible to objective judgments about its being decent or indecent depending on how it interacts with the memories and desires of the viewer.[58]

Francés de Urrutigoyti's compressed argument against Ferrantino can be understood in two different ways. The first way is that Francés de Urrutigoyti is saying that lovers' portraits, as obscene paintings, are not indifferents. On the assumption that only indifferents can be excusable, these paintings are therefore inexcusable.

If this is Francés de Urrutigoyti's strategy, he is confusing two different senses of 'indifferent'. In the primary sense, 'indifferents' are simply things or actions that can be used for either good or bad ends while 'non-indifferents' are things or actions that in the vast majority of cases are used for bad ends (call this sense 1). In another sense, an action is non-indifferent when it is intrinsically bad, for example because it constitutes cooperation in sin (sense 2). The production of non-indifferents as understood in sense 2 is inexcusable. But Francés de Urrutigoyti at best

---

[56] F. Lucius Ferraris, *Prompta bibliotheca canonica, juridica, moralis, theologica, nec non ascetica, polemica, rubricistica, historica*, vol. 3 (Paris. J.-P Migne, 1861) p. 83.

[57] Navarrus, *Enchiridion*, cap. 16.

[58] Thomas Francés de Urrutigoyti, *Consultationes in re morali* (Toulouse: Guillelmus Ludovicus Colomerius and Hieronymus Possuet, 1682) cons. 37 n. 5, 6 at p. 283 'Aequo ergo lance Philosophandum in amasio concubinam petente pingendam in imagine; etsi enim hic obscenae delineatam non videat, concubinam ad ejus memoriam reducit per inhonesta quae ipsi evenerunt & probabili periculum consensus, seu pollutionis videbatur ... sed pictura, seu sculptura in casu consulto res obscena determinate erat.'

establishes that lovers' portraits are indifferent only in sense 1, which is not enough to show that painting these portraits is inexcusable.

Francés de Urrutigoyti was not alone in attributing an undue moral significance to the distinction between indifferents and non-indifferents (sense 1). Diana, for example, asserts that if something is indifferent in the sense that it can be used for good and for bad, then its production or selling can in principle be excusable.[59] Yet this merely presses the question why treat in morally different ways the selling of something that could be used for a good end but which one knows with certitude will be used for a bad end and the selling of something that *cannot* be used for a good end. Either both types of selling are excusable or neither of them. This is precisely Suárez's point in insisting that the distinction between indifferents and non-indifferents does not make a real moral work. In Suárez's view, for the production and sale of portraits of lovers to be morally inexcusable, it must be the case that the painter cooperates in the sins of the purchaser of the portrait, which Francés de Urrutigoyti does not show.

But Francés de Urrutigoyti's response to Ferrantino can be understood differently. According to this second understanding, what does the work of rendering the painting of lovers' portraits inexcusable is not its being non-indifferent but rather, contrary to Ferrantino's view, that painters *induce* sins which the person who commissioned the painting is *not* predisposed to commit. True, the purchaser is predisposed (*paratus*) to buy the painting, but he is not predisposed, and for reasons specific to the mechanism connecting images to lust, cannot be predisposed, towards sins of lust. The induction of lustful thoughts is brought about by the sight of the portrait. For an analogy consider gluttony. You may plan to order an irresistible meal without being at the time of ordering bent on indulging in unrestrained eating. Gluttony as such will be induced by the actual sight and smell of the irresistible dishes (at the point of ordering the meal you at most have a second-order desire to eat unrestrainedly: you may want to want to eat in this fashion). This case is unlike that of a person who buys a knife in order carry out a murderous plot. Here, unlike in the case of portraits and of the irresistible food, providing the knife does not normally have any motivational or psychological effect on the buyer.

Francés de Urrutigoyti's view is that lovers' portraits are not mere means of carrying out sinful purposes but, rather, that the sight of them moves the viewer to have lustful thoughts and carry out deeds that he would not

---

[59] In the 1639 *Resolutionum moralium* (pars 5 tract. 7 res. 5 at p. 175), Diana says because painting the portrait is indifferent in the sense of indeterminacy of use, it is excusable.

otherwise carry out. This view, although incomplete and sketchy, is not entirely implausible. Note that the painter is acting on the request of the lover, so the painter seems to be a means of the purchaser's self-induction. Self-induction is an interesting idea that Francés de Urrutigoyti fails to develop. But he certainly makes a plausible point: a person cannot simply decide to experience lust in the same way he decides to go for a walk. He must elicit the required sensual and imaginative responses through an indirect method, in this case through using images to trigger erotic memories. This is reminiscent of Augustine's view in *City of God*, book 14, that, after Original Sin, 'even those who delight in this pleasure [lust] *are not moved to it by their own will*'. The mechanism requires the assistance of image producers. So essentially artists are co-inducers of sin rather than merely givers of the occasion of sin, and so their portraits are inexcusable.

5.8 Summary

Portrait painting for the purpose of initiating and sustaining illicit relationships fell within the scope of the general doctrine of scandal. This doctrine attempted to solve the problem of the over-demandingness of scandal, namely the problem that almost anything we do or produce could be an occasion of sin, by examining the question of in which cases one could be excused for giving occasion of sin. The level of burden that the agent, the creator or the seller should be ready to shoulder in order not to furnish an occasion of sin depended on a number of factors. But the very principle that the production and sale of indifferent objects could be excused, opened the door to increasingly lenient views on the excuses available to portraitists painting lovers.

Francés de Urrutigoyti sought to counter this and to show that these portraits are inexcusable. One way in which he sought to do this was by removing these paintings from the category of indifferents. In the hands of lovers, the paintings cannot serve other than lustful ends. This argument fails, however: non-indifferents need not be intrinsically bad, and only intrinsically bad actions and things are inexcusable. From a Suarezian perspective, Francés de Urrutigoyti had to prove that to paint portraits of lovers is to cooperate in the sins of the lovers, which he does not attempt to show. The second way Francés de Urrutigoyti uses seems more plausible. Because paintings operate *on* the viewer (rather than the viewer on them), and because lustful deeds and thoughts are only indirectly voluntary, it makes sense to say that the painter is co-inducing sins by creating the stimulus required for the awakening of lust.

The controversy about portraits provides a good illustration of the fact that, on the one hand, the doctrine of scandal imposed heavy burdens on moral agents, but on the other hand gave significant leeway for excusing the producing or selling of things foreknown to result in others' self-harmful sins.

Thinking about the production of images added to the standard application of the principles of the doctrine of scandal by introducing the hybrid category of productive actions that combine features of the induction of sins and of the occasioning of sins. Images are not mere means to carry out pre-existing sinful designs (as are weapons, for example), but are *causes* of those sins. The image is acting on the agent; the agent is not merely acting by means of it. Because of this, it was argued that the production and sale of obscene images, or images that were similar to obscene images in effect, were less excusable than the production and sale of other objects which are merely the means of sin.

PART II
War

CHAPTER 6

Conscientious Objection in War: From Duty to Right

6.1 Introduction

We have a duty to fight for our community when summoned to do so by the public authority, but at the same time we have a duty – or perhaps a right – to follow our own moral convictions, which may condemn the war we are called on to fight. While the question of the limits of the subject's obedience, and obedience in general, was never absent from Christian theology, and particularly from medieval theology, this question attracted renewed attention from the late scholastics. To no little extent this should be credited to Adrian from Utrecht – later Pope Adrian VI (1459–1523) – and his strong view on the duty to adhere to one's moral conscience even when this means disobeying someone whom we ought to obey. In this chapter, I survey the unfolding of the controversy on the subject of obedience ignited by Adrian's seemingly subversive view.

Here 'conscience' should not be understood so much as a faculty, but as one's determinate judgment about how one ought to act in one's particular circumstances.[1] The scenarios that attracted the most interest were those in which the agent is uncertain about the right thing to do, either because he is in doubt, or because, while not in doubt, he has preference for one option over the others but lacks complete confidence that he is right. Theologians were split on the right rule to apply to these cases. Tutiorists argued that one must act in such a way so as to minimize moral danger, because this is the safer (*tutior*) option. So if I find ten dollars and I am in doubt about whether it is mine or yours, I should give it to you, thereby avoiding the moral danger of misappropriating your

---

[1] On the development of notions of moral conscience, see Timothy Potts, 'Conscience', in N. Kretzmann, A. Kenny and J. Pinborg (eds.), *The Cambridge History of Later Medieval Philosophy* (Cambridge: Cambridge University Press, 1980) pp. 687–704.

money. Other theologians recommended focusing on the plausibility or the verisimilitude of the moral opinions in dispute (*probabilitas*), which does not correlate with their moral safety in the sense given to this term by the tutiorists. Among these theologians, the probabiliorists believed that one must follow the most probable of the opinions, while the once dominant but later much derided and condemned probabilists thought that any sufficiently probable opinion can be followed in practice. Some theologians combined elements of more than one of these approaches.

In most moral theologians' treatises on conscience and probable opinion, discussion of the more abstract and hefty questions about moral certainty was followed by a more practically oriented section presenting implications for the dilemmas confronting different types of profession and roles. Borrowing from what was customary in confessional and penitential manuals, these theologians addressed separately the moral uncertainties confronted by lawyers, judges, confessors, priests, theologians, rulers, surgeons, apothecaries, physicians and soldiers.[2]

Many of these persons operate within hierarchical institutions, so the question of the moral demands of obedience presented itself. In these theologians' works, the term 'subjects' as used in the controversy about obedience referred not only to political subjects but to all those who owe obedience to a superior in a legitimate hierarchical institution. So 'subject' also covers members of religious orders who owe obedience to their prelate.

One of the frequently discussed cases was that of subject soldiers (as opposed to non-subject mercenaries) who doubted the justice of the war they were called on to fight or who plainly believed it to be unjust. Attention was also given to subject soldiers whose uncertainty concerned not so much the justice of the war as the authority of the ruler declaring it.

---

[2] Navarrus in his *Manual* (pp. 517–97) discusses the dilemmas of 'kings and lords', 'judges and others under a superior', advocates, prosecutors, plaintiffs, defendants, witnesses, notaries, masters and doctors, students, physicians and surgeons, will executors, tutors of minors, administrators and purveyors, clergy, preachers and church beneficiaries. For other examinations of cases of conscience according to walk of life, see, for example, Juan de Salas, *Disputationum Ioannis de Salas Castellani in Primam Secundae Divi Thomae, tomus primum* (Barcelona: Gabriel Graells and Giraldo Dotil, 1607) pp. 1220–9; Tomás Sánchez, pp. 60–5; Castro Palao, *Operis moralis*, tract. 1 d. 1–2 at pp. 6–15; Thomas Tamburini, *Explicationes in decalogum et alias opera moralia* (Lyon: Ioannes-Antonius and Marci-Antonius Ravaud, 1659) pp. 24–8; and João de São Tomás, *Cursus theologici in primam secundae Thomae pars prima, tomus quartus* (Cologne: Wilhelm Metternich, 1711) q. 18 a. 5 at pp. 534–72.

Most of the theologians surveyed here attempted to find a way to firmly reconcile the moral duty to abide by one's conscience with the presumptive duty to obey the superior. As we will see, the controversy bridges two very different conceptions of justifiable disobedience. One view, which was defended by Adrian, admits the prima facie duty to obey authority but argues that it is trumped by the duty to follow one's conscience. The other view holds that the force of the prima facie duty to obey the superior depends on the degree of the perceived justice of the superior's command. When we believe that a ruler's command is probably unjust, it is not the case that our duty to abide by conscience trumps our duty of obedience, but rather, that no duty of obedience is in place.

6.2 Adrian's Challenge

Obedience was the subject of a public disputation delivered in Leuven in 1491 by Adrian of Florisz or of Utrecht.[3] In this lecture, which reignited a discussion on the duty to abide by one's conscience, Adrian addressed three key questions. The first was whether, when one is in doubt about whether the authority of the superior extends to oneself or to the act prescribed, one must obey. The second was whether it is a mortal sin to obey when one is in the grip of probable doubt about the licitness of what is commanded. The third was whether, when in probable doubt, learned persons (*doctorum*) can obey the commands of the ruler against their own opinion or whether they should consider illicit doing the act thus commanded.[4]

Concerning the second of these questions, Adrian provocatively argued that subjects may not obey their superior when in doubt, for in doing so they expose themselves to the moral danger of acting against their own conscience. In support of his view, Adrian drew from St Paul saying to the Romans (14:23), 'All which is not from faith [*ex fide*] is sin'.

Adrian takes something being *ex fide* to be commonly interpreted as its 'not being against faith' – and he clarifies – 'that is, faith or conscience'. So the view he attributes to St Paul is that 'everything we do is a sin if we do not believe it to be permitted.'[5]

Bona fide in its traditional legal context had two main functions. The first was to determine a person's rights and liabilities. A second traditional function of *bona fide* was to excuse deeds committed whilst

---

[3] Pope Adrian VI, *Quaestiones quodlibeticae XII* (Paris: Nicolaus Savetirius, 1531) first published 1515.
[4] These can be found in *Quodl.* q. 2 fols. 24B, 32A and 38B, respectively.   [5] *Quodl.* 2 q. 2 fol. 38A.

bona fide was present. So it is one thing to inquire whether my *bona fide* occupation of a plot of land generates acquisitive rights after a statutory prescriptive period, and another to inquire whether it excuses me from the very act of occupation. Adrian was well aware of the Roman legal concept of good faith (*bona fides*). Indeed, in his earlier *Commentary on the Sentences*, he discussed in some detail the interaction between doubt and good faith within the treatise on restitution.[6]

Adrian's use of 'faith' and 'good faith' in his later work, however, confers a more expansive meaning to these terms by equating them with moral conscience itself. By equating acting *ex fide* (and thus in *bona fide*) with acting in accordance with conscience, Adrian made *bona fide* an ingredient in the agent's practical deliberation. Following one's conscience is a duty that should stand before the eyes of the agent in deciding how to act, and therefore he should ask himself whether he is acting in good faith before proceeding.

The subject of war is prominent throughout Adrian's discussion. He is quick to present a possible objection to his view: for the king to be able to wage war he must arrange things so that when military leaders or captains entertain doubts about the precise nature of the king's orders, the opinion of 'the majority of the greatest experts [*expertorum*]' prevails over theirs.[7] If each of the latter follows his own opinion on the contents of the king's orders, the army will be divided against itself and unable to act collectively. Therefore, says the objection, victory requires acting against one's own opinion about the true content of the king's orders and deferring to the view of these experts (by which, one assumes, Adrian means some government officials). Adrian's response concedes the necessity of internal unanimity and concord for the successful waging of war but claims that what we must conclude from this necessity is that, in order to avoid dissension, the king must take care that war orders will be easy in the consciences of the military leaders and 'cause no harm'.[8]

The military example is built on a parallel between the king and God. Just as I may doubt that what ecclesiastical officials tell me that God commands me to do is really what God commands me to do, I may doubt that what political officials tell me that the king commands me to do is really what the king commands me to do. In both cases it is the responsibility of the officials to interpret the superior's order in ways that

---

[6] Pope Adrian VI, *Quaestiones in quartum sententiarum praesertim circa sacramenta* (Leuven: Jocobus Dassoneville, 1516) 66r-67v.
[7] *Quodl.* 2 q. 2 fol. 39A.   [8] *Quodl.* 2 q. 2 fols. 42A.

Conscientious Objection in War: From Duty to Right

conflict as little as possible with what the subordinates take these orders to be. When conflict persist between what most people believe the orders to be and what one believes them to be, we should, according to Adrian, remember that God ('the celestial king') ordered that we should not allow ourselves to be dragged by the mobs to do evil.

6.3 Vitoria on Doubt and Good Faith

Vitoria discussed the doubt affecting initiators and participants in war both in his lectures on the *Summa* from 1535 and in his better-known *Relection on the Law of War* from 1538.[9] There are two noticeable differences between the two texts. First, the *Relection*, unlike the *Lectures*, contains a detailed discussion of Adrian's view on the effects of doubt on good faith. Second, in the *Relection* alone we find a short passage that seems to admit the possibility of wars that are just on both sides at the level of the subjects.

Against Adrian, Vitoria argued that a subject combatant could fight in good faith even when he remained in doubt about the justice of the war. The mistake he imputes to Adrian is to think that 'if I am in doubt about whether the cause of war is just, I must therefore doubt whether I may lawfully fight in that war'.[10] Doubts about the justice of the war need not transform into doubts about the permissibility of one's participation in the war. In putting forward this view Vitoria surely had in mind the distinction between 'speculative' and 'practical' doubts. Speculative doubts are doubts about whether there is a just cause. Practical doubts are doubts about whether it is permissible *for me* to fight in this war.

The view that these two sorts of doubt need not entail each other was possibly introduced by Cajetan. We find it in a *responsa* signed 9 February 1521.[11] Cajetan writes that 'according to some' for the action to be licit you need certain *fides* (*fidem certam*), excluding all hesitation,

---

[9] Vitoria, *Comentarios a la Secunda Secundae de Santo Tomás de Caritate et Prudentia (qq. 23–56)*, q. 40 a. 1 at p. 282–3.

[10] Vitoria, *IB*, q. 2 a. 3 n. 31 at p. 312. Translations from *IB* are by Jeremy Lawrance in 'On the Law of War', *Political Writings*, Anthony Pagden and Jeremy Lawrance (eds.) (Cambridge: Cambridge University Press, 1991).

[11] Cajetan, *Opuscula Omnia* (Lyon: Gulielmus Rovillius, 1588) tom. 1, tract. 31 resp. XIII lines 67–80 (col. A), 10–50 (col. B) at p. 134. Cajetan considers the example of jesting on a holy day and argues that you can have doubts about its licitness when the thing is considered in itself without having doubts about the licitness of your own doing so and vice versa. He adds that if we were to require speculative certitude this would expose to sin not only the simple lay people but also the learned, for there are innumerable doubts which offer reasons on both sides.

otherwise you expose yourself to the danger of sinning.[12] It seems that it was Adrian whom Cajetan had in mind when advancing this view, as revealed by Cajetan's use of Adrian's idiosyncratic use of *fides* in the context of the discussion of conscience.

Cajetan distinguished between speculative and practical certitude. Speculative certitude is hard to come by. If this was a moral requirement, most of us would be exposed all the time to sin. But conscience, properly understood, is an *application* of our cognition or understanding. Therefore, the only doubt which goes against conscience properly understood is the doubt against application itself, that is, against one's judgment that a certain action can be done here and now.

Roughly around the time in which Vitoria was considering the implications of Adrian's view of war, Adrian was being engaged by Juan de Medina in his discussion of prescription in *Codex de restitutione et contractu*.[13] If you are in possession of real estate for a statutory period, you may then acquire ownership rights over it. The good faith of the possessor, at least at the time of possession, is crucial in order to acquire these rights. Suppose the possessor paid for some land to a person posing as the legitimate owner. In order to grant ownership to the possessor after the statutory period, the judge may want to make sure that she thought she was purchasing it from its legitimate owner. So good faith was a requirement for the acquiring of moral and legal rights. Medina asked whether doubt on the part of the possessor, whether at time of possession or after, eliminated the good faith required for prescriptive acquisition.

As Vitoria's, Medina's move was to preserve good faith, by distinguishing between two types of doubts, speculative and practical, and by making good faith immune to one type of doubting, namely speculative doubting.[14] Soto disagreed and argued alongside Adrian that positive doubt – that is actual suspicion that the thing may not be mine – destroys good faith and thereby impedes full acquisitive prescription.[15]

6.4 Tutiorist Defences of Obedience

Adrian relied on the principle that in moral matters it is always the safer course (*tutior*) that should be followed.[16] Soto explained that this tutiorist

---

[12] Ibid., p. 134. col. A lines 75–6.
[13] Juan de Medina, *Codex de restitutione* (Alcala de Henares: Juan de Brocar, 1546) q. 17 fol. 58b-61a
[14] Medina, *Codex de restitutione*, fol. 59 col. A.   [15] Soto, *II*, lib. 4., q. 7 a. 2 at p. 369.
[16] On the roots of tutiorism, see Kantola, *Probability and Moral Uncertainty*, pp. 82–84; and Deman, 'Probabilisme' cols. 424–5.

principle operates lexically. We first weigh the gravity of the two sins that we risk committing. Then we should choose to do the act that, if it should turn out to constitute a sin, will be the lesser sin of the two. We should do that act even if the alternative act presents less of a risk to turn out to be sinful. If the two sins we risk committing are of equal moral gravity, the difference in the likelihood of each of the actions turning out to be a sin can determine what should be done.[17] So what matters in the case of war is whether the sin we risk committing by disobeying the ruler's call to arms in a just war is worse than the sin of fighting in an unjust war.

Adrian seems not to acknowledge that failure to fight can also involve a moral risk. In his presentation of the case of war, it is only following your prince into a possible unjust war that presents a moral danger.[18] This is perhaps a consequence of his closely following medieval theologian William of Auxerre. Odon Lottin regarded William of Auxerre as well as Stephen Langton as precursors of tutiorism.[19] They defended the principle that in cases of doubt about whether a planned action constitutes moral sin, one should abstain from action. In the words of *Ecclesiasticus* 3:26, 'He that loveth danger shall perish in it'. Auxerre proposed the rule: 'if someone doubts whether something is a mortal sin and does that thing, he sins mortally'.[20]

Vitoria, by contrast, notes that refraining from fighting for your king can also be morally dangerous. Since no option is without dangers, these *two* moral risks must be compared. In the *Relection*, the risks to be compared are characterized as 'assisting the enemies of the commonwealth by disobeying' and 'fighting these enemies while in doubt' (*pugnare contra hostes cum dubio*), which he considered to be worse.[21] It seems that Vitoria was drawing the wrong comparison. The combatant should be troubled because he may end up killing innocents, not because he may be acting against his own conscience (which comparatively should be a negligible and even inappropriate worry). However, we may interpret Vitoria differently in light of his saying in the *Lectures* simply that 'it is less bad to harm

---

[17] Soto, *DRTDS*, membr. 3 q. 2 concl. 2 at p. 457.
[18] Suárez (*De fide, spe et charitate*, VI.9 at p. 828) says that, for Adrian, the moral danger involved in fighting in case of doubt is 'the peril of unjust slaughtering and plundering'. Adrian, however, only mentions the risk of killing the innocent. *Quodl.* q. 2. f38v.
[19] Odon Lottin, *Psychologie et morale aux XIIe et XIIIe siècles* (Leuven: Abadie du Mont César, Gembloux: J. Duculot, 1948) vol. 2 pp. 407–11; and also his 'Le tutiorisme du trèizieme siècle', *Recherches de théologie ancienne et médiévale*, 5(1933)292–301.
[20] William of Auxerre, *Summa aurea in quattuor libros Sententiarum* (Paris: Philippus Pigouchet, 1500) f92v. The rule is invoked in *Quodl.* Q. 2 fol. 27r.
[21] Vitoria, *IB*, q. 2 a. 4 n. 32 p. 313.

enemies than to harm one's one republic [by not fighting]'.[22] So the sin involved in *pugnare contra hostes cum dubio* should be taken to be the very fighting against (innocent) enemies, rather than doing so in *doubt* (*cum dubio* should be read as a mere adjunctive).

Suárez drew a close comparison. What is at stake if we refrain from fighting is not just a violation of a duty of obedience but one of justice, since, by failing to fight, subjects are rendering their princes (and commonwealths) unable to defend their rights.[23] The thought is that it is a morally worse outcome to leave your innocent compatriots defenceless than to cause the deaths of innocent foreigners.[24]

This is not an implausible view. Even if we bear less responsibility for allowing the death of innocents than for causing it, allowing the death of your innocent compatriots may, all things considered, be worse than killing foreign innocents. This is so if you have an agent-relative duty to put ahead the interests of those specially related to you. This duty may offset the comparative moral worseness of doing harm over allowing harm. Suppose that your son and a stranger are fighting over car keys, and you do not know who the car belongs to. It may be morally worse to refrain from acting in a way that will reduce the likelihood that your son will be a victim of theft (if he turns out to be the legitimate owner) than to act in a way that increases the likelihood that a stranger will be a victim of theft (if he is the legitimate owner). As a parent you may even have a *duty* to aid your son in these circumstances. Notice that the argument thus formulated no longer rests on duties of obedience. Even if you are not summoned to fight by your ruler, you have a moral duty qua citizen to privilege the doubtful claims of your compatriots over the doubtful claims of foreigners when these claims are in conflict, so long as it is clear that one of the parties will act and the other will resist.

6.5 The Doubtful Soldier: Obliged *and* Excused

As we have seen, Vitoria allowed that subject combatants may licitly fight not only when they mistakenly believe their war to be just, but also, by

---

[22] Vitoria, in *ST II-II* q. 40 n. 8 at p. 282.
[23] Suárez, *De fide, spe et charitate*, VI, n. 9 at p. 832–3.
[24] As Soto writes, 'Even though there is the danger that innocents will be killed (if the war is unjust) this danger is not more weighty than the alternative. For citizens have a duty towards their own republic and not towards a foreign one. But the prince cannot defend and care appropriately for the republic if each time he goes to war he must explain to each citizen the reasons for doing so.' Soto, *DRTDS*, membr. 3 q. 2 concl. 4 at p. 467. For a discussion, see my 'Late-Scholastic Just War Theory' in Seth Lazar and Helen Frowe (eds.), *Oxford Handbook of Just War Theory* (Oxford: Oxford University Press, 2018), pp. 122–44.

applying tutiorist reasoning, when they *doubt* that this is the case. This seems to imply that subject combatants on both sides may justly fight each other.

Because of this, some scholars interpret Vitoria as marking the inflexion point between the medieval just war theory paradigm and the regular war paradigm.[25] The latter paradigm affirms the view dubbed 'the moral equality of combatants' according to which combatants have the same licences, rights and immunities regardless of whether they fight for the just or unjust side.[26]

Vitoria, however, was not the first moral theologian to entertain scenarios in which combatants on both sides fight each other licitly.[27] The Scottish theologian John Mair (whom Vitoria knew from his Paris studies) strikingly wrote this in a work published some thirty years before Vitoria's *Relectio de iure belli*:[28]

> It could be argued that it follows from my view that the same war can be in one respect just and in another unjust, since as regards the superior [the commanders] it is unjust but as regards the inferior [the subordinates] it is just. This is problematic [*inconveniens*], because for the side for whom the war is just, or is considered to be so, there is no obligation to restitute the things taken, otherwise however [i.e. if unjust] they must restitute, and the same can be claimed by the opposite side. In response: I concede this, for it could happen that two opposing armies suffer from probable ignorance, sometimes affecting the superiors and inferiors and sometimes affecting only the subjects and, so Lucan seems to say in the first book of his *Civil War* [(*Pharsalia*), bk. 1–126-7], about the war between Caesar and Pompey:

---

[25] For example, Stephen C. Neff, *Just War and the Law of Nations: A General History* (Cambridge: Cambridge University Press, 2005) pp. 75–6. Similar claims were made by Alfred Vanderpol in his *La doctrine de la guerre juste* (Paris: A. Pedone, 1919) p. 182–5; and Alex J. Bellamy, *Just Wars: From Cicero to Iraq* (Cambridge: Polity, 2006) p. 55.

[26] Graham Parsons, 'Public War and the Moral Equality of Combatants', *Journal of Military Ethics*, 11 (2012)304; and his response to Reichberg, 'What is the Classical Theory of Just Cause? A Response to Reichberg', *Journal of Military Ethics*, 12(2013)366. Gregory Reichberg, 'The Moral Equality of Combatants – A Doctrine in Classical Just War Theory? A Response to Graham Parsons', *Journal of Military Ethics*, 12(2013)184–5. The attribution of the moral equality thesis to Vitoria is also rejected by Peter Haggenmacher, 'Just War and Regular War in Sixteenth-Century Spanish Doctrine', *International Review of the Red Cross*, 290(1992)442. A general defence of Vitoria is found in Robert Hubert Willem Regout, *La doctrine de la guerre juste, de Saint Augustin a nous jours* (Paris: Pedone, 1935) pp. 182–5.

[27] I am not the first to notice this. See, for instance, Haggenmacher, *Grotius et la doctrine de la guerre juste* (Paris: Presses Universitaires de France, 1983) pp. 208–9. Among humanist jurists the view defending the possibility of just war on both sides was more common, notably present in the works of Andreas Alciatus and Raphaël Fulgosius.

[28] According to some, Vitoria may have been Mair's student. See Ricardo García Villoslada, *La universidad de París durante los estudios de Francisco de Vitoria* (Rome: Gregorian University, 1939) pp. 95–6, 163–5.

'Which had the fairer right for warfare we may not know: each has high authority to support him.'[29]

Gregory Reichberg and Graham Parsons have engaged in a lively exchange on whether for Vitoria the just and unjust but ignorant subjects are moral equals. Parsons has argued that for Vitoria objectively just and objectively unjust fighters are moral equals: they have the same rights and liabilities.[30] Reichberg countered that objectively unjust fighters are not 'wholly justified', but are merely excused on account of invincible ignorance.[31]

Vitoria's phrasing certainly seems to support both views. On the one hand he says that these soldiers are not just permitted to fight but *must* do so. The reason, as explained above, is that it is better to fight against innocent enemies than to fail to defend your homeland against culpable ones. We have a moral duty to minimize moral risk. If you had taken the more dangerous option and by luck ended up doing the objectively right thing you would *still have sinned*, because it is a sin to take unnecessary moral risk. So in case of doubt, you are not only permitted to follow your king but *must* do so. To fight for your prince is to abide by the outcome of a binding moral rule of risk reduction.

On the other hand, the view that Vitoria *excuses* doubtful soldiers seems to be supported by a revealing clarification made in his *Lecture*s. There he observes that just as there is 'probable' ignorance (a designation for insurmountable or justified ignorance) as opposed to voluntary or crass ignorance, there are also probable doubts and doubts that are voluntary.[32] Voluntary doubts, says Vitoria – those are that are preserved by refraining from acquiring further knowledge – do not excuse.[33] Vitoria wants to make it clear that when he affirmed that subject combatants can follow the prince when in doubt, he meant only those in the grip of insurmountable doubt. This passage seems to convey that when we follow the prince and are in the grip of insurmountable or justified doubt we are excused.

---

[29] 'Contra tertiam conclusionem cum parte quartae arguitur sic: ex illis duabus conclusionibus sequit quod aliquid bellum est in parte iustum et in parte iniustum: cum ex parte superioris sit iniustum et ex parte inferiorum iustum. Consequens est inconveniens quia quibus bellum est iustum vel tale putatum, non tenentur restituere ablatum et idem potest esse ex parte opposita. Respondet concedendo illatum: potest esse ex parte duorum exercituum oppositorum probabilis ignorantia: interdum quo ad superiores et inferiores, interdum quod ad subditos tamen. Ut Lucanus de bello inter Caesarem et Pompeium dicere videtur primo Pharsaliae "Quis iustus induat arma Scire nefas: magno se iudice quisque tuetur."' Mair, fol. 120v.
[30] Parsons, 'Public War', p. 303.   [31] Reichberg, 'The Moral Equality of Combatants', p. 185.
[32] This terminology comes from the twelfth-century canonist Huguccio of Ferrara. See Kantola, *Probability and Moral Uncertainty*, p. 28 n. 7 and references there to Lottin where the relevant texts are found.
[33] Vitoria, *In ST II-II* q. 40 a. 1 n. 8 at pp. 282–3.

Note that in Vitoria the idea of justification does not play a role; only obligation and excuse do. In fact, late scholastic discussions of conscience never contrast obligation with justification. Consider de São Tomás. He asks, 'How does an erring conscience oblige or excuse?'[34] We should not understand João as positing that an erring conscience either excuses *or* obliges. Rather he is asking how is it that conscience does both these things. In formulating the question thus, João is not pretending to make a novel or controversial point; he is presupposing that his readers believe that conscience excuses *and* obliges. If this presupposition was shared by Vitoria, it would be wrong to ask about whether Vitoria thinks doubtful soldiers are justified *or* excused. It would also be wrong to ask about his view whether doubtful soldiers are obliged to fight *or* excused for doing so. They are both obliged to fight and excused for doing so. How can this be?

João explains: the force of erroneous conscience to oblige comes from the fact that it is a sin to act against the dictum of conscience.[35] So Vitoria's main claim ought to be simply interpreted as saying that the doubtful soldier who fights does not violate the obligation to act according to his conscience. Contrary to Adrian's charge, he does not incur the sin of acting against his conscience. So when Vitoria says that they can (*possunt*) fight, he means that they are not committing the sin imputed to them by Adrian.[36]

So what is it that is excusable in a soldier's conduct? To be excused is to be liberated from sin by some circumstance, such as duress or ignorance. Fighting subjects do not stand in need of being excused from the sin of disobeying their conscience because – and this is Vitoria's point – no transgression *of this rule* is taking place.

Vitoria says that what invincibly ignorant soldiers are excused for is the sin of *killing innocent enemies*. Doubtful soldiers belong within the class of people in the grip of invincible ignorance. The doubtfulness involved in seeing probable reasons supporting both the justice and injustice of the same war requires lack of certitude. Ignorance is precisely a lack of certitude. And since, as Vitoria made clear in the *Lectures*, the doubt that excuses soldiers must be of the kind that is invincible, then it must be the case that the ignorance from which this doubt results is invincible. And this is precisely the kind of ignorance that excuses. So the referred passage from the *Lectures* should be understood in light of the view that invincibly

---

[34] de São Tomás, *Cursus theologici in ST I-II*, q. 18 a. 2 n. 11 at p. 511.
[35] de São Tomás, *Cursus theologici in ST I-II*, d. 12 a. 2 n. 11 at p. 513.
[36] Vitoria, *in ST II-II*, q. 40 a. 1 in n.8 at p. 282.

doubtful soldiers are excused for their killing of enemy innocents because of the invincible ignorance that is the root of their doubtfulness.

To recast, Vitoria seems to be saying that, when fighting their prince's unjust war, doubtful soldiers are not sinning *against the obligation to follow their conscience*. Their fighting is the fulfilment of an obligation rather than something that needs to be excused. However, as regards *the duty not to kill innocents*, these soldiers are doing something objectively wrong. Yet they are excused from this sin by the invincible ignorance that is the source of their doubtfulness.

For these reasons, it seems to me that the dispute between Reichberg and Parsons on whether Vitoria justifies or excuses some of the objectively unjust soldiers results from trying to impose on Vitoria a question that is central in recent discussions of just war theory, namely whether unjust soldiers are justified or merely excused. As I have argued, Vitoria's analysis of the situation of the doubtful soldier fighting an unjust war resists this disjunctive posing of the question. The reason is that for him there is more than one obligation at play. The normative status of these soldiers' unjust fighting must be analysed separately in reference to each of these obligations, namely, the obligation to follow your conscience and the obligation not to kill innocents.

Reichberg is entirely correct, however, in saying that unjust doubtful soldiers are moral unequals to their just opponents. Their cause is objectively wrong and their killings are a sin that needs to be excused, whereas their opponents do not sin in killing them.

6.6 Probabilist Defences of Obedience

The development of the question of the doubting soldier is intimately tied to the development of theories of moral conscience. As treatments of conscience grew larger and more elaborate, the taxonomy of conscience grew more complex. In his important treatise on conscience (1569), Franciscan theologian Antonio de Córdoba distinguished between what we may call different degrees of confidence in the dictum of conscience: these are faith, opinion, scruple and doubt.[37] In Juan Azor's *Institutiones* (1602), this distinction is treated as one between types of conscience: so we may speak of erroneous, opinative, doubtful and scrupulous conscience.[38] In Gregory Sayer (1560–1602), we already find the taxonomy that would

---

[37] Antonio de Córdoba, *Quaestionarium theologicum* (Ziletti: Venice & Ayala: Toledo, 1569–70) lib. 3 qq. 2–3 at pp. 155–8.
[38] Juan Azor, *Institutionum moralium in quibus universae questiones ad conscientiam recte, aut prave factorum pertinentes, breviter tractantur* (Cologne: *Antonius Hierat*, 1602) lib. 2 c. 8 at p. 90.

become standard: conscience can be rightful, erroneous, doubtful, probable (instead of 'opinative') and scrupulous.[39]

As types of conscience branched off so did the analysis of the subject soldier's conscience. In addition to the soldier in doubt – that is, the soldier who has no determinate judgment about the justice of the war he is called to fight, we now have the soldier who believes that there are probable (plausible) arguments for the view that the war is unjust. The view that you have to obey even when you believe that there is a good, if inconclusive, reason to regard the war as unjust, rightly awoke more resistance, and therefore more controversy, than the view that you have to obey while in doubt. In what follows, I will focus on the former question.

Vázquez's treatment of probable conscience is a good place to start. He was the first Jesuit on record to endorse probabilism, and his treatment was followed by most other late scholastics (more so than Suárez's rather concise discussion on the matter, for example). Vázquez was interested not only in the obedience of the subject called on to bear arms, but in the more general question of obedience to superiors. He thought that while tutiorist reasoning may be able to deliver the desired result insofar as obedience in the case of soldiers was concerned, this may be just because of the specifics of war and that there was no guarantee that tutiorism would deliver the right results in all of the cases in which it seems that obedience is due.

Vázquez asked whether it was permissible to act against one's opinion when one believed that what had been commanded is unjust.[40] The key here is 'acting against one's own opinion', which for Adrian meant acting against one's own conscience and for this reason was impermissible.

Before surveying Vázquez's solution we should inspect the reasons why he was unsatisfied with earlier defences of the duty of obedience, mainly with that provided by Antonio de Córdoba.

Córdoba, against Adrian's view that it is never permissible to act against one's own opinion, advanced a hybrid of tutiorism and probabiliorism. Córdoba regards his view as the accepted view and references a little known work, *Relection on the Variety of Opinions*, published in Valencia in 1540, by the Hieronymite eremite Bernabé de Rosales.[41]

---

[39] Gregory Sayer, *Clavis Regia Sacerdotum* (Venice: Baretius Baretius, 1605) lib. 1 c. 3 n. 6 at p. 4.
[40] Vázquez, *Commentariorum ac disputationum in primam secundae S. Thomae, tomus primus* (Alcalá de Henares: Widow of Juan Gracián, 1614) d. 62 c. 6 at p. 396. Adrian, *Quodl.* 2, q. 2 fol. 38B: 'an in probabili dubio doctorum licet obedire contra propriam sententiam seu opinione?'
[41] See Bernabé de Rosales (or Roses), *Relectio fratris Barnabae a Rosalibus ordinis divi Hieronymi de tribus poenitentiae partibus atque opinionum varietate, quae videlicet tenenda sit* (Valencia: Juan Mey,

According to Córdoba, the more probable opinion should be preferred when it is not the same as the safer one.[42] When two opinions appear as equally probable we should go for the safer one.

Despite Córdoba's probabiliorism, his take on obedience is tutiorist. If one must necessarily choose between two moral evils, the less bad of these evils becomes a good. So if we have to choose between the moral evil of disobedience and the moral evil of acting against one's own opinion, acting against one's own opinion becomes a moral good, since disobedience is morally worse.

Vázquez is not persuaded. He provides an argument that aims to demonstrate that following the superior's command acting against one's own opinion is inconsistent with Córdoba's tutiorism. He asks: if the command of the superior is unable to change the opinion of the subject, how will it be able to move him to act against his own opinion? If it does so, this must be because of the 'extrinsic principles' capable of producing the subject's judgment that in this case he can act against his own opinion. By 'extrinsic principles' Vázquez seems to have in mind those considerations alien to whether the superior's command is just or unjust. But if, according to Vázquez, the extrinsic principles of this sort can bring the subject to form the judgment that he can act against his own opinion, so can the subject reach a similar judgment based on the extrinsic principles provided by the authority of the learned, absent any commands. That is, he can form a judgment that he can act not on the merits of the case but, rather, because the opinion contrary to one's own is supported by reputable authorities. But tutiorism, Cordoba's doctrine, concludes Vázquez, cannot allow going against one's own opinion on the basis the extrinsic principles supporting obedience to command.[43]

Moreover, says Vázquez, Córdoba's procedure fails to deliver the desired result, namely to invariably support the duty of obedience. After all, it could happen that, in a particular case, going against one's own conscience by obeying the superior is sometimes morally riskier than disobeying.[44] When this happens, Córdoba should actually recommend disobeying. For example, says Vázquez, it may be one's own opinion that

---

1540). De Rosales defends probabiliorism [fol. 86B] and says that if the opinions are of equal probability the safer should be followed [fol. 97A]. Córdoba cites him in *Quaestionarium*, lib. 3 q. 9 at p. 189.

[42] Córdoba, *Quaestionarium theologicum*, lib. 2 q. 3 at p. 12.
[43] Vázquez, *Commentariorum in ST I-II*, d. 62 c. 6 n. 31 at pp. 396–7.
[44] Vázquez, *Commentariorum in ST I-II*, d. 62 c. 6 n. 30 at p. 397.

Conscientious Objection in War: From Duty to Right 135

that which has been ordered constitutes a violation of natural law. In such a case, it would be worse to act against one's own opinion and obey than to fail to obey. It could also happen that failing to follow one's own opinion involves a violation of a more important virtue than the one that would be violated by disobeying a precept.[45] So that Córdoba's reasoning may sometimes support the duty to obey, but sometimes the duty to disobey. For these reasons, Vázquez believes that a sound defence of the duty of obedience cannot be firmly established on the basis of tutiorist reasoning.

In order to understand Vázquez's probabilist defence of the duty of obedience, some background of probabilism must be provided. Although he did not invent probabilism, it was the Dominican Bartolomé de Medina who gave it its standard formulation in 1577 by asserting that 'when an opinion is probable it may be followed even when the contrary opinion is more probable'.[46] The view is that if two conflicting opinions about the moral status of an action satisfy a certain threshold of probability, then it is sometimes permitted to follow the less probable one.

Opinion, unlike doubt, involves assent to a proposition. The assent is not firm and certain; it includes the fear (*formido*) that the opposite proposition might be true. An opinion is probable if 'it is sufficiently supported by reason to be held to be true by a rational person'.[47] Or, more simply, if it has the appearance of truth; so 'probability' was sometimes used interchangeably with 'verisimilitude'.[48]

To assess the probability of an opinion, one must assess the grounds supporting it. Two conflicting opinions may be both probable and held as probable by one and the same agent without him incurring a contradiction. This is the sort of probability involved in judicial practice. The claim that Manfred is the killer and the claim that he is not may both be well grounded ('probable'). The epistemic probabilities of two conflicting propositions, unlike aleatory probabilities, need not satisfy the complementational principle for negation (if

---

[45] Ibid.
[46] Medina, *Expositio in ST I- II*, p. 309a. The doctrine is also defended in his *Breve instrucción de como se ha de administrar el sacramento de la penitencia* (Huesca: Juan Pérez de Valdivieso, 1581) p. 21. Blic, in his 'Barthélémy Medina et les origines du probabilisme', *Ephemerides Theologiae Lovaniensis*, 7 (1930)46– 83, 264– 91, 481– 2, convincingly demonstrates that probabilism was not Medina's innovation.
[47] Schüßler, 'On the Anatomy of Probabilism', p. 93.
[48] The term was used frequently as the equivalent of 'probable'. See for example Molina, *II*, lib. 1 tract. 2, d. 103.7.

the epistemic probability that p is true is 1/x then the probability that not p is true need not be 1–1/x).[49]

The probability of an opinion could be intrinsic or extrinsic depending on the type of cause (*principia*) of assent.[50] Assent to an opinion derives from intrinsic *principia* when one demonstrates the proposition, for instance, by showing the opposite opinion to be absurd or impossible.[51] The extrinsic *principia* of assent are expert authorities, such as theologians and legal experts. Juan Azor, for example, listed 182 different authorities grouped according to field of expertise and historical provenance.[52]

Vázquez argued that one may act against one's own opinion in the following case. After examining the merits of intrinsic principia supporting each opinion, one assents to one of them. However, one may then consider the extrinsic sources of probability and discover, say, that many respected authorities support the other opinion. These extrinsic grounds allow one to give one's assent to the proposition that the contrary opinion is probable, although we still regard the opinion inferior as far as its intrinsic merits are considered (yet satisfying the threshold of intrinsic probability). The assent based on extrinsic authority is not an assent to the opinion contradicting the one that we assented to on the basis of its intrinsic merits but, rather, an assent to the proposition that the opinion is probable. So the assent based on intrinsic probability and the assent based on extrinsic probability do not strictly contradict each other.[53]

So Vázquez's view is that, in the matters contested, when two opinions are probable, one can either follow the one that seems the most probable, assenting to it based on its intrinsic merits, or assent to the proposition that the contrary opinion is probable and follow it in practice, thereby acting against one's own opinion (but not against one's own conscience). So whenever a good number of respected authorities hold an opinion contrary to one's own, practical deference becomes permissible.

Like Córdoba, Vázquez notes that the opinion assented to can be the less safe of the two. There is no correlation between moral safety in the tutiorist sense and the degree of probability of an opinion.[54]

---

[49] See Blic, 'Les origines', p. 78.
[50] Vázquez, *Commentariorum in ST I-II*, d. 62, c. 3, n. 8 at p. 391.
[51] Vázquez, *Commentariorum in ST I-II*, d. 62. c. 3. nn. 10–11 at pp. 391–2.
[52] Azor, *Institutionum moralium*, pp. 104–7.
[53] Vázquez, *Commentariorum in ST I-II*, d. 62 c. 3 n. 10 at p. 392.
[54] Vázquez, *Commentariorum in ST I-II*, d. 62 c. 1 n. 1 at p. 389.

Vázquez's take on the problem of obedience is an application of the doctrine that one can follow *any* probable opinion, not just the more probable one. If the action commanded by the ruler's precept is supported by probable reasons, one can follow it. He argues that if there is what we may call a prima facie duty to do something, and there is a way of doing this licitly, then it is morally necessary to do this. Therefore, the subject has a moral duty to obey, by going against his own opinion, whenever this can be done licitly.[55]

Vázquez is clear that the extrinsic probability of the ruler's precept cannot derive from his status as ruler, but rather from the fact that moral experts believe the precept to be binding (accidentally, it could happen that the ruler is a moral expert, but he would not be a moral expert just because he is the ruler).[56]

So, for Vázquez, probabilism is able to offer a more successful defence of the general duty to obey than tutiorism. While the morally safer opinion may not inevitably be that one must obey the ruler, it is always the case that if there is a perceivedly probable case for the justice of the war, the subject can fight, even when his own opinion is that the war is unjust. It suffices, as he says, that the subjects believe that the king is asking and following the counsel of wise and saintly men.

It may be noted that the doctrine does not allow for disobedience when the ruler declares war on a whim or is acting in such a patently unjust way that no authority can be presumed to back him. There was much discussion and little agreement as to what confers extrinsic probability on an opinion: does one author suffice or do we need the majority of them? Does it matter who the author is? What if the authors are merely following one another: do they then count as one or many? What if the opinion in question has became antiquated? It was hard to give definite answers to these questions, and very easy to plausibly claim extrinsic probability for almost every non-outlandish claim that the war was just. So, in effect, by making extrinsic probability a sufficient condition of the subject's obedience, Vázquez makes obedience virtually invulnerable to the opinions of subjects and soldiers about the justice of the ruler's command. It is worth remembering, however, that this applies only to *opinions* – that is, judgments that involve uncertainty and fear of getting things wrong. For Vázquez, it remains the case that the subject or soldier who feels certain

---

[55] Vázquez, *Commentariorum in ST I-II*, d. 62 c. 6 n. 32 at p. 397.
[56] Vázquez, *Commentariorum in ST I-II*, d. 62 c. 6 n. 33 at p. 397.

about the injustice of what he is being commanded to do would act wrongly against his conscience by obeying.

6.7 The Freedom to Disobey

Although Vázquez's view was followed by the vast majority of authors, it was not without opponents, prominent among whom were Castro Palao[57] and, very extensively, Juan Sánchez (†1624?).[58]

In both Castro Palao's and Juan Sánchez's treatments, the principle of the condition of the possessor plays a pivotal role. As we have seen, this is the principle that, in cases of doubt, the condition of the possessor prevails.[59] So if two persons contend about a disputed piece of land and doubt is equal on both sides, the judge should favour the party in actual possession. The same principle was applied to analyse disputes over relations of subordination. There is a presumption in favour of obedience, because when there is doubt, the superior is in de facto possession of some aspects of the subject's freedom. This was a standard argument to defend a subject's obedience in cases of doubt.

Castro Palao and Juan Sánchez make two central moves. The first move is to limit the applicability of this principle to doubt as opposed to opinion. While in cases of doubt the condition of the de facto ruler prevails, they argued that this should not be so in cases in which the subject holds as probable that the ruler is not to be obeyed.[60] This doctrine was taken from Tomás Sánchez, although Tomás did not go as far as to present the views advanced by Juan Sánchez and Castro Palao.[61]

The second move was to deny any substantial difference between uncertainty about the licitness or justice of the ruler's command and uncertainty about his having jurisdiction over the agent. Earlier standard treatments asserted that, when in case of doubt about whether the ruler is acting within or without his powers, I may be morally allowed to disobey because I need not assume that the presumption in favour of the possessor applies. However, it was standardly argued that when ordered to do that

---

[57] Castro Palao, *Operis moralis*, tract. 1 d. 2 punct. 6 n. 6 at pp. 10–11.
[58] Juan Sánchez, *Selectae illaeque practicae disputationes* (Venice: Bertanos, 1639) d. 33 n. 32 and following at p. 201 et fol.
[59] On this, see Rudolf Schüßler, 'Moral Self-Ownership and *Ius Possessionis* in Late Scholastics' in Virpi Mäkinen and Petter Korkman (eds.), *Transformations in Medieval and Early-Modern Rights Discourse* (Dordrecht: Springer, 2006) pp. 160–4.
[60] Sánchez, *Selectae et practicae*, d. 33 n. 30, *in fine* argues that the condition of possession is a tutiorist principle that applies only in cases of doubt.
[61] Tomás Sánchez, *Opus morale*, lib. 1 c. 10 n. 66 at p. 93–4.

which I doubt to be licit or just, this presumption in favour of the ruler applies and so I must obey.[62] Castro Palao and Juan Sánchez thought that there was no substantial difference between the ruler possibly exceeding his authority and the ruler possibly commanding something illicit or unjust. In the latter case, not less than in the former, I have reason to doubt that the ruler is in condition of being the possessor. So if I do not have a duty to obey in the former case, neither do I in the latter.[63]

Juan Sánchez gives an expansive and intricate exposition of this view in eleven dense pages containing a very large number of references. He argues that, while the probable judgment that the superior's order is illicit as such is not enough to ground the permission to disobey, one cannot have this probable judgment without also judging it probable that one need not obey, and *this* judgment does ground the permission to disobey. He goes so far as to say that a subject is permitted to disobey not only on the basis of his own opinion that the ruler's command is illicit, but also by following the probable opinion of some authority that believes so, *even if he personally does not believe the command to be unjust.*[64]

Sánchez tackles Vázquez's argument that there is a duty to obey simply because every probable opinion can be safely followed and so the probable opinion that the command is not illicit removes any obstacle in the fulfilment of our duty of obedience. Sánchez replies that this may be true when there is zero risk of sin, but not when there is probable risk of sin.[65]

Like Castro Palao, Sánchez takes his view to be intimated by Suárez who, perhaps tendentiously, he appoints his patron. In the section from *De censuris* referred to by Sánchez, Suárez takes a stand in favour of obedience and against the inference that because it is safe to follow one's probable opinion, one may disobey the law whenever one believes it unjust. Suárez says that because the ruler is in the condition of possessor, the probabilities of the opinion that the law in question is just and that it is not are not to be assigned the same weight. If the probabilities are equal, the presumption must be in favour of the ruler.[66] Yet Suárez calls 'very plausible' the opinion that one would be excused from observing the law if one regarded the probability of the opinion that the command is unjust as *manifestly* more probable than its opposite.[67] Note, however, that Suárez's view remains

---

[62] For example, Vàzquez, *Commentariorum in ST I-II*, d. 62 c. 6 n. 34 at p. 397.
[63] Castro Palao, *Operis Moralis*, d. 2 punct. 6 n. 5 at p. 14; Sánchez, *Selectae et practicae*, d. 33 n. 37 at p. 202.
[64] Sánchez, *Selectae et practicae*, d. 33 n. 46 at p. 205.
[65] Sánchez, *Selectae et practicae*, d. 33 n. 44 at p. 205.
[66] Suárez, *De censuris*, d. 4 sect. 6 n. 6 at p. 110.   [67] Suárez, *De censuris*, d. 4 sect. 6 n. 7 at p. 111.

different from Sánchez's, who argues that one may disobey a command whenever the opinion that the command is unjust is merely probable, regardless of how its probability compares to the probability of the opposite view.

Let me consider Sánchez's instructive replies to some foreseeable objections against his view. Concerning the objection that his view is scandalous, he replies that scandal requires that the scandalous action be bad, or intrinsically bad, which is not the case in permissible disobedience.

He devotes more space to the objection that his doctrine, if applied, would encourage civic unrest, rebellion and sedition.[68] He argues – puzzlingly – that no civic unrest needs to follow if the opinions of the ruler and the subjects are known to each other, for no one should be surprised if the inferior strives to keep his right intact.[69]

There is the fear that the superior may interpret as contempt (*displicentia*) the non-execution of the command, but, he says, the fact that this is a natural reaction does not make it just. The subject must make his opinion known to the superior before disobeying, so that the superior will not interpret the non-execution of the command as an act of mere contempt. Moreover, says Sánchez, in comparative terms, the opinion of other authors that the subject may not obey when he considers that the superior is illegitimate or acting beyond his authority is bound to cause much more unrest than his own opinion, as such cases are bound to be more frequent than cases in which a particular command of the legitimate superior is considered illicit.[70] So, comparatively speaking, the latter accepted doctrine has more noxious consequences to the civic order than Sánchez's.

Finally, Sánchez raises the objection that, in civil law cases, it is rightly considered scandalous and wrong to use private violence to deprive a person whom we regard as mispossessing one's property. However, he argues that in the case at hand, the subject does not deprive the superior of something that he – rightly or wrongly – possesses (namely, the subject's liberty) but merely defends his liberty, a liberty that he has because of his probable opinion that the action commanded is illicit.[71] The subject is defending his own possession, which is neither scandalous nor seditious.

---

[68] Sánchez, *Selectae et practicae*, d. 33 n. 42 at p. 202 (note that 204 has been misprinted as 202).
[69] Ibid.: 'quilibet ius suum illaesum conservare contendat, quod fieri iure naturale concessum est' 'Anyone, whoever it may be, would strive to keep his own right undamaged, which is granted to take place by natural law'.
[70] Ibid. [71] Ibid.

Sánchez concludes that even when the superior is right and the command that is disobeyed was not in fact illicit, he cannot rightly punish the disobedient subject, for there is no blame or guilt (*culpa*) in what the subject did.[72]

6.8 Domestic War That Is Just on Both Sides

Suárez forewarned that the sort of view that would later be defended by Sánchez would allow the possibility of a domestic war that is just on both sides, which would make it impossible to govern the republic.[73] Suárez believes that his view avoids this. When the ruler and the subjects have the same assessment of the probability of the opinions concerning the justice of a given law, they will reach the same conclusion about whether it must be obeyed or not. Of course, there may be many cases of actual civil insurrection and its repression, in which both sides *consider* themselves to be just, but this will be because at least one of them got the probabilities of the opinions about the justice of the law wrong.

Sánchez denies Suárez's implication that his view commits him to allowing the possibility of a war between subjects and rulers that is objectively just on both sides.[74] The subjects assent to the opinion that their disobedience is probably right and they assent that the opinion of the ruler that it is not, is probably wrong. So, at least from the point of view of the subjects, their enemy is not as just as they are.[75] The king is not their moral equal. In the eyes of God, moreover, and as to the truth of the matter, one of the parties fights justly and the other does not.

Sánchez's characterization of the insurrectionary conflict taking place seems baffling. If probable opinion suffices to fight licitly, then the subjects could believe that their reason for insurrection is as probable as the reason that the king has to coercively enforce his command.

What Sánchez must have in mind is that while subjects may indeed believe that these two opposite opinions can be equally probable, they give practical assent only to one of two opposites or to the other. But then this 'assent' cannot follow from an appraisal of the superior epistemic reliability of their opinion (since these opinions may be equally probable), but must be simply an act of will embracing the opinion in favour of rebelling as a practical guide (*sed solum secundum assensus opinativus contrarius*).[76]

---

[72] Sánchez, *Selectae et practicae*, d. 33 n. 43 at p. 205.
[73] Suárez, *De censuris*, d. 4 sect. 6 n. 6 at p. 111.   [74] Ibid.
[75] Sánchez, *Selectae et practicae*, d. 33 n. 42 at p. 205.
[76] Sánchez, *Selectae et practicae*, d. 44 n. 60 at p. 296.

So Sánchez's claim that there is no subjective assessment of the war being just on both sides on the part of the subjects is suspect. What is really going on is that the subjects can say that both conflicting opinions about who is right and wrong in the confrontation between subjects and ruler are embraceable but decide to assent to only one of them.

What we find troublesome about the thesis that a war can be just on both sides – a subject to which I return in Chapter 8 – is not only the belief that this cannot be objectively correct, but that there is something disturbing about someone trying to kill somebody whom he regards as no less just than he is. Sánchez's saying that one cannot practically embrace the two conflicting opinions simultaneously does not remove this source of uneasiness, because the uneasiness is about the *assessment* of the moral situation by the subject and not about his acts of will (i.e. his acts of giving assent).[77] In Sánchez's view, the subject can assess the ruler and subject as equally just even if he can choose to embrace only one of the sides.

6.9 Two Conceptions of Subject Disobedience

The itinerary of the controversy about the duty of obedience paints a very interesting picture. On the surface, the discussion makes a full circle. We start from Adrian's strong view for sticking to one's own belief, then we have tutiorist rationales in favour of obedience by Vitoria and Soto to be replaced with probabilistic defences of the duty of obedience, such as those of Vázquez, to end with Castro Palao's and Juan Sánchez's defence of disobedience.

However, it is easy to see the great chasm between the defences of subject disobedience offered by Adrian and Castro Palao and Juan Sánchez. While for Adrian there is a real duty of obedience which is trumped by the duty to adhere by one's conscience (which in his view requires adhering to one's opinion), for Castro Palao and Sánchez the probability of the opinion that one may not obey extinguishes any presumptive duties of obedience.

It is not only the reasons behind the positions defended by Adrian, Castro Palao and Sánchez that are very different but also their substance. Adrian defends the duty to disobey as part of the duty to be loyal to one's conscience. By contrast, as Sánchez expressly puts it, the latter defend the freedom of the subject not to carry out illicit orders, a freedom that he has as a natural right.

[77] Ibid.

These are two entirely different views of subject disobedience (or as we would call it now 'civil' disobedience). In the first case, what matters is sticking to one's own judgment of right and wrong, which prevails over other prima facie duties, whereas, in the latter, what matters is the conditions under which you can blamelessly consider yourself to be free of the moral duty to obey the ruler. It was the development and endorsement of probabilism which caused the transition from one conception to the other.

The question of obedience is intimately connected with the question of the possibility of war that is just on both sides. As we will see in Chapter 8, probabilist arguments in favour of the prevailing of the duty of obedience over the subjects' moral doubts seem to lead to the upshot that subjects from two enemy polities may both justly fight each other, thereby being moral equals. Arguments in favour of disobedience based on probabilist doctrine of the sort explored in this chapter seem to lead to the conclusion that rulers and subjects may both fight *each other* justly, again as moral equals. It would seem, therefore, that the moral cost of avoiding wars just on both sides between political communities by weakening the subjects' duty to obey their rulers has the effect of relocating war just on both sides to the domestic arena.

CHAPTER 7

Patriotic Collaborationism: Demosthenes and Alexander

7.1 Genesis of the Controversy

What kinds of sacrifice can the political community rightfully demand from its citizens? Most agree that it can demand that they risk their lives to defend it by opposing an unjust enemy. But can it also demand that they sacrifice their lives for its sake when this entails cooperating with the wrongful designs of the enemy? The answer depends partly on the sort of right that the community has over its members and partly on the moral restrictions against the infliction and self-infliction of intentional harm.

Catholic moral theology upholds an absolute prohibition on the intentional killing of the innocent. The late scholastics discussed many cases that put this prohibition under pressure. One of these cases was raised by Vitoria in his Commentary on Aquinas' *Summa Theologiae*, where he discussed one possible exception to the prohibition. '[I]f the King of the Turks were to ask for a Christian preacher [to be delivered to him] so that as a consequence everybody else would be spared, is it licit to deliver him to the King?'[1] When Soto, a few years later, took up the same question, he used a story told by Plutarch as an illustration.[2] According to the Greek historian, Alexander the Great offered to spare besieged Athens on the condition that Demosthenes, the leader of the anti-Macedonian party, and seven of his fellows be handed over to him. Were the Athenians morally permitted to deliver Demosthenes and his friends to face certain death at the hands of Alexander?

This question engaged not only a great number of late scholastic moral theologians (with the interesting exception of Suárez), but also humanist

---

[1] Vitoria, *In ST II-II* q. 64 a. 6 n. 2 at p. 299.
[2] Plutarch, *Plutarch's Lives*, Bernardotte Perrin trans. (Cambridge, MA: Harvard University Press, London: William Heinemann, Loeb's Classical Library) 'Demosthenes' 23.3–5, vol. 7, p. 57. Soto, *II*, lib. 5 q. 1 a. 7 at p. 399.

jurists such as Fernando Vázquez de Menchaca (1512–1569), finally reaching Hugo Grotius and his Protestant commentators, such as Johann Adam Osiander and Kaspar Ziegler.

As we will see, the vast majority of the late scholastic moral theologians felt that the right answer must be that the republic is morally permitted to surrender the innocent citizen. However, they had a hard time showing how this could be compatible with the absolute prohibition on intentional killing of the innocent. The moves available to these authors were either to try to construe the harm resulting to the innocent from his being surrendered as *unintentional* harm, or to find a way to remove his innocent status. Both strategies met many obstacles. This led to an unexpected upshot: the view, held by a minority of theologians, that an innocent person is not morally permitted to voluntarily surrender himself to the tyrant.

There are other historical instances of cases such as that of Demosthenes. Antonio Tomasso Schiara in his *Theologia Bellica* gave an example from his own time – the case in which Ethiopian monophysite rebels demanded five Jesuit Fathers to be surrendered to them as condition for refraining from attacking the forces of the Emperor's brother, the Catholic neophyte Sela Krestos.[3] Polemists sometimes used arguments from the Demosthenes controversy to support or impugn the legitimacy of killing and handing over of purported innocents, for instance, in the case of the Portuguese Prince Duarte of Bragança who died in Spanish captivity in 1649.[4]

Situations like the one discussed by Vitoria and Soto presented themselves in more recent times. In 1943, the Gestapo threatened to raze the Vilna Ghetto unless the Partisan commander Itzhak Wittenberg be surrendered. The head of the local Judenrat set a trap to catch Wittenberg, which ultimately failed. Riots by the Ghetto population demanding Wittenberg's delivery to the Nazis followed. He surrendered himself and then killed himself while in Nazi captivity.

Vitoria's answer to the question concerning surrendering the innocent is not entirely clear. He ruled out the direct killing of an innocent person at a tyrant's behest but failed to pronounce on the question of surrendering him. Vitoria considered the argument: 'If the Turkish sultan were to ask

---

[3] Antonio Tomasso Schiara (†1718), *Theologia bellica* (Rome: Ioannes Francisci de Buagnis, 1702) vol. 1. lib. 1 diff. 19 at p. 71, on the basis of a letter from Tomás de Barros to the Jesuit General Muzio Vitteleschi (26 June 1622). This letter was digitally retrieved from http://bdlb.bn.br/acervo/handle/123456789/47475.

[4] See Francisco Velasco de Govea, *Perfidia de Alemania y de Castilla en la prisión, entrega, acusación y proceso del serenísimo infante de Portugal Don Duarte* (Lisbon: Craesbeek, 1652) lib. 1. tit. 2 a. 5 at p. 99.

for one Christian preacher in order to kill him, with the result that all others would be saved, it would be lawful to give the man to him. Therefore it would also be lawful to kill him.'[5] Although Vitoria rejected the consequent, he never directly disproved the antecedent. Salón and others after him (such as de São Tomás) understood Vitoria as allowing the view that the innocent *can* be surrendered or at least be made to leave the republic. Perhaps it was Vitoria to whom Soto was alluding when he wrote, 'There are those who held that the republic cannot kill the man but it can surrender him to the tyrant, but these are the same thing and if one is forbidden then the other is also forbidden'.[6]

7.2 False Leads

7.2.1 *The Organicist Analogy*

As the controversy unfolded, a number of grounds for and against were floated, only to be put aside relatively quickly. First, there was the organicist analogy, which suggested that the relationship between a citizen and the republic was analogous to the relationship between a part of the body and the whole. Just as the part exists for the sake of the body, so does the citizen exist for the sake of the republic. Vitoria, Soto and everybody after them believed the analogy could not hold: the individual citizen has an existence of his own, his own goals and ends, and his own set of rights, as opposed to a hand, which, as an organ, derives its being from the whole body, has no ends other than those that belong to the preservation and functioning of the body, and is not a right holder.[7] So, while all of the authors involved in the controversy mentioned this argument, none of them believed it could really justify the surrendering of an innocent citizen.

7.2.2 *Artificial Causality*

An argument that played a role in the initial stages of the controversy was that there is no difference between surrendering a citizen to the enemy and

---

[5] Vitoria, *In ST II-II*, q. 64 a. 6 n. 2 at p. 299. Translation from John P. Doyle, trans. intro. and notes, On Homicide & Commentary on Summa theologiae IIa-IIae q. 64 (Thomas Aquinas) (Milwaukee: Marquette University Press, 1997) p. 187.
[6] Soto, *II*, lib. 5 q. 1 a. 7 at p. 400. Followed by Córdoba, *Quaestionarium theologicum*, lib. 1 q. 37 at p. 303.
[7] Soto, *II*, lib. 5 q. 1 a. 7 at p. 400.

sending soldiers to certain death in the battlefield, something the republic was certainly allowed to do.

Soto, however, insisted that there is a great difference between sending someone to a foreseeable death as a result of resisting the enemy and cooperating with and facilitating the enemy's evil designs.[8] Salón gave the following case as illustration: a mugger threatens a passerby, saying that unless he gets a hundred gold coins he will be killed on the spot.[9] You happen to witness the situation and have enough money in your pocket. The common view of the scholastics was that while you were allowed to give the money to save the passerby, you were not obligated to do so. In contrast, if you could, with little cost to yourself, forcefully repel the criminal and set him off running then you were obliged to do that. If you save the passerby by giving the money your act achieves its purpose because of the criminal's readiness to keep his promise. This is why, said Salón, Demosthenes (absent any legislation compelling him to do so) had no duty to surrender himself to the enemy in order to save the republic, just as you do not have a duty to give money to the mugger (Alexander) so that the lets his victim (Athens) go. Demosthenes was obliged to help defend Athens from Alexander but he was not obliged to save Athens by playing into Alexander's plan. Thus, in this view, it would be wrong for the republic to compel him to do what he has no duty to do. In the same way, in the case of surrendering an innocent person, the defensive effect of this action is not achieved directly, as it would be if you punched the criminal, but through the criminal's intervening agency.

Molina, on the other hand, and Salón before him, convincingly argued that it makes no moral difference whether the infliction of harm to save someone is made necessary because of 'natural' causes or because of an intervening malicious agency which creates an artificial causal link between two events. Soto thought that if a tyrant says, 'Cut off your hand or I'll kill you', you are not morally permitted to cut off your hand. Yet you would be allowed to do so if, say, gangrene had developed in your hand and cutting it off were the only way of saving your life.[10] Molina argued that you can cut off your hand in both cases, regardless of what it is that makes it the case that if you fail to do so you die.

For Molina, the real reason that the republic cannot kill an innocent citizen directly is not that his death is a condition for saving the republic only because of the ill will of the tyrant, but rather, because, as noted, the

---

[8] Ibid. [9] Salón, *II*, q. 64 a. 6 concl. 2 at p. 398. [10] Molina, *II*, lib. 4 tract. 3 d. 10 at p. 30.

relation between the republic and the citizen is fundamentally different than the relation between one's hand and oneself.[11]

7.2.3 The Scope of the State's Authority

Vitoria floated, though stopped short from embracing, the view that since it is the citizen's patriotic duty to sacrifice himself for the republic, he can be intentionally and directly killed by the republic.[12] Soto, reflecting on the citizen's duty to surrender himself to the tyrant, affirmed that, although there is a patriotic duty to sacrifice oneself for the community, this is not one of the duties that the state can legitimately compel citizens to discharge because it is not required by justice.[13] In advancing his view Soto offered no principled ground for why the state should restrict the scope of legislation to duties of justice. Soto's view was rejected by the majority of authors as both untenable and at odds with actual practice. Leonardus Lessius noted that the magistrates may and do oblige their subjects to do many things that they are not obliged as a matter of strict justice (*iustitia particularis*) to do, such as giving alms in times of hunger, being compelled to selling the fruits of their trees in times of scarcity, avoiding immodest dress, not getting drunk, not fornicating,[14] or, as Molina added, going to war or sweeping the patch of sidewalk in front of their doorstep.[15] It is no wonder that Soto's adherents in later stages of the debate made no use of this particular argument.

7.3 Overview of Leading Views

The dispute reached its maturity in the writings of Salón, de São Tomás and Molina. Around this time, three main views became distinguishable within the controversy, while a fourth rather interesting view was never quite incorporated into the fray.

The first view, originating in Soto and defended by Aragón, de São Tomás and others, flatly denied the moral permissibility of surrendering the innocent.[16] Aragón added that handing over the innocent to the tyrant constitutes *positive* cooperation with an intrinsically evil act:[17] to surrender the innocent is not just refraining from defending him, it involves positive

---

[11] Molina, *II*, lib. 4. tract. 3 d. 10 n. 1 at p. 29; Giavanni Bosso, *Moralia varia* (Lyon: Phillip Borde and Laurence Arnaud, 1649) pars 1 tit. 1 sect 29 n. 936 at p. 234.
[12] Vitoria, *In ST II-II*, q. 64 a. 6 n. 2 at p. 303.   [13] Soto, *II*, lib. 5 q. 1 a. 7 at p. 400.
[14] Leonardus Lessius, *II*, lib. 2 cap. 9 dub. 7 at pp. 82–3.
[15] Molina, *II*, lib. 4 tract. 3 d. 10 n. 4 at p. 30.   [16] Aragón, *In ST II-II*, q. 64 a. 6 at p. 268.
[17] Aragón, *In ST II-II* q. 64 a. 6 ad 3 at p. 269.

action: you must seize Demosthenes, handcuff him and physically hand him over. But, notes Aragón, as St Paul says in the *Letter to the Romans*, 'One may not do evil so that good may come'.[18]

Molina found Soto's position to be inconsistent: if there is no difference between surrendering the innocent and killing him, why assume, as Soto did, that there is any difference between the innocent person voluntarily surrendering himself, which Soto held to be permissible, and his killing himself, which Soto did not consider permissible?[19] As we will see below, this criticism pressed de São Tomás to shed some of Soto's grounds.

A second view, attributed to Vitoria and defended by the likes of Molina and Lugo (and before him Luis López [1530–1595] and Pedro de Navarra [fl. 1570]), held that the republic is morally permitted to surrender the innocent even if he remains morally and legally innocent.[20]

A third view, defended by Báñez, Lessius and Salón, asserted that it is permissible to surrender the innocent so long as there is a law in place that the citizen would be breaking by not surrendering himself to the enemy.[21]

A fourth view, which did not ultimately gain much ground, came from Vázquez de Menchaca who held that surrendering the innocent would violate the tacit contract on which political society is based.[22]

I shall briefly present the last two of these views first, to clear the way for the first two views, which, I think, constitute the core of the controversy.

7.4 The Legal Way Out

Salón, following the footsteps of Báñez and Lessius, strove to offer what he presents as a middle way. He pointed out, somewhat misleadingly, that there was a general consensus among the authors around five principles: (1) that, in the case under discussion, the republic is not bound to defend the citizen if the tyrant tries to apprehend him; (2) that, on the other hand, the republic may not kill the citizen itself; (3) that the citizen is not morally required to preserve his life by defending himself against the tyrant's agents; (4) that the citizen has a duty of charity to surrender himself; (5) that the republic has the authority to legislate that any innocent citizen

---

[18] *Letter to the Romans* 3:8 (King James Version); the Vulgata reads: 'Faciamus mala, ut veniant bona?'
[19] Molina, *II*, lib. 4 tract. 3 d. 10 nn. 4–5 at p. 30.
[20] Luis López, *Instructorii conscientiae* (Lyon: Petrus Landry, 1591) c. 60 p. 310; Pedro de Navarra, *De ablatorum restitutione in foro conscientiae* (Lyon: Iuntarum, 1593) vol. 1 lib. 2 c. 3 n. 119–28 at pp. 204–5.
[21] Báñez, *II*, in *ST II-II* q. 64 a. 6 at p. 217.
[22] Fernando Vázquez de Menchaca, *Controversiarum illustrium* (Venice: Franciscum Rampazetum, 1564) lib. 1 c. 13 at p. 45.

demanded by a tyrant in the stipulated circumstances should surrender himself or be punished by death if he fails to do so.[23]

On the basis of (4) and (5), Salón argued that the republic may surrender the requested citizen to the tyrant so long as there is a law or command in place requiring him to do so, for if he fails to comply he is no longer innocent. He then becomes punishable by death, and surrendering him is just another way of administering this punishment.[24]

In Salón's words:

> [T]he republic does not have the power to take the wealth of rich men in order to relieve grave or extreme necessities that would bring common harm, but only has the power to command the rich men themselves to give. But if they won't do it, then, since [the republic] was looking to the common good, by just command it has the power to take their money from their homes as punishment for their cruelty and disobedience, and to use their goods to help the poor. Similarly, in the case we are investigating, the public authority does not have the power to kill an innocent man, since he is neither an evildoer nor an invader. Nor [does it have the power] to simply hand him over absolutely to the tyrant, since it does not have the power to hand him over to death when he has done nothing wrong, but since he would be considered guilty under the rule of charity, and moreover according to legal justice ought to prefer the common good over his own life, and in this case to hand himself over to [the tyrant] to free his fatherland. The republic has the power and ought to command him to do this, and if he does not obey, then he is already guilty, and by just command the republic has the power to hand a disobedient man over to a tyrant. In this way we avoid all the difficulties of Vitoria's and Soto's opinions, and we offer the governors of these places a lawful means, apart from any doubt, by which they are able to liberate their republics.[25]

There were a number of objections to this view, which, interestingly, was the one followed by Grotius. Torres objected that this form of punishment is as inhuman as requiring a lawbreaker to slay himself with his sword as punishment and this is something which the republic cannot demand.[26] Salón did not make much of this claim, responding that commanding soldiers to remain in a position that the commander knows will be overrun by the enemy is no less inhuman and yet the republic is authorized to issue that command.[27]

---

[23] Salón, *II*, q. 64 a. 6 at p. 399.   [24] Ibid., p. 400.   [25] Ibid., p. 399.
[26] Luis Torres, *Disputationum in secundam secundae D. Thomae* (Lyon: Iacobi Cardon and Petrus Cavellat, 1621) d. 26 dub. 2 n. 15–16 at p. 258.
[27] Salón, *II*, q. 64 a. 6 at p. 400.

Molina was unsympathetic to Salón's legal solution. He inquired: how is it that the republic is not authorized to surrender the innocent to the tyrant but it is authorized to order his surrender and to punish him for not doing so?[28] It is fair to say that Molina and de São Tomás both saw Salón's legal way out not only as contrived, but as a distraction from the main issue: whether the act of expelling Demosthenes from the republic constitutes an instance of intentionally murdering the innocent or not.

7.5 Vázquez de Menchaca's Contractualism

Another distracting but very interesting move was that of the humanist jurist Fernando Vázquez de Menchaca.[29] Unlike the late scholastic authors, whom he read and quoted, he was not interested in the question of whether the act of surrendering a citizen was intrinsically evil or not. Rather, he thought the right question to ask was whether surrendering an innocent citizen was in accord with the very rationale of political association. In many ways anticipating Hobbes, who was influenced by him, he understood political association to rest on a good faith contract for the sake of each other's increased security and well-being. This social pact did not include the duty to sacrifice oneself for society (or to be willing to face certain death on the battlefield), which would betray the very point of entering political society. Vázquez de Menchaca compared the republic to travellers who decide to journey together for better protection against bandits. The bandits say, 'Give us this one person and we'll let the others go'. To accept this would be vile and perfidious: it would be violating the tacit or explicit good faith promise to defend each other.[30] Consequently, the republic must face danger to one citizen as if it were danger to all.

Vázquez de Menchaca's argument, if taken at face value, is not compelling. It may not be irrational to enter into a contract that contemplates a very low, evenly distributed statistical probability that one citizen may be surrendered to save the rest.

In his *De iure belli ac pacis*, Grotius offered a softened and, in his eyes, charitable reading of Menchaca.[31] According to Grotius, Menchaca did not mean that the state may never surrender the innocent to the enemy, but rather that while there is even a small hope of successful defence of the innocent, such defence should be offered. Grotius had little of his own to

---

[28] Molina, *II*, lib. 4 tract. 3 d. 10 n. 5 pp. 30–31.
[29] Vázquez de Menchaca, *Controversiarum illustrium*, lib. 1 c. 13 at p. 45. [30] Ibid., p. 46.
[31] Hugo Grotius, *The Rights of Peace and War*, Richard Tuck (ed. and intro.) (Indianapolis: Liberty Fund, 2005) book 2, ch. 25 pp. 285–6.

add, except to second the view – without providing an argument – that the sovereign is capable of legislating laws enforcing duties that are not duties of strict justice, including the duty of the innocent to surrender himself. Grotius' critical commentators, such as Ziegler, would side with Menchaca.[32]

In the end, the late scholastics, with very few exceptions (Giovanni Bosso [†1655], for example), failed to engage or even acknowledge Menchaca's argument.[33] That is not to say, however, that the late scholastics failed to see that the state has contractual duties and duties of reciprocity to defend its citizens. Molina went to great lengths to explain that the state is under obligation to sacrifice the lives of many soldiers to save just one citizen and not just for prudential deterrent reasons. This is the duty of the republic in virtue of the citizen's paying his taxes, obeying the law, and his reverence in doing many works for it, and so the republic must be there when the citizen is in need. Further, this policy redounds in the common good, because each citizen may find himself in a situation where his life is demanded by a tyrant, and it is for everyone's benefit that the standard policy is to risk the many for the sake of one (which could be anyone). For Molina, the only case in which trading the innocent may be permissible is when defending him even at great expense of lives would be hopeless.[34]

7.6 Why the City Is *Not* Intentionally Killing the Innocent: Molina, Wiggers and Valencia

Molina compares the case of the republic's surrendering of the innocent to that of Christian prisoners used as rowers by the Ottoman Navy in its wars against Christian nations.[35] At that time, there was much controversy over what Christian prisoners of war were morally permitted to do, partly because of the papal bull *In Coena Domini* excommunicating those who cooperate with infidels in war. Molina's view was that Christian prisoners were permitted to row and perform other tasks for the Turks, not, of course, with the aim of killing other Christians, but in order to avoid their own death. Rowing under the order of the Turks is not an intrinsically evil action. Rather, this is an 'indifferent' act. As discussed in Chapter 5,

---

[32] Kaspar Ziegler, *In Hugonis Grotii de Jure Belli ac Pacis* (Frankfurt and Leipzig: Quensted & Schumacher, 1686) in c. 25 at p. 509.
[33] Bosso, *Moralia varia*, pars I, tit. 11 sect. 29 n. 950–1 at pp. 236–7. He says that Menchaca implicitly agrees that if there is no hope of defending the innocent then the innocent can be surrendered. He also criticizes Menchaca's view that the republic exists only for the utility of each private individual.
[34] Molina, *II*, lib. 4 tract. 3 d. 10 n. 4 at p. 30.   [35] Ibid.

indifferent acts are acts that are neither good nor bad in their nature, but that derive their moral properties only from the ends that they are made to serve. The prisoner rows for a good end: that of saving his life. The Turks use this act to attack Christians. By parity of reasoning, says Molina, surrendering the innocent is neither a good nor a bad action in itself.[36] Rather, it is an indifferent action. While it is true that the tyrant requests the innocent to be delivered to him for a bad end (killing him), the republic hands him over for a good end: that of saving the republic.

The thought is then that, since indifferent actions are made good or bad by the ends they are made to serve, two different agents may put one and the same action to the service of different and conflicting ends – one of a morally wrong end and the other a morally right end.

Note that Molina also gives weight to the fact that what is at stake are the rowers' lives. According to him, it would not be licit for the Christian prisoner to row in a Turkish boat just in order to avoid some minor discomfort or monetary loss. Similarly, if the republic surrenders the innocent, not out of fear of being destroyed, but only in order to avoid paying a small tribute, then it would not be morally allowed to turn over the innocent citizen.[37]

However, distinguishing indifferent actions from intrinsically evil actions is by no means an easy task. While everyone agreed that it would not be morally acceptable for a Christian prisoner on a Turkish boat to steer the boat or to shoot at fellow Christians in the other boat, at the time there was no agreement on whether the typical tasks of prisoners of war, which included taking care of the gunpowder and shells, digging trenches, and carrying ladders to scale fortifications, constituted indifferent or intrinsically evil actions.

As Suárez noted, while Molina's motives are praiseworthy – namely, the relief of the moral anxiety of Christian captives – his argument cannot actually do the job of excusing these captives, for undiscriminating reliance on indifferent acts opens the door to every type of cooperation with depraved pursuits. The accomplice will almost always be able to say that the act was indifferent and that his intention in cooperating was not the intention of the principal agent.[38] So, if a person is intent on setting a house on fire and compels someone to help him carry the torch, the helpers should not be able to excuse themselves by saying that carrying a torch is in

[36] Ibid.   [37] Molina, *II*, lib. 1 tract. 2 d. 115 n. 15 at p. 424.
[38] Suárez, *de Censuris*, d. 21 sect 2 n. 61 at p. 525 in *Opera Omnia*, vol. 23. Also Francisco de Toledo (1534–1596), 'Explicatio casuum in bulla coena domini reservatorum' in *De instructione sacerdotum libri septem cum bulla coena* (Lyon: Horatius Cardon, 1599) p. 1056.

itself an indifferent act. Suárez believed that actions suspected of constituting cooperation with evil are to be judged one by one in their specific circumstances, *hic et nunc*, and not by appealing to the general category of 'indifferent action'.[39] In the case of the Christian rowers, as commentators at the time said, it does matter to the permissibility of their rowing, for instance, whether refraining from rowing would lead to a general mutiny or would, by contrast, lack any effect on the other rowers.[40]

Beyond the theory of indifferent acts, other arguments were advanced to demonstrate that the republic would not be intentionally killing the innocent by handing him over to the tyrant. Flemish Theologian Jan Wiggers (1571–1639) presented this objection to his own view: if the republic can expel the citizen knowing that he will be killed by the tyrant, it can also thrust an innocent into an arena full of lions foreseeing that he will almost certainly be killed. But the second act clearly counts as killing the innocent. His answer is that the tyrant, unlike the lions, acts freely and is guided by understanding; his act of killing is not a mechanical reflex. As a consequence, he says, the death of the innocent does not follow as a matter of necessity from the expulsion of the citizen.[41]

The answer seems to convey two different thoughts: one is that the rulers of the republic, knowing the tyrant is free and guided by understanding, cannot foreknow what he will do; it is possible he will spare the expelled innocent. But this contradicts the particulars of the case. What makes the question interesting is that you *know* the citizen will be killed. If you think there is a good chance the innocent will not be killed, then the dilemma waters down or is at least weakened.

The second thought is that the tyrant is morally responsible (as opposed to the lion) for the innocent's death in a way that would reduce or altogether eliminate the responsibility of the republic. This thought, although natural, is hard to defend. A person's responsibility for a murder does not decrease when the killer acts in concert with another criminal.[42] In the end, this rationale is not very helpful in defence of the view that the republic is not killing the expelled innocent.

---

[39] Suárez, *de Censuris*, d. 21 sect 2 n. 61 at p. 525.
[40] Rutilio Benzoni, *Speculum Episcoporum & Curatorum* (Venice: Minima Societas, 1595) lib. 1 d. 1 at pp. 102-3B.
[41] Ioannes Wiggers, *De iure et iustitia* (Leuven: Cyprianii Coenenstenii & Georgii Lipsii, 1661) tract. 2 c. 2 dub. 12 n. 84 at p. 102.
[42] So, Italian theologian Paolo de Bianchi, in discussing the case of the Jews surrendering Jesus Christ to Pontius Pilate as an example of surrendering the innocent to a tyrant, says: 'the Jews sinned no less in surrendering Christ to Pilate than Pilate himself, in fact they sinned more given the sentence suffered by Christ'. *Disceptationes de difficilioribus materiis casuus* (Venice: Evangelista Deuchinus,

Another thought floated by Wiggers is that we can think of the case of the innocent citizen in terms of the Doctrine of Double Effect.[43] What the innocent aims at is to save the republic, which he does by exiting it. However, his exit also has the undesired effect of getting him murdered by the tyrant. Yet the innocent could say that it is his leaving the republic that saves it from destruction, not his death, so his death is not a means for saving the republic, and that the saving of the republic is a great enough good to justify the undesired, evil outcome of his death. Yet this presentation by Wiggers hardly does justice to the specifics of the case, for as it is clear, the death of the innocent is not an accidental feature of his exiting the republic, but the tyrant's reason for demanding him being surrendered in the first place; it is the death, not the expulsion or exit of the citizen, which constitutes the means of saving the republic.

Valencia was closer to the mark when he saw that the crux of the problem is whether the innocent can will to exit the republic without willing to die. If he can, then this act would be permissible or even obligatory and the republic could command it. As Valencia puts it, what must be explained is why the citizen is not to be regarded as 'the moral cause of his death'.[44] If this can be shown, it can also be shown that the republic is not the moral cause of the citizen's death either. According to Valencia, the innocent citizen is not the moral cause of his death because it is possible for him to will to leave the republic for the sake of saving it, while at the same time to will not to die at the hands of the tyrant. And this is because saving the city 'is accidentally conjuncted with the death'. In other words, for Valencia, it is the malice of the tyrant that creates the causal link (the 'accidental conjunction') between these two events (saving the city; the innocent's death). Because there is no natural connection between them, one can be willed without the other being willed too.[45]

The idea is that the scope of the intention to bring about X includes the bringing about of event Y only if X and Y are naturally connected in the sense that they are always or almost always concomitant. The causal connection between being in the vicinity of lions and being attacked by them is a natural one so one cannot seriously be intended without the other. However, arguably, there is no similar, natural, close causal connection between being in the vicinity of the tyrant and being attacked by him.

1630) at p. 441. According to John (18:14) Caiaphas surrendered Jesus in the belief that otherwise the whole nation would be destroyed by the Romans: 'Now Caiaphas was he, which gave counsel to the Jews, that it was expedient that one man should die for the people' (King James Version).

[43] Wiggers, *De Iure et Iustitia*, tract. 2 c. 2 dub. 12 n. 84 at p. 102.
[44] Valencia, *Commentariorum*, d. 5 q. 8. punct. 2. col. 1315. [45] Ibid.

This notion of closeness plays a role in some of the modern literature on the Principle of Double Effect, but it has also been more or less demolished by Warren Quinn in his classic article on the matter.[46] By presenting a number of double effect cases, Quinn argued that the presence or lack of closeness between the intended effect and the secondary effect of an action does not correlate with our moral intuitions about the moral permissibility of the actions producing these effects. Note in addition, the idea that one has authority over the scope of one's intention is suspect. If I know with complete certainty that, when X happens, Y will also occur, how can I really confine my intention to X without my intention also propagating to Y?[47]

7.7 Why the Citizen Is Committing Suicide by Exiting the Besieged Republic: João de São Tomás

João de São Tomás was not alien to war. As confessor of Felipe IV, he accompanied him and his army to Aragón in his war to quash a French-supported Catalonian uprising.[48] He thought we should focus on the root of the problem: either surrendering yourself, an innocent, to the tyrant to face a certain death is intrinsically evil or is not. If it *is* intrinsically evil then you can neither surrender yourself nor can you be coerced to do so by the republic.[49]

For de São Tomás, this act *is* intrinsically evil. The act of surrendering yourself to the tyrant is 'ordered out of its very nature' (*ordinatam ex natura sua*) to a bad end (your own death) and under a proper account of action specification this action should be described as the act of killing an innocent (yourself). The fact that the ulterior motive is to save the community does not alter this. Since you ought not to kill an innocent, you ought not surrender yourself (the innocent). A law that compels you to do what is intrinsically evil cannot be binding. Therefore, the republic should

---

[46] Warren Quinn, 'Actions, Intentions, and Consequences: The Doctrine of Double Effect', *Philosophy and Public Affairs*, 18(1989)334–51.

[47] This is Rodrerick Chisholm's 'principle of diffusiveness of intention'. See Roderick Chisholm, *Person and Object* (La Salle, Ill.: Open Court, 1976) p. 74. Also in 'The Structure of Intention,' *Journal of Philosophy* 67(1970)639–41.

[48] On João de São Tomás' actual war experience, see Orietta Filippini, 'Aspetti della direzione della coscienza regale e dell' operato di un confessore regio durante le campagne militari. Juan de Santo Tomás, O. P. e Filippo IV in Aragona nel 1643 e nel 1644' in Enrique García Hernán and Davide Maffi (eds.), *Guerra y sociedad en la monarquía hispánica. Política, estrategia y cultura en la Europa moderna (1500–1700)*, vol. II (Mapfre, Laberinto and C.S.I.C.: Madrid, 2006) pp. 743–64.

[49] João de São Tomás, *Cursus theologici in secundam secundae Divi Thomae, tomus sextus* (Cologne: Wilhelm Metternich, 1711) q. 64 a. 2 n. 10 at p. 255.

not command you by law or by decree to leave. Your non-compliance with a law that is not binding cannot change your moral status from innocent to non-innocent.

de São Tomás says:

> But this action [leaving the city] truly is killing oneself, and cannot have the character of defending the republic and as such is causally tied to the death of that innocent [*causalitatem in ordine ad mortem ipsius innocentis*], and even though that action seems to be a defensive one, nevertheless it is primary in it that the innocent is surrendered to be killed, and thus what is formally salient and what specifies the action is the killing of the innocent. Thus under no heading can he do so [leave the city], insofar as this action is bad in both species and in form.[50]

Here de São Tomás is relying on a distinction present in the early works of Aquinas, which is also central to his own works: that between the end of the act (*finis operis*) and the ends of the agent (*finis operantis*).[51] Some actions have their purpose built in. So, for example, an act of almsgiving, in its very nature, is an act aimed at relieving the distress of the poor (*finis operis*). João says that the *finis operis* comes from the very nature and tendency of the act (*ex propria natura, et tendentia actus*).[52] A person can give alms in order to be admired or to feed his vanity or to further some other end (*finis operantis*). So the act takes its species qua act of almsgiving from the *finis operis*, and not from the end to which it is made to serve by the agent.[53] In doing some actions, one cannot but will certain ends that come along with it, regardless of one's avowals of intention.

A good way of describing de São Tomás's move is to say that he accepts Molina's challenge that if handing over the innocent is intrinsically evil, so is surrendering oneself, but decides to bite the bullet and accept this inference. The view that one may not surrender oneself to save the republic was an innovative and provocative view and one that did not attract much support. Among the very few supporters of de São Tomás we should mention Andrés de la Madre Dios (1622–1674), a Carmelite at Salamanca.[54]

---

[50] de São Tomás, *Cursus theologici in ST II-II*, q. 64 a. 2 n. 13 at p. 256.
[51] Aquinas, *In II Sent.*, d. 131 q. 2 a. 1 c.
[52] João de São Tomás, *Cursus theologici in ST I-II*, q. 17 a. 3 n. 2 at p. 332.
[53] de São Tomás, *Cursus theologici in ST I-II*, q. 17 a. 3 n. 3: 'finis vero operis vocatur etiam proximus, extrinsecus et specificans quia objectum actus est'.
[54] See Andrés de la Madre de Dios, *Cursus theologiae moralis* (Venice: Nicola Pezzana, 1750) tom. 3 tract. 13 c. 2 punct. 4 sect. 1 n. 57 at p. 165.

The view seems to defy a long entrenched idea of patriotic self-sacrifice inspired by Greek and Roman sources (e.g. Horace's '*Dulce et decorum est pro patria mori*'). It also seems to fly in the face of Christian veneration of genuine martyrdom. Moreover it was at odds with the scriptural story of Jonah, often alluded to in the controversy (however, not by de São Tomás) as an example of virtuous self-sacrifice for the common good.[55] In the story of Jonah, a terrible storm appears at sea, which Jonah believes is his fault for disobeying God. He tells the ship's crew to throw him into the sea, thus saving the ship by placating God and ending the storm.

In addition, it could be argued against de São Tomás that his doctrine entails that a soldier cannot expose himself or be ordered to expose himself to certain death in the battlefield. If he accepts this, de São Tomás is contradicting himself, given that he argues elsewhere that soldiers can be exposed to a certain death, so that, for instance, a soldier would be allowed to throw himself on a grenade in order to save his comrades.

De São Tomás, on the other hand, could reply that there is a difference between a combatant and the non-combatant who surrenders himself or is surrendered to the enemy. In the case of the non-combatant, his action is surrendering himself *for the sake of him being killed*. This is not the case with the combatant. The success of the latter's plan in the grenade case does not depend on his being killed and his death plays no useful causal role. His action is a truly defensive one. By contrast, for de São Tomás, in the case of the non-combatant surrendering himself, his being killed is precisely what he aims to achieve by surrendering himself, for it is this that will save the city.

7.8 Taking Stock

As it unfolds, the controversy exhibits a gradual refining in which some of the elements considered essential by the first contributors of the debate are gradually driven to the periphery. The controversy boiled down to whether trading over an innocent person to face a certain death at the hands of a tyrant constitutes intentionally killing him or not. Soto believed that a citizen who surrendered himself to face a foreseeable death at the hands of a tyrant was not intentionally killing himself but that the republic that compelled the citizen to surrender himself was intentionally killing him. Salón and Molina pointed out that you cannot have it both ways, and that

---

[55] See for example Salón, *II*, q. 64 a. 5 at p. 393; Sayer, *Clavis Regia Sacerdotum*, lib. 7 c. 10 n. 6 at p. 470; Trullench, *Operis moralis tomus secundus*, lib. 5 c. 1 dub. 3 n. 6. at p. 6.

one of these two beliefs must go. De São Tomás reached the right conclusion when he suggested that it is more reasonable to believe that the citizen is intentionally killing himself by exiting the city than that the republic is *not* intentionally killing the citizen by surrendering him.

Each of the answers to this question takes a different moral intuition as fundamental. For Molina, the fundamental intuition is that the innocent citizen is permitted (or has a duty, or it would be praiseworthy of him) to leave the republic. For de São Tomás, the basic intuition is that a republic that forcefully surrenders an innocent is intentionally killing him.

Whatever moral intuition they use to ground their argument, there is a price to pay. De São Tomás has to deny the permissibility of the citizen's voluntarily surrendering himself while Molina has to attempt to defend the implausible view that the republic is not intentionally killing the innocent by sending him into the hands of the tyrant. While de São Tomás's view is philosophically sounder in the end, it departs drastically from ordinary moral intuition insofar as it denies the moral permissibility of altruistic self-sacrifice.

At the methodological level, de São Tomás accepts the principle that whether a harmful action involves intentional harm or not will not depend on whether the victim of the harm is the harmer or some other person. If Demosthenes would be intentionally harmed by the Athenians by being expelled, he would also be intentionally harming himself by exiting of his own accord. This methodological principle has also been used by modern philosophers interested in questioning the principle prohibiting intentional harm. Shelly Kagan, for instance, has discussed the case of the soldier ('Manfred') who throws himself on a grenade to save his fellows.[56] Kagan believes that it is specious to argue that, in this case, Manfred only intends to save his comrades, and his death is a foreseeable and unintended side effect of an action aimed at some other end. The test that Kagan employs to show this is that if Manfred's comrade Annette were to throw him onto the grenade with the same goal of saving the others, we would unequivocally say that Manfred's death was intended. The point is that either Annette and Manfred intend to harm Manfred, or neither does. The identity of the agent cannot determine whether the harm is intended or not.

---

[56] See Shelly Kagan, *The Limits of Morality* (New York: Oxford University Press, 1989) pp. 145–6. As he points out: 'advocates of the constraint against intending harm – far from considering his reaction meritorious – must condemn Manfred's [the soldier that throws himself on the grenade] act as morally forbidden, for it apparently violates the constraint. Manfred harms himself as a means of protecting his fellow revolutionaries. But this means that he intends harm – and this is forbidden by the constraint.'

One main philosophical upshot of this controversy, other than clearing out many false leads and distracting moves, was to make it clear that some forms of admirable self-sacrifice are in fact cases of intentionally killing the innocent. So long as we stick to the principle that intentionally harming the innocent is always wrong, these self-sacrifices are morally impermissible. The consistent application of moral principles led to the purging of a revered moral intuition. If de São Tomás is right, to quote Kagan, 'Countless saintly, heroic, and altruistic deeds will not be the living examples of moral ideals which they are normally taken to be, but will rather be examples of acts which are morally forbidden'.[57]

[57] Ibid., p. 145.

CHAPTER 8

War and the Boundaries of Punitive Jurisdiction

8.1 Introduction

The late scholastics conceived just war as the sovereign's enforcing of a just ruling over non-subjects. Under this then-predominant judicial model of war, the king assumes the position of a judge in charge of determining and then enforcing restitution, compensation, punishment and preventive measures.

To fight a just war, you need a just cause. Examples of just causes of war are the persisting, unpunished violation of the rights of the subjects by non-subjects or unjust land seizures by a foreign state. An important question concerned the degree of certainty in the justice of one's cause that one is morally required to have in order to initiate war. Is one permitted to launch war with less than complete confidence in the justice of one's cause?

The view that the king does not need absolute certainty to permissibly go to war can already be found in the work of Vitoria. But it was emergence of the doctrine of probabilism that triggered the controversy over the implications of relaxing the king's need for moral certainly before initiating war. The permissibility of going to war on the basis of mere probable opinion seemed to present two main dangers. On the one hand, it conjured up the spectre of a war that is objectively just on both sides. Each of the two rival kings, it would seem, may act on his probable opinion and seek to take over the disputed territory while resisting similar attempts by the adversary. The late scholastics had no trouble admitting this possibility in cases in which at least one of the sides was in the grip of 'invincible ignorance', that is cases in which that side's belief in the justice of its war resulted from an insurmountable error. However, cases involving probable opinion were construed as involving no epistemic gap between the adversaries: each side had equal access to the complete set of reasons and evidence and the same assessment of the probability of these reasons. Under probabilism, it seemed, each could say: 'I am fighting justly because I fight on the basis of probable opinion and so is my enemy.' This was a problem because the idea that a war could be objectively just on both sides was universally resisted as absurd by the late scholastics. There were different explanations of the nature of this absurdity, one of them being that one and the same thing cannot belong in its totality in an exclusive way to each of two persons at the same time.[1]

Another perceived danger posed by the permissibility of going to war on the basis of probable opinion is that it seems to leave both sides morally free to fight each other. This in turn may be taken to confer legal or moral validity to the military outcome. But mere military superiority should not be allowed to settle an issue of right. Might is not right.

The late scholastic moral theologians who thought that a probable just cause of war sufficed to make war permissible had to find ways of closing off the possibility that their view allowed wars just on both sides. To this end, moral theologians such as Vitoria, Navarrus, Suárez and Molina proposed a number of moral rules for adjudicating a conflict between two sovereign adversaries each with probable just causes of war.[2] These rules would determine who has an all-things-considered just case of war.

In this chapter, after discussing these adjudication rules, I turn to two critical responses. Some moral theologians, such as Vázquez, thought the proposed rules of adjudication to be incapable of entirely precluding the possibility of the two sovereigns retaining an actionable cause of war.[3] Vázquez, and followers such as Castro Palao, Luis de Montesinos (1552–1620) and Juan de Salas (1553–1612), proposed a different approach, one which territorially restricted the judicial jurisdiction of sovereigns.[4] According to his approach, instead of producing rules of adjudication, the important thing is to have only one person deciding on the justice of each contested case. A later theologian, Juan Sánchez, disagreed on the diagnosis.[5] He thought that the moral permission to go to war on the basis of merely probable opinion need not, as charged, generate the specific

---

[1] Valencia, *Commmentariorum*, vol. 3, q. 16 punct. 2 ad 3 at cols. 971–2.
[2] Vitoria, *IB*, q. 4 a. 1 at pp. 309–12. Navarrus, *Manual*, c. 25 n. 4 at p. 520. Suárez, *De Fide, spe, et charitate*, d. 13 sect. 6 in *Opera Omnia* (Paris: Vivès, 1858) vol. 12. I am using the bilingual edition *Luis de Molina y el Derecho de Guerra*, Fraga Iribarne (trans. and ed.) (Madrid: C.S.I.C., 1947) covering disputations 98–121 from *II* (Cuenca: Juan Maselini, 1593).
[3] Vázquez, *Commentariorum in ST I-II*, d. 64 c. 3 pp. 406–9.
[4] Castro Palao, *Operis moralis*, tract. 1. d. 2 punct. 7 n. 10 at p. 10. Luis de Montesinos, *Commentaria in Primam Secundae Divi Thomae Aquinatis* (Complutense: Widow of Juan Gracián de Antisco, 1621) d. 29 q. 5 sect. 5 at pp. 794–802. Salas, *In ST I-II*, q. 21 tract. 8 d. unica. sect. 13 at pp. 1223–7
[5] Sánchez, *Selectae illaeque practicae disputationes*, d. 44 at p. 296

sort of wars just on both sides that are morally problematic. Even without adjudicating rules or restricting the sovereigns' judicial jurisdictions, they could pursue through war probable just causes without thereby fighting the sort of wars just on both sides that we ought to reject.

8.2 The King as Judge

Vitoria and most other late scholastics endorsed the judicial model of just war formulated by Cajetan. In this view, wrongs perpetrated by a king or by his subjects on another king or his subjects should not remain unpunished. Therefore, it falls on kings to fulfil the function of a judge. In this view, war is the carrying out of a judicial sentence.

> That [the prosecutor of a just war] functions as a judge of criminal proceedings is clear from the fact that a just combat is an act of vindicative justice [*actus vindicativae iustitiae*], which is properly within the power of a prince or judge. A private person is not empowered to seek vengeance ... It is clear that he who has a just war is not a party [to the litigation], but becomes, by the very reason that impelled him to make war, the judge of his enemies.[6]

Thus the king, in deciding whether war is to be waged or not, must be guided by the same considerations and principles that should guide a hypothetical supranational judge.

In his *Relectio de iure belli* delivered on 18 June 1539, Vitoria asked, 'What must be done when the just cause of war is doubtful given that there are apparent and probable reasons on both sides?'[7] Note that here Vitoria is not discussing a case of doubt merely inhabiting the minds of the kings, but rather a case in which the truth of the disputed matter is objectively hard to know and there are probable reasons on both sides. Importantly, in the scenario described by Vitoria, the rival kings may be in agreement about the contents of the set of available reasons and the relative force of each. If we hold the opinion that probable reason suffices for initiating war, it would seem that each of the kings can go ahead and use force to fulfil his territorial ambitions, both being equally just.

---

[6] Cajetan, *Peccatorum summula*, 'bellum' n. 6 p. 32, trans. in Gregory M. Reichberg, Henrik Syse and Endre Begby (eds.), *The Ethics of War: Classic and Contemporary Readings* (Oxford: Blackwell, 2006) pp. 245–50.

[7] Vitoria, *Relectio de iure belli, o paz dinámica: escuela española de la paz, primera generación 1526–156*, Luciano Pereña, Vidal Abril Castelló, Carlos Baciero, Antonio García and Francisco Maseda (eds.) (Madrid: C.S.I.C., 1981) 8. 'quid faciendum est cum quando iusta causa belli dubia est, cum ex utraque parte sunt rationes apparentes et probabiles'. The paragraph numbering follows Pagden and Lawrance's edition. Note that this question was not discussed by Vitoria in his lectures on war of 1534.

8.3 Breaking the Stalemate

Late scholastic treatments of war and probable opinion focused on two main cases: the case where one of the parties is in possession of the disputed territory, and the case where neither is. Let me first consider the former case. According to a long-standing legal and moral rule, when there is a dispute about who owns a realm, the presumption is in favour of the side which has actual possession (*in dubio melior est conditio possidentis*).[8] Molina gives the example of the Moluccas (now part of Indonesia), which were conquered by João III of Portugal but claimed by Carlos V of Spain under the Treaty of Tordesillas.[9] According to Molina, João did not have a duty to surrender the islands, neither did Carlos have the right to forcefully dispossess João. Instead, the cases were mutually presented to each other, eventually culminating in the Treaty of Zaragoza of 1529, by which Portugal retained possession (but monetarily compensated Spain).

Although the case in which there is a possessor seems relatively uncomplicated, it did give rise to some discrepancies. First there was the question of the type of certainty required of the possessor to privilege from this condition. According to Vitoria, the king cannot benefit from the condition of being the possessor if he fails to conduct a careful examination of the grounds for his purported claim. If, after the examination, some doubt persists, he may still enjoy possession in good faith (but not if the doubt can be surmounted).[10] In saying this, Vitoria restates his view – pitched against that of Adrian of Utrecht – that doubt and good faith are compatible, so long as the doubt is not deliberate and does not follow from neglect.

Can the *bona fide* possessor ever be legitimately forcefully dispossessed? According to Castro Palao, Vitoria, who at first reading seems to be a staunch defender of the principle of possession, opens the gate for forceful dispossession.[11] This accusation is not without truth, for Vitoria argues that forceful dispossession is wrong 'for so long as the case remains unresolved'.[12] This suggests that if, on the basis of the evidence available, the judge decides that it is more probable that the territory belongs to the plaintiff, then he may forcefully dispossess the defendant of it. But since each of the kings

---

[8] On this see Schüßler, 'Anatomy of Probabilism' and his '*Moral Self-Ownership and Ius Possessionis*', pp. 160–4.
[9] Molina, *II*, lib. 1 tract. 2 d. 103, n. 3 at p. 304.   [10] Vitoria, *IB*, q. 4. a. 1 n. 29 at p. 310.
[11] Vitoria, *IB*, q. 4. a. 1 n. 26 at pp. 308–9.
[12] Castro Palao suggests the same in *Operis moralis*, tract. 1 d. 2 punct. 7 n. 4 at pp. 11–12. Also Villalobos, *Summa de la theología moral y canónica, primera parte*, tract. 1 diff. 17 n. 7 at p. 14. Pace Nicole Reinhardt, *Voices of Conscience*, p. 109: 'This containment [of war] through *ius possidentis* remained strong [from Vitoria] until Molina'.

involved is acting in the capacity of judge, the pretender also can, after consulting with his legal advisors, pass sentence that the territory belongs to him, thereby also morally enabling forceful dispossession.

Suárez is much more explicit than Vitoria. He directly argues that when the pretender finds his own claims more probable than those of the possessor, he may forcefully dispossess.[13] For him the principle of possession holds only when the probability of the opinions is equal on both sides.[14] Molina criticizes Suárez on this score and argues that the principle of the possessor precludes forceful dispossession even when the reasons supporting the non-possessor have greater probability than the reasons supporting the possessor's claim.[15] The possessor could be obligated to relinquish part of the territory or be forced to do so only in the rare case in which *he himself* regards his claims as less probable than those of his rival, and, in addition, the rival is in no doubt as to the truth of his territorial claims.[16]

The really tricky case was that in which the disputed territory had no possessor and there were probable opinions on both sides. According to Vitoria, each side should be open and ready to negotiate a division of the disputed land (or to set a compensation for the surrendering thereof), should the other side be equally disposed. If the claims on both sides were equal in force then the territory should be divided into equal parts.[17] Suárez suggests that there may be other acceptable means to settling this case, such as casting lots or reaching an agreement on the basis of some other rationale (*ratione*) (i.e. a rationale other than luck).

Molina notes that if one side rejects the division, the other side could justly wage war to seize its share.[18] However, the other side's refusal does not entitle that side that proposed the division to try for the *entire* disputed territory. Otherwise, one would be admitting the possibility of a war that is just on both sides (one side justly aiming to take the entire territory while the other side is fighting to take only its share). Suárez, however, believes that if one side wrongly attempts to take the entire territory, the other side would have the right not only to take its own share, but the entire territory.[19]

---

[13] Suárez, *De fide, spe et charitate*, sect. 6 n. 2 at p. 749.
[14] Suárez, *De fide, spe et charitate*, sect. 6 n. 3 at p. 749.
[15] Molina, *II*, lib. 1 tract. d. 103 n. 8 at p. 230.   [16] Molina, *II*, lib. 1 tract. d. 103 n. 10 at pp. 230–1.
[17] Vitoria, *IB*, q. 4 a. 1 n. 28 at p. 310.   [18] Molina, *II*, lib. 1 tract. d. 103 nn.10.
[19] Suárez, *De fide, spe et charitate*, sect. 6 n. 4 at p. 749.

8.4 Duties of Arbitration?

Is there sometimes a moral duty to negotiate with the enemy or resort to arbitration? Vitoria does not mention the possibility of arbitration as such, but believes that even if you are in a stronger military position, you may have a duty to negotiate a division of the disputed territory. He fails to say whether if, after honest attempts to reach a deal, negotiations break down, you are relieved from any constraints on war making.

According to Navarrus, a Christian king sins when he refuses to engage in peacemaking negotiations with another Christian king when the conflict (1) cannot be decided on the basis of justice (for example, because the disputed relevant rights and facts are very difficult to assert given their antiquity and contestable status), and (2) should not be decided by means of arms because, given the size of the armies, the conflagration would make the Church more vulnerable to infidel attacks.[20] However, Navarrus says nothing about the parties' duties in the event of failed negotiations.

Suárez discusses the presumed duty of arbitration in some detail. As noted, he believes that when there is no possessor and the doubt is equal on both sides, the kings must divide the territory or, if division is impossible, negotiate some form of compensation for the territorial loss to one of them. Suárez asks whether 'in this case the kings have a duty to leave [*relinquere*] the decision to good men',[21] namely, arbitrators. By 'this case' he must mean a case in which the kings do not directly reach an agreement on the fair division of the territory or on a fair compensation for territorial loss.

Suárez's answer is that the view that there is such duty is very probable because there is a duty to avoid war when this can be done by morally permitted means. If there is no fear that by resorting to arbiters the sovereign risks being a victim of injustice, he must embrace arbitration. He adds:

> This opinion is confirmed as follows: it is impossible that the Author of nature should have left human affairs, governed as they are by conjecture more frequently than by any reason, in such a critical condition that all disputes [*lites*] between kings and states should be decided only by war; for such a condition would be contrary to prudence and to the general welfare of the human race; and therefore it would be contrary to justice. Furthermore, if this condition prevailed, those persons would as a rule possess the greater rights who were the more powerful; and thus such rights

---

[20] Navarrus, *Manual*, c. 25 n. 4 at p. 520.   [21] Suárez, *De fide, spe et charitate*, sect. 6 n. 4 at p. 749.

would have to be measured by arms, which is manifestly a barbarous and absurd supposition.[22]

But why should Suárez believe that resorting to war instead of arbitration would amount to endorsing the view that might is right? True, of two king-judges, the one with the greatest army will be more capable of enforcing his ruling, but this is very different from saying that it is the successful enforcement that creates the right. It is extremely strange that Suárez would admit an assumption which seems to run against the very foundation of the model of judicial war.

As we will see, Suárez's passage was exploited by Vázquez and others as a purported concession by Suárez that his doctrine leaves room for war as a way of creating rather than merely enforcing rights. As noted in the Carmelite *Course of Moral Theology* edited by Sebastián de San Joaquín (1672/3–1719), this view reminds us of those cannons engraved with the motto '*ultima ratio Regum*' (the last or ultimate argument of the kings).[23]

The problematic passage should be read in its argumentative context. Suárez is presenting reasons supporting the sovereign's duty of arbitration before going on, as we see below, to significantly qualify the existence of such duty. Even though Suárez recognizes the force of these reasons, he does not necessarily endorse them. The scenario that Suárez has in mind is one in which the justice of a dispute cannot be established on the basis of the merits of the case and so we need to pick a decisory mechanism to terminate the conflict. There are a number of mechanisms we could go for, for example, flipping a coin. The pick of the decisory mechanism must be guided by moral considerations; dishonest or immoral means must be avoided. The candidate mechanisms considered are war or arbitration. The important thing to see is that war qua decisory mechanism is not the same as war as the enforcement of a just ruling, rather it is a sort of military contest. So when Suárez argues that, faced with a choice of decisory mechanisms, we have a moral duty to pick arbitration rather than war because selecting war would allow might to determine right, the 'war' that is being referred to is *not* just war, but rather a military contest. Suárez's view is entirely consistent with the fundamental belief that *just war* is the

---

[22] Suárez, *De fide, spe et charitate*, sect. 6 n. 5 at p. 749.
[23] Sebastián de San Joaquín (Salmanticensis), *Cursus theologiae moralis, tomus quintus* (Venice: Niccolo Pezzana, 1715) c. 8 punct. 3 n. 26 at p. 173. The story goes that Louis XIV demanded this motto to be inscribed in some of his artillery pieces. Louis Figuier, *Les merveilles de la science: ou Description populaire des inventions modernes* (Paris: Furne et Jouvet, 1869) p. 391.

use of violence to enforce pre-existent rights. Or, in other words, that *just* might does not create rights.

Let us examine Suárez's qualification of the king's moral duty to accept arbitration. For the rulings of these arbitrators to be binding on the king, who has no superior, they must be consented to by him. With a note of realism, Suárez points out that it would be most rare for both kings to agree on the same set of foreign arbiters.[24] Since this is unlikely to happen, the substitute is for the king to consult 'prudent and learned men', namely his own counsellors and advisors. If he does this, he is exempted from the duty to appoint or abide by the arbiters.[25]

Further, Suárez explains – drawing from the judicial paradigm – that the court has two aims: to determine the truth of the contended matter and to enforce its ruling through an exercise of jurisdiction. The king can meet both aims. Being supreme, he has the jurisdiction needed to enforce the ruling. The king's counsel can get to the truth of the matter. This is a good answer to the criticism that failure to rely on arbitration means conceding that might is right. If the king follows the opinion of unbiased truth-finders and on that basis wages war, he would be enforcing his rights, rather than creating them by force. Setting aside the option of arbitration does not mean that the king is free to fight as he wishes or that the dispute will be decided by a military contest.

True, as Castro Palao says, in practice the king's appointees are much more likely than foreign arbitrators to decide so as to please him.[26] This indeed may be a very bad method of pursuing justice. Yet even if the advisors are no more than yes-men, it would not follow that Suárez is saying that whoever wins in the battlefield has a right to the territory as a consequence of his victory. If the advisors misadvised, the only thing that would follow is that the war was unjust as a consequence of either an involuntary or a complacent mistake, not that force is creating rights.

In order to understand Suárez's scepticism about duties of arbitration, it is important to say something about how arbitration was conceived in his time. Consider Suárez's intriguing statement, 'Since war does not aim at this [i.e. the examination of the judicial action and knowledge of the rights of both parties] but rather should be based on this, there is no occasion to call any arbitrator [*non est cur arbitris sit committendum*]'.[27]

---

[24] Suárez, *De fide, spe et charitate*, sect. 6 n. 6 at p. 749–50.   [25] Ibid.
[26] Castro Palao, *Operis Moralis*, tract. 1 d. 2 punct. 7 n. 5 at p. 12.
[27] Suárez, *De fide, spe et charitate*, sect. 6 n. 6 at p. 750 'examen causae et cognitio iuris' with Pereña Vicente.

The key here is to see that arbitration was considered to be about peacemaking, not about justice. Juan Machado de Chaves (†1653), in a short treatise on arbitration, distinguishes between *árbitro/juez-árbitro* ('arbiter'/'judge-arbiter') and *arbitrador* ('arbitrator'). The former have to decide the matter according to right, whereas the latter look for concord and peace and decide in accordance with 'what is good and equitable', which allows them 'to take the right of one person and pass it on to the other as befits the pursuit of peace'.[28] For this reason, while the decisions of arbiters can be appealed on the basis of judicial reasoning, the decisions of arbitrators cannot be appealed.[29] Arbitrators are essentially peacemakers rather than legal truth-finders. So the problem with arbitrators, as far as Suárez is concerned, is not merely the unlikelihood of the rival kings agreeing to them, or their challenging royal supremacy, but rather that arbitration is a way of bypassing the requirements of justice. Avoiding war may sometimes justify taking this step, but it depends on how much one is compromising on justice and how harmful the alternative, namely war, is. In a sense, arbitration decides issues of right by relying on considerations foreign to the merits of the case, and, in this sense, it has some similarity to the dice of Mars.

This seems also to be Molina's view. He believes that when both parties hold the territory to be theirs without entertaining any doubt then they have no duty to appoint arbitrators or to settle the issue by negotiation. They would have this duty only if the ensuing war is expected to bring extraordinary destruction or if each party is persuaded that the other side acts in good faith, that is, without fault.[30]

To recast: the doctrine probabilism held that a sovereign can, in principle, permissibly wage war on the basis of a merely probable cause of just war. However, authors also suggested a number of criteria limiting the moral licence to fight on the basis of a probable cause of just war. Although these criteria blocked many avenues for war, they did not rule out entirely fighting merely on the basis of a probable cause. Although arbitration seemed as a procedure capable of blocking this option definitively, authors like Suárez felt that positing an absolute duty of arbitration would entail too much of a compromise on justice for it to be acceptable.

---

[28] Juan Machado de Cháves, *Perfeto confessor i cura de almas* (Barcelona: Pedro Lacavallería, 1641) vol. 2 lib. 6 part. 2 tract. 4. documento 1 n. 1 at p. 509.
[29] Machado de Cháves, *Perfeto confessor*, doc. 4 n. 3 p. 511.   [30] Molina, *II*, lib. 1 tract. d. 103 .10.

8.5 Vázquez's Revisionist View

8.5.1 Vázquez's Critique of the Traditional View

According to Vázquez, the view of Navarrus and some more contemporary authors (*recentiores*) is that, if after due examination by the experts of his choice, and mutual presentation of the cases, each of the kings concludes that the opinion supporting his right is more probable than that of the adversary and that he is likely to win the war, he may permissibly proceed to wage war.

Vázquez thinks that this view has two seriously problematic implications. The first is that, preposterously, it seems to allow that matters of right can be settled by the force of arms. 'All controversy between opinions regarding some right is to be decided by judgment, not by power and arms; it is a barbaric custom to consider the right to rule as better pertaining to the stronger party.'[31] He adds, 'To allow the settling of a contentious issue by means of arms is unheard of.'[32]

The second alleged implication of the traditional view, according to Vázquez, is that it seems to allow for wars that are just on both sides. Each side fights inculpably on the basis of probable opinion.[33] Vázquez believes just war on both sides to be a conceptual impossibility.

> If a war is just for one side, there has to be injustice in some way on the other side and a fault or at least a legally presumed fault. Here, however, [in a war fought on the basis of probable opinion] there is neither injustice nor fault, even if only legally presumed, on either side. This is so because none of the kings has a duty to submit to the other's sentence, but can judge the cause himself, and this each of them must realize (and realize that the other realizes) because it is self evident, as each knows of the other that he is also led by what in his judgment and that of his experts is the more probable opinion. It follows that neither of them will be guilty of any fault if each, following his own opinion, attempts to obtain the [disputed] kingdom, nor can one legally presume a legal fault of the other. Therefore the rationale for

---

[31] Vázquez, *In ST I-II*, d. 64 cap. 3 n.13 at pp. 407–8. [32] Ibid., p. 408.
[33] Vázquez's twelve-page *Parecer sobre la Conquista de Portugal* (henceforth *Parecer*) is contained in a manuscript volume of 506 pages titled *Opera theologica* at the Archivo Nacional de Madrid (ES.28079.AHN/1.2.2.1.9/Universidades, L. 1197) fols. 60-64v from which I am citing. The full title is: *Si el Rey de Portugal es verdadero y legítimo juez de la Magestad del Rey Catholico pretensor de aquel Reyno para citarle, para que comparezca en juicio y alegue su derecho, que tiene como heredero al Reyno de Portugal, despues de muerto el Rey don Henrique*. The volume's discovery was reported by Luciano Pereña Vicente in his 'Importantes documentos inéditos de Gabriel Vázquez', *Revista Española de Teología*, 16 (1956) pp. 193–213, fol. 62. Datos. For a fuller analysis, see my 'Probabilism, Just War and Sovereign Supremacy in the Work of Gabriel Vázquez', *History of Political Thought*, 34 (2013)177–94.

a just war is destroyed, which consists in the punishment by vindictive justice of the person who merits punishment for a fault or at least a legally presumed fault.[34]

True, says Vázquez, the idea of just war on both sides was entertained by Vitoria, Covarrubias and Alonso Tostado (Abulensis) (1410–1455). But 'none of the cited doctors has until now dared to concede that this war is just [on both sides] except accidentally, that is, because of the invincible ignorance of something that the other knows with certainty. Such ignorance is not considered to arise from the contrariety of probable opinions.'[35] So when opposite sides adhere to contrary probable opinions, they cannot use ignorance to excuse their fighting. They are acting on the basis of the probability of their opinion, but they are not mistaken or ignorant about the opinion followed being probable or not. And it is this probability that licenses their war acts.

Vázquez's criticism is to some extent warranted, at least as it concerns Navarrus. For Navarrus, it is not a sin to resort to force and refuse negotiations when there is a judicially unresolvable case that can be swiftly decided in the battlefield without much harm to the *res publica christiana*. This author is in effect conferring moral and legal effects to mere military victory, to the dice of Mars.[36] Moreover, Navarrus may also be intimating the idea of just war on both sides when, as Vázquez notes, he says that failure to accept negotiations would be against concord between Christian nations, but fails to make clear whether in this case, by waging war on each other, the kings do injustice *to each other*.[37]

Do Vázquez's criticisms apply to Suárez and Molina? Vázquez's claim is that the non-exhaustiveness of the adjudicating rules for cases in which both kings have probable cause of war allows for situations in which each of the kings may permissibly wage war on each other. They are left morally free to fight each other. Should two epistemically equally positioned king-judges be provided with an exhaustive set of adjudicating rules, then the possibility of this troublesome scenario would be eliminated. The two king-judges would reach the same conclusion about who has and who has not a just cause of war. There would still, of course, be cases in which both *believe* their war to be just, but at least one of them would do so as consequence of mistake or ignorance so that the war would not truly be just on both sides.

---

[34] Vázquez, *Parecer*, fol. 62.   [35] Váquez, *In ST I-II* d. 64 cap. 3 n. 16 at p. 408.
[36] Suárez, *De fide, spe et charitate*, VI. 4–5 at p. 830. See Juan Cruz Cruz, 'El caso del juez árbitro en caso de guerra, según los Maestros de Siglo de Oro' at http://leynatural.es
[37] Vázquez, *Commentariorum in ST I–II* d. 64 cap. 3 n.10 at p. 407.

However, if this is indeed Vázquez's criticism, he fails to locate the root of the problem. The problem with the view of Suárez and Molina is not that the rules of adjudication are non-exhaustive, but rather that there is a need for them in the first place. Vázquez's claim should be that since a war that is just on both sides is not conceptually possible, there isn't in principle any permission to go to war on the basis of probable opinion. He should argue that the problem is not the non-exhaustiveness of the adjudicating rules charged with blocking the troublesome possibility of war that is just on both sides but, rather, that it is the very idea that probability gives you an in-principle permission to proceed to fight.

Could this in fact be the claim that Vázquez is making? It cannot. Vázquez maintains the belief that in principle the king could wage war on the basis of probable opinion. What he does instead is propose a different kind of solution to the alleged problem of non-exhaustiveness that he identifies as the flaw in Suárez's and Molina's theory.

8.5.2 *Vázquez's Jurisdictional Solution:* Rei sitae

According to Vázquez, the tacit concession of the possibility of a war that is just on both sides by Navarrus and some 'more recent doctors' is rooted in their understanding of the king's supremacy. In this understanding, to be supreme means not having to stand before the judgment of another. The result is overlapping jurisdictions: two judges hearing the same case and executing conflicting sentences. Each king, being judge to himself, can sentence and blamelessly carry out by arms his own ruling, which the other king is under no duty to submit to.

It is plausible to assume, as some scholars have done,[38] that by 'recent doctors' Vázquez is alluding to Suárez.[39] In his pioneering work, Javier Antonio García Vilar suggests that it is more likely that Vázquez is alluding to the various *pareceres* ('expert opinions') on the succession to the crown of Portugal after the elderly cardinal Henrique was crowned on the death of Sebastião I.[40] These *pareceres* were commissioned by Felipe II, the Castilian

---

[38] Manuel Fraga Iribarne, *Luis de Molina y el derecho de guerra* (Madrid, 1947) p. 99; Regout, *La doctrine de la guerre juste*, p. 230; and in the same vein, Peter Haggenmacher, *Grotius*, p. 220.

[39] On this rivalry, see Raoul de Scorraille, *François Suárez de la Compagnie de Jésus* (Paris: Lethielléux, 1914) vol. 1 pp. 282–314.

[40] José Antonio García Vilar, 'Teoría de la guerra y arbitraje internacional en Gabriel Vázquez' in Manuel Medina, Roberto Mesa and Primitivo Mariño (eds.), *Pensamiento Jurídico y Sociedad Internacional: Estudios en honor del profesor D. Antonio Truyol Serra* (Madrid: Centro de Estudios Constitucionales, 1986) 2 vols. pp. 461–482. In his 'El maquiavelismo en las relaciones internacionales. La anexión de Portugal a España en 1580', *Revista de Estudios Internacionales* 2(1981)599–645,

pretender, from various theologians acting individually and collectively. Written under tight deadlines, the theologians responded to a number of set questions on the accession of Felipe to the Portuguese throne. Vázquez himself wrote a commissioned *parecer* in 1579 that remains in manuscript form. His is the only one of the eight *pareceres* surveyed by García Vilar that denies Castilian royal ambitions.

To settle the succession dispute, Henrique, the successor of the Portuguese monarch Sebastião, proposed in 1578 to hold a judicial process in which he would act as judge, assisted by the realm's experts. Each of the pretenders would be summoned to litigate the case. But as the anonymous theologian of the town Burgo de Osma asserted in his *parecer*, because the Spanish monarch is 'prince and head of the perfect republic, he has no superior from whom to judicially demand the right to the crown of Portugal, because if he was under a superior judge he would not be a prince of a perfect republic'.[41]

The collective *parecer* of the Theology Faculty of Alcalá (which in its prologue curiously presents itself as unanimous, despite Vázquez being in attendance) argues that King Felipe 'is exempt from any judicial tribunal having no other obligation than following the guidance of God and of the wise and to show extrajudicially to the Republic of Portugal the true right that he has to succeed the crown after the death of their most serene king'.[42] 'Because he is the King of Castile, this King is supreme, independent and by divine right the natural authority to deal with and examine and juridically define the rights that belong to him and to avenge and punish grievances and wrongs against him.'[43]

It is exactly the views of the authors of these and other *pareceres* – those favourable to Felipe – that Vázquez criticizes in his treatise on conscience and war in the *Commentary* on Aquinas's *Prima Secundae*.

> Some modern doctors consent to this doctrine only for this reason: that because the king is supreme and has no superior he need not stand before the judgment of any other king, and so he must judge his cause himself: because

---

García Vilar mentions and discusses eight such *pareceres* produced between 1579 and 1580. I am using a copy of latter titled *Examen Theologal que el Catholico Rey Don Felipe mando hacer para seguridad de su consciencia, antes de apprehender la possession de los Reynos y señorios de la Corona de Portugal* (Archivo General de Simancas, Signature PTR, LEG 51, DOC. 2.) (digital copy retrieved online).

[41] In García Vilar, 'El maquiavelismo ... ', p. 629. 'Perfect republic' in the Aristotelian tradition designates a self-determining and self-sufficient polity.

[42] *Examen Theologal*, fol. 11v. Exactly the same view on the issue of the Portuguese succession is taken by Molina, lib. 1 tract. d. 103 n. 14 at p. 231.

[43] *Examen Theologal*, fol. 13v.

were he to find out by himself or by the doctors of his kingdom that it is more probable that he has the right to the disputed kingdom, he could pronounce sentence in his favour and execute it by means of arms, and if necessary declare war on the other king and fight against him.[44]

As Vázquez says in the *parecer* on Portugal, to have two kings deciding on the same dispute is almost like having two gods judging the same case.[45] The judicial stalemate resulting from the conjunction of conflicting probable opinions and overlapping jurisdictions must be referred to a higher judge. 'A controversy of opinions should be defined by judgment, not by arms. Therefore it necessarily follows that the matter will be decided by someone else's judgment.'[46] But who will be the judge?

8.5.3 Suzerainty and Jurisdiction: Flanders

Vázquez distinguishes between two types of case. Either (1) both of the litigants lack a superior or (2) one of them is subject to some superior authority. In the latter case, we have a dispute between the king of a subordinate polity (such as a principality, marquisate or dukedom) and a supreme king. The marquis or duke is not supreme; he is subject to a king. He must therefore subject himself to the judgment of this superior king:

> Because of his regal status the supreme prince is not the subject of the king under whose jurisdiction is this marquisate. However, because the marquisate is subject to this king and the laws by which the realm is governed, the cause [*causa*] and the right to that [marquisate] should be judged and defined by the laws of the kingdom ... This reason proves that ... an otherwise non-subjected prince is rendered a subject by reason of the territory [*ratione territorii*] which is in dispute. It is not just that without the judgment and consent of the king under whose dominion that territory is others would occupy it. By reason of that territory, the prince remains the subject of such a king, as for example when the kings of Spain, insofar as the County of Flanders was concerned, were subject to the Kings of France.[47]

The test case refers to a period stretching from the Treaty of Senlis (1493) to the Treaty of Cambrai (1529), during which the Habsburg monarchs were

---

[44] Vázquez, *In ST I-II* d. 64 cap. 3 n.11 at p. 407 [45] *Parecer*, fol. 62.
[46] Vázquez, *In ST I-II* d. 64 cap. 3 n.18 at p. 408.
[47] Vázquez, *In ST I-II* d. 64 cap. 3 n.19 at p. 409.

also Counts of Flanders while France retained its suzerainty over Flanders, thus making the Habsburgs vassals of France, because the county was a vassal entity of the kingdom.[48]

According to Vázquez, the kings of Spain lacked the jurisdiction necessary for ruling on the case of Flanders and executing the sentence by means of war. Consider the analogous case of Queen Elizabeth claiming ownership rights to a house in Greece. She could litigate for the house but must do so both before a Greek court and by interpreting Greek law to defend her claims. This would not change even if Greece was also in the position of a litigant claiming the house as state property (and hence acting as judge and party). The reason is that the house is in Greek territory. Queen Elizabeth cannot occupy the house by force based on the argument that she is not a subject of Greece and hence need not abide by the decisions of a Greek court. So while the claims of Greece and Queen Elizabeth that they each have exclusive property rights to the house may both be probable, the fact that the house is within Greek territory gives Greece the right to adjudge the matter. This makes sense because having jurisdiction over something is different from having ownership rights. Therefore Greece can say that by asserting jurisdiction over the case it is not yet deciding the issue of property rights on the house, which will be decided by its court.

For Villalobos, Vázquez's solution expresses the general legal maxim *actor sequitur forum rei*, meaning that the plaintiff must have his case heard by the court of which the defendant is a subject.[49] This is the general principle in Roman Law for determining the competent judicial forum. One idea behind the maxim is to avoid 'forum shopping', for instance by the suitor establishing domicile in the most convenient territory.[50]

Why does Vázquez appeal to *ratione territorii*? Roman lawyers distinguished between four main constituting grounds for deciding the forum: the domicile of the defendant (*ratione domicili*), the location of the disputed thing (*rei sitae*), the place in which the tort was committed

---

[48] García Vilar, 'Teoría de la Guerra ... ', p. 475. See Wim P. Blockmans, 'La position du comté de Flandre dans le royaume à la fin du XVe siècle' in B. Chevalier and P. Contamine, *La France de la fin du XVe siècle: Renouveau et apogée* (Paris: CNRS, 1985) pp. 71–89.

[49] Villalobos, *Summa, primera parte*, tract. 1 diff. 17 at p. 15.

[50] Well explained by José de Vicente y Caravantes, *Tratado crítico filosófico, histórico de los procedimientos judiciales en material civil* (Madrid: Gaspar y Roig, 1856) p. 224 section 242. On the use of the principle in cases of conflict of laws, see Joseph Story, *Commentaries on the Conflict of Laws Foreign and Domestic* (London: A. Maxwell, Dublin: A. Milliken, Edinburgh: T. Clark, 1841) p. 767, section 577.

(*ratione delicti*), and the place in which contractual obligations must be discharged (*loci contractus*).[51]

The notion of *ratione delicti* was useful to justify offensive wars because aggressive actions normally involve the commission of a wrong within the victim's territory. Vázquez concedes that one acquires punitive jurisdiction over the defendant by being victim of a wrong. Yet he must think that no such wrong was committed on Spain by Flanders such that would confer to Spain punitive jurisdiction over Flanders. This is exactly what Vázquez thought concerning the Portuguese case: by summoning the pretenders to the throne, Portugal does no *iniuria* to them and therefore cannot be judged or punished by the King of Castile.

8.5.4 Vacant Thrones: Aragón and Portugal

This takes us to the second type of case: that involving two supreme kings litigating a succession to the vacant throne of a supreme kingdom. It may be argued that Vázquez's theory, focusing as it does on the case of the vacant throne, has little to offer the case that occupied Vitoria and most other authors, namely the case of disputed unpossessed territories, which one may take to refer primarily to the newly discovered lands overseas. A close reading of Vitoria's text, however, disproves this. For Vitoria declares to be discussing the case in which a 'city or province which is the subject of doubt lacks legitimate possessor — as in the case in which it is left vacant *because of the death of the legitimate lord* — and it is doubted whether his successor is the king of Spain or the king of France' (my italics).[52] So the vacant kingdom that Vázquez is referring to is what Vitoria had in mind when talking about unpossessed territory. Vázquez's discussion of the cases of Aragón and Portugal are directly relevant to the discussion initiated by Vitoria.

According to Vázquez, in these cases, matters must be decided according to the laws of the kingdom concerned as interpreted by its courts. Vázquez praises the solution reached at the Compromise of Caspe that decided the successor to the crown of Aragón in 1412:[53]

---

[51] See ' De foro competente' in *Corpus juris canonici emendatum et notis illustratum* Gregorii XIII. pont. max. iussu editum (Rome: In aedibus Populi Romani, 1582) *Liber II Decretales d. Gregorii papae IX*, Tit. II c. XX. See also Thomas Carlevalius, *Disputationum de iuris variarium* vol. 2, *De foro competente et legitima iudicum potestate, tomus prio* (Madrid: Typographia Regia, 1656) d. 2 qq. 1–4.

[52] Vitoria, *IB*, q. 4 a.1 n. 28 at p. 310; my trans.

[53] On this, Ramón Méndez Pidal, 'El Compromiso de Caspe: Autodeterminación de un Pueblo' in *Historia de España* (Barcelona, 1965) vol. XV pp. IX-CLXIV; and Enrique Cantera Montenegro, 'El

If the controversy is regarding the succession of some supreme reign, I think that all the litigants, whether they are both supreme princes or whether one is supreme and the other is not, must stand trial before the realm, [and] by 'realm' I mean the people who after the death of the prince have the right to govern by the power of the towns' election. And in our Spain, we've seen this in the time of Saint Vicent from the Order of the Dominicans in the kingdom of Aragón: the contenders and disputants were all forced to stand before the realm's judgment. The reason is obvious, since it is the right of succession which is disputed and must be decided by some rule; however, the rule can be no other than the laws of the realm itself, regarding which there is controversy. Nobody is a legitimate interpreter of its laws but the realm itself, once the king has died. Nor can the legitimate interpretation pertain to foreigners; therefore all the pretenders must stand before the judgment of the king.[54]

As interpreted by Vázquez, the pretenders to Aragón's throne were summoned to litigate their case before the *Cortes* of Aragón according to its laws of succession.[55] The role of the litigants and their representatives (the *compromiseros*) was to argue for different interpretations of these laws. The disputed realm remains a self-standing jurisdiction even while the succession remains undecided. By reason of territory, pretenders to the throne are, as it were, subjects of the disputed realm in this matter, and their role is reduced to that of litigant rather than judge.

The case of Aragón shaped Vázquez's thinking about Portugal.[56] The King of Portugal had appointed eleven persons to a tribunal to judge on this matter.[57] Vázquez was asked 'whether the King of Portugal is the true and legitimate judge of his Majesty the Castilian king, pretender of that kingdom, so as to summon him so that he stand before the judicial process and allege the right that he has as successor to the Kingdom of Portugal after the king of Portugal, Don Henrique, dies.'[58] His answer was yes. The King of Portugal is the only legitimate interpreter of the succession laws of the kingdom. This interpretative authority has been given to him by the 'realm and republic' (*reino y república*).[59] Hence, the Spanish king must submit to the judgment of the King of Portugal on the matter of succession. Although Felipe, insofar as he is absolute king of his realm, 'has no superior or temporal judge in the land to rule Castile and the rest of his domains',[60] as far as Portugal is concerned, Felipe is in the same situation as the other pretenders, for Castile cannot give him jurisdiction over

Compromiso de Caspe' in Vicente Ángel Álvarez Palenzuela (ed.), *Historia de España de la Edad Media* (Barcelona: Ariel, 2008) pp. 707–27.
[54] Vázquez, *In ST* I-II d. 64 cap. 3 n.19 at p. 409.   [55] *Parecer*, fol. 60v.   [56] Ibid.
[57] *Examen Theologal*, fol. 12v.   [58] *Parecer*, fol. 60.   [59] *Parecer*, fol. 61.   [60] Ibid.

Portugal.[61] The King of Castile is demoted by Vázquez from the role of judge to that of mere litigant. Portugal (and Aragón) had a right to decide its successors under the *rei sitae* ('location of the thing') rationale.

The theologians defending Castilian pretensions went out of their way to deny these grounds of Portuguese jurisdiction over the issue of succession.[62] As they argued, 'The objection that, because this is a matter of Portugal, it must be judged in Portugal according to the law that establishes that the actor must follow the forum where the thing is under litigation has little force because the ruling of civil and canonic law clearly refers to private persons (as opposed to sovereigns) who, because of their condition and state, are under a superior judge.'[63]

In legal terms, Vázquez is proposing the use of choice-of-law rules, which assign each case to one forum. Vázquez thinks that standing before the judgment of a foreign court need not imply having a superior so long as the foreign court asserts jurisdiction merely *sub ratione territorii*, or according to *forum rei sitae*. The king appearing before the foreign court is recognizing only the exclusive jurisdiction of the court over a limited territory.

The main innovation resulting from Vázquez's endorsement of probabilism was his territorially limited conception of the king's supremacy. But there is another, less conspicuous, innovation. In the traditional view espoused, for example, by Vitoria, each king assumes a judicial role, not in that he judges the presumed offence according to the law of his realm, but rather in that he decides on the justice of his case as a matter of natural law. This is a *moral*, not a legal determination. In Vázquez's scheme, by contrast, the competent forum decides the case according to positive municipal law. In this way, recognizing the authority of another state implies not seeing oneself as free to act directly as instructed by natural law in matters falling within that state's jurisdiction. Kings are no freer than private persons from having to respect the decisions of foreign courts on these matters. The only exception is when a king justifiably believes that the judge appointed by the disputed realm is partial, in which case he can justly ask for the judge's recusal. If his petition is unjustly rejected he is entitled to wage war.[64]

---

[61] *Parecer*, fol. 61v.
[62] See *pareceres* by de la Fuente, the anonymous theologian from Burgo de Osma, 'many professors of Alcalá', in pp. 623, 630, 633, respectively, and the *Examen Theologal*, fol. 14v.
[63] *Examen Theologal*, fol. 14v.
[64] The same point is made concerning the case of Portugal in *Parecer*, fol 63b-63bv ('63b' designates a non-numbered folio between folios 63 and 64).

8.6 Juan Sánchez and the Possibility of War That Is Just on Both Sides

Juan Sánchez, in typical fashion, begins his treatment of the question of launching war on the basis of probable reasons with a twenty-name-long list of authors and works that can be consulted on the matter, headed by Vázquez.[65]

Sánchez resorts to the view, defended by Suárez and other authors, that attaches different moral significance to doubts about facts as distinguished from doubts about law.[66] One reason proposed for believing that doubts about the law release us from the duty to act in conformity with law has to do with the fact that doubt about a particular law can be evidence of the imperfect promulgation of that law; promulgation or publicity being a requisite for law's bindingness. So the risk to violate binding law is significantly diminished by the presence of doubt. However, when you doubt about facts, for instance, about whether a certain medicine will cure you or kill you, your doubt about this fact has no influence on the risk of being killed if you take the medicine.[67]

Sánchez argues that Vitoria's traditional position, which places many restrictions on the launching of war on the basis of probable opinion (conducting an impartial investigation into the truth of the matter, giving priority to the rights of the possessor, etc.), is correct only when the probable opinions involved concern matters of fact, for example the authenticity of wills and testimonies relative to the ownership of the disputed territory.

However, in Sánchez's view, when the probable opinion concerns purely legal matters, such as when the king sees that, on the basis of all available and undisputed factual evidence, he has a probable (but not certain) legal case, that suffices for justly going to war, overruling the *bona fide* possessor's right.[68] Sánchez's belief is that, since the king is both litigant and judge, he can rule on the basis of probable but inconclusive right in his favour and then proceed to dispossess the possessor.[69]

Regarding Vázquez's objection that such war undermines the very rationale that justifies it, because if both sides are inculpable and are so mutually regarded, none is allowed to punish the other, Sánchez says,

---

[65] Sánchez, *Selectae illaeque practicae disputationes*, d. 44 n. 55 at p. 317.
[66] Suárez, *De bonitate et malitia humanorum actus*, d. 12 s. 6 n. 8, n. 10 at p. 452.
[67] On this see, Schwartz, 'Probabilism Reconsidered', p. 387–8.
[68] Sánchez, *Selectae illaeque practicae disputationes*, d. 44 n. 57 at p. 317.
[69] Sánchez, *Selectae illaeque practicae disputationes*, d. 44, n. 58, p. 318.

relying on Suárez, that only aggressive wars require punitive aims, not defensive ones. So his claim is that there is no obstacle to there being a defensive war that is just on both sides. It seems difficult, however, to envisage a case in which two countries at war against each other are only defending themselves. One can think of situations in which each side can plausibly *regard itself* as engaged in defence. Think about two people pulling in opposite directions a blanket each claims as her own. Each believes she is defending her right to the blanket, which the other is infringing.

For Sánchez, the sort of war that is just on both sides that is problematic is that in which each side can tell itself, 'I am fighting justly and so is my enemy'. It is war that is just on both sides in this subjective sense that must be avoided. Sánchez argues that his view avoids this implication. Considering the case in which the disputed territory has a possessor, Sánchez notes that there may be probable reasons supporting the claim that he is a just possessor and probable reasons supporting the claim that he is not. Conversely, there may be probable reasons to think that the would-be dispossessor is a just dispossessor and probable reasons to think that he is an unjust dispossessor. The possessor can resist forceful dispossession and say to himself, 'I am probably just and the enemy is probably unjust', and, conversely, the dispossessor can say to himself, 'I am probably a just dispossessor and the enemy is probably an unjust possessor'. So the dreaded scenario in which each side believes the other no less just than itself is avoidable.[70]

Sánchez, relying on a view already discussed in Chapter 6, argues that each of the belligerents can avoid the belief that he is morally on a par with his opponent by giving 'opinative assent' to the reasons favouring the justice claim. Sánchez may be taken to be making a stronger claim: that on his view one side *cannot* believe himself and the enemy to be fighting equally justly. This may be because one cannot simultaneously assent to two contradictory opinions. So suppose it is probable that a man is married and it is also probable that he is single. Then if I assent to the belief that he is married, I cannot at the same time assent to the belief that he is single. Equally, if I assent to the belief that my war is just, I cannot simultaneously assent to the belief that my war is unjust (and conversely that my enemy's war is just). However, Sánchez cannot really use this sort of argument to exclude the possibility of the subjective perception of moral equality by the belligerents. The reason is that in his own

[70] Sánchez, *Selectae illaeque practicae disputationes*, d. 44, n. 60 at p. 319.

presentation of his view probability is part of the contents of the belief that is assented to. There is no contradiction in believing that 'I am probably just' and that 'my enemy is probably just' (where probability indicates that set of reasons supporting each of these claims surpass a threshold). So there is nothing preventing one from giving simultaneous assent to these two beliefs. The most that Sánchez can say for his view is that it does *not necessitate* that each belligerent believes himself morally on a par with the adversary.

8.7 Summary

The judicial model of war requires the king to act in the capacity of a judge. Just war is the enforcement of a just ruling. Starting with Vitoria, the doctrine of probabilism, as applied to the judicial model of war, significantly expanded the occasions for just war. If a judge can rule a case based on probable opinions and two conflicting opinions can be probable simultaneously, it follows that two judges can simultaneously attempt to enforce two conflicting rulings about the same case.

Probabilism as it relates to war not only expanded very considerably the set of actionable conflicting judgments by the kings, but it also greatly increased the room for discretion on the part of each of the king-judges, thereby creating a need for rules limiting this room for discretion.

This was the purpose of the rules proposed by Vitoria, Navarrus, Suárez and Molina to decide cases in which there are probable opinions on both sides, the most important of which was to favour the condition of the possessor. Although these authors thought it plausible that there may sometimes be a duty to decide cases by resorting to external arbitrators, they fell short of affirming a general duty to do so. The reason, for Suárez, was that arbitration is a peacemaking mechanism that often involves some sacrifice of rights. Avoiding war sometimes justifies giving up some rights, but not at any price.

Vázquez thought that the adjudication rules proposed by the other authors to deal with disputed cases were not exhaustive. He thought that this opened the way to the conceptual impossibility of wars that are objectively just on both sides and to the morally repugnant view that in some cases matters of right can be decided by mere military superiority. These perhaps unwarranted criticisms led to Vázquez's fundamental revision of the judicial war paradigm, which was shaped by his thinking on the Portuguese succession. In this view, the king is no longer universally supreme. His supremacy and jurisdiction reaches only as far as the boundaries of his realm. When the matter under dispute belongs to a different jurisdiction, the king acts not in the capacity of international judge but only as a private litigant. Vázquez's theory indirectly drew from legal principles governing the determination of the competent judicial forum.

Juan Sánchez both disagreed and agreed with Vázquez's criticism of the traditional view. He did not dispute the charge that the traditional view results in wars that are truly just on both sides, that is, without ignorance affecting the judgments of the belligerent sides. Nevertheless, unlike Vázquez, he did not think these wars to be either conceptually impossible or morally problematic. What is morally problematic about war is a situation in which each side thinks that the enemy is no less just than he is. He believed that this is not what happens when each side wages defensive war on the basis of probable reasons. In these cases, each side can believe itself to be probably just and the enemy to be probably unjust. However, Sánchez is hardly convincing in attempting to put moral disquiet to rest, for it is perfectly possible to give assent to the view both that the enemy is probably just and that we are too.

CHAPTER 9

Justice After Victory

9.1 Introduction

The *ius post-bellum*, as it came to be called, has become an increasingly popular subject among just war theorists in the last ten years or so.[1] Just war theorists feel there is an urgent need to provide ethical guidelines for 'day-after' questions such as, what are the duties of the just victorious state concerning the reconstruction of the vanquished state? Does the victor have a right or duty to set up new political institutions? What are the duties of the defeated state in terms of reparation to the unjustly attacked state? Does it have a duty to punish and lustrate all or some of those responsible for the unjust war? Can the occupation of the defeated state be just, and for how long?

World events abundantly demonstrate the relevance of these day-after questions. The disastrous post-war realities in Iraq, Afghanistan and Libya, for example, make clear that winning presumptively just wars can be much easier than ensuring stable peace and security.

In the late scholastics one can find, often intermingled with other subjects, many discussions on the ethics governing the post-victory phase. In this chapter, I put some of these discussions in the spotlight. After outlining the reach and conceptual scope of post-victory justice, I present the various opinions on the rights of the just victor to kill, despoil and enslave the defeated unjust enemy.

---

[1] On the latest developments in *ius post bellum* research, see Jens David Ohlin, 'Justice After War' in Seth Lazar and Helen Frowe (eds.), The *Oxford Handbook of the Ethics of War* (Oxford: Oxford University Press, 2018) pp. 519–37; and the comprehensive Carsten Stahn, Jennifer S. Easterday and Jens Iverson (eds.), *Jus Post Bellum: Mapping the Normative Foundations* (Oxord: Oxford University Press, 2014).

9.2 Post-Victory Justice: Conceptual Issues

Before we engage the texts, it is useful to introduce a number of important conceptual distinctions suggested by the reading of the late scholastics. Post-victory justice can be understood first in a purely temporal sense as comprising the requirements of justice applying to the victor's actions after victory has been accomplished.

In the late scholastic approach to war, victory itself is not the goal of the just war. Victory is primarily a physical event, not a moral one (although it may have legal consequences). It is simply the end of the enemy's obstruction to the pursuit of the just war goals (such as recuperation of land and property and satisfaction for wrongs). Some goals of just war become fully feasible only after the enemy has put down its arms, for example, the judgment and punishment of those culpable for the wrong that the war aims to repel and rectify.

Note that the late scholastic focus was not on post-*war* but on post-*victory*. War may end with the victory of either side through an armistice, a peace agreement, or simply by coming to a standstill. The late scholastics were interested in only one of these scenarios, when the just side finally faces no short-term danger from the enemy and can act unimpeded to secure the just war goals.

It is customary among just war theorists, if only for presentational reasons, to consider questions about justice in the course the war (*ius in bello*) apart from questions about the justice of launching the war (*ius ad bellum*). It is natural to understand *ius post bellum* as covering the temporally subsequent phase after the war. However, if we look at Vitoria and the authors who used Vitoria's treatment as a useful platform for expansion and criticism, we find that the questions we usually consider to belong to *ius post bellum* actually feature within his discussion of how it is licit to fight (*ius in bello*).

There is a good reason for this. While the formal capitulation that marks the definite victory over the enemy takes place at the end of war, this definite victory results from many piecemeal victories, city after city, siege after siege. So, if we ask, for example, whether the just side can execute the besieged troops once they surrender, this is an *ius in bello* question as much as a post-victory question.

Of course, we also find Vitoria speaking about '*the* Victory', as referring to the final outcome of the war rather than local victories. So in late scholastic just war theory, the *ius* post-victory does not cover a period subsequent to those covered in *ius ad bellum* and *ius in bello*. The 'post' in post-victory is sometimes used in relation to local or interim victory and some other times in relation to total or definite victory.

In a second sense, post-victory justice may refer not so much to the temporal location of war actions as the temporal location of their goals. Importantly, a war action conducted with a view to the day after may be performed before victory, that is, in parallel with the fighting to defeat the enemy. So an army may take a hill not because it is necessary for victory but because it is necessary for a secure peace afterwards. Post-victory justice taken in this sense concerns the justification of actions made during war that are aimed at goals that will become fully realized after victory.

In short, post-victory justice, as understood here, concerns both actions undertaken before victory in the pursuit of post-victory goals and actions undertaken after victory (whether local or final).

What are the just goals that become easier to realize once the enemy has been defeated? For the late scholastics, just war aims at recuperating unjustly seized property or land, defraying the cost incurred in having to carry out the just war, exacting satisfaction from the enemy for its wrongs (which includes the punishment of the offending state), and establishing a secure peace.

Killing, despoiling and enslaving the enemy are among the available means of pursuing some of these just war goals. I shall discuss them in turn, focusing on the liability of enemy innocents to these harms.

Since I use the term 'innocent' repeatedly, I feel it is necessary to include some clarifications. First, 'innocent' is not the equivalent of 'non-combatant'. Contrary to its etymology, 'innocent' is used not only to designate the person who does not endanger us (the non-*nocens*), but also to designate the person who is free of sin. Indeed the English word 'innocent' and its cognates in other languages are the terms that have been chosen to translate *Exodus* 23:7 as 'the innocent and righteous slay thou not'.[2] The Hebrew word that is translated as 'innocent' is נקי (*nakih*), which means 'clean' (as in 'clean of sin'). The Vulgate has *insontem* ('guiltless') and the Septuagint has ἀθῷον (*athoon*), meaning both 'harmless' and 'undeserving of punishment'. It is not implausible that the cause of the slippage from *insontem* to *innocentem* both in scholastic Latin and in the vernacular is the phonetic closeness between the words. The twofold

---

[2] Medieval Spanish bibles translated directly from the Hebrew do not make this mistake and provide 'libre' (free, free from sin) rather than 'inocente'. Américo Castro, Agustín Millares Carlo and Àngel José Battistessa, *Biblia medieval romanceada según los manuscritos escurialenses I-j-3, I-j-8 y I-j-6* (Buenos Aires: J. Peuser, 1927) p. 101.

meaning of 'innocent' as 'free of sin' and 'not harmful' has been preserved in ordinary language.

9.3 Killing

9.3.1 Punitive Killing

It was agreed by all the late scholastic authors that after victory no innocent, either enemy or otherwise, could be intentionally killed. But could non-innocents be killed after victory?

Vitoria asks 'whether after victory [*parta victoria*], when there is no longer any danger from the enemy, those who bore arms against the victor [*nocentes*] can be killed'.[3] The scenario that Vitoria appears to be considering is that of the taking of a besieged city. Vitoria discussed in a different place the case of captured combatants and the case of those who surrendered themselves voluntarily. These categories seem exhaustive, so it is not clear who are the non-innocents that Vitoria has in mind when discussing post-victory killing. Later authors such as Hurtado de Mendoza and Francisco de Oviedo (1602–1651) helpfully suggest that Vitoria's question may be about non-captives, for example, defeated survivors who are fleeing, having left behind their weapons.[4]

Vitoria, Suárez and Molina proposed different answers to this question but they agreed on two points. First, they agreed that, *in principle*, all enemy combatants who fought culpably (that is who had no good-faith excuse for fighting) are liable to be punitively killed even when they do not pose a future threat, so long as such punishment is proportionate to the gravity of their crimes.[5] Second, if killing all culpable enemy combatants is necessary in order to ensure lasting peace and security to the unjustly attacked republic, this may be done.[6]

---

[3] Vitoria, *IB*, q. 3 a. 4 n. 45 at pp. 319–320.
[4] Hurtado de Mendoza, *Scholasticae et moralibus disputationibus*, d. 169 sect. 10 n. 97 at p. 1423; Francisco de Oviedo, *Tractatus Theologici, Scholastici & Morales De virtutibus fide, spe et charitate* (Lyon: Philippus Borde, Laurentius Arnauld and Claudius Rigaud, 1651) contr. 12 punct. 7. num. 89 at p. 433. This connection between the question on killing the fleeing enemy and post-victory killing of the enemy is present also in Vitoria's lectures where he runs the two situations together. *In ST II-II*, q. 40 a. 1 n. 10 at p. 283.
[5] Vitoria, *IB*, q. 3 a. 3 n. 46 at p. 320; Molina *II*, lib. 1 tract. 2 d. 123 n. 3 at p. 251; Suárez, *De fide, spe et charitate*, q. 13 sect. 7 n. 7 at p. 753.
[6] Vitoria, *IB*, q. 3. a. 3 n. 48 at p. 321; Molina *II*, lib. 1 tract. 2 d. 123 n. 4 at p. 251; Suárez, *De fide, spe et charitate*, q. 13 sect. 7 n. 7 at p. 753.

What the authors disagreed about is how many of those liable to be killed can actually be killed and for what reason, when it is *not* the case that killing all of them is indispensable for future peace and security.

The punitive goal of war seems to justify killing all the culpable enemies. Vitoria identifies two constraints on this course on action. The first is that this magnitude of killing may be disproportionate to *their state's* wrongs and therefore unjust. The second is that unrestricted killing is inhuman, cruel and 'opposed to the public good'.[7] For Vitoria, the need for peace and security, however, overrides both these constraints and justifies the killing of all. Like Molina and Suárez, Vitoria, in saying this, had in mind incorrigible infidels who he believed would tirelessly resume their attacks as soon as they were able to do so. In the case of Christian enemies, he writes, it is very unlikely that peace and security will ever require the killing of all the culpable.[8]

Let us look at the first constraint to the killing of enemy combatants, namely proportionality. Note that proportionality is not an external consideration limiting the operation of justice, but rather it is internally generated by justice itself. So Vitoria says that 'only in order to punish the wrong [*ad vindicandam iniuriam*] it would not be permissible to kill all'.[9] Why would killing all be disproportionate? Vitoria resorts to the example of a crime committed by everyone in a city, or a city that unjustly rebels against the king.[10] In such cases, he says, killing all involved would not only be against the public good of the republic but also disproportionate.

After reminding the reader of Ambrose of Milan's excommunication of Emperor Theodosius for the Massacre of Thessalonica, in which thousands of the city's inhabitants were killed after rebelling against what they considered to be an injustice, he notes that to calculate the satisfaction owed by the enemy after victory we must take into account 'the wrong, the damages, and all the other crimes inflicted according to their gravity, and

---

[7] Vitoria, *IB*, q. 3 a. 4 n. 47 at p. 319. Vitoria does not use the word state but rather *hostibus*, translatable as 'the enemy' (as it features in both in the Spanish and English translations) or 'the enemies'. 'Oportet ergo habere rationem iniuriae ab hostibus acceptae et damni illati et aliorum delictorum'. In *IB*, q. 3 a. 9 n. 58 at pp. 325–6, however, Vitoria writes in connection to the deposition of rulers as punishment that 'punishment should not exceed the crime … Therefore, although the harm done by the enemy [hostibus] may be a sufficient cause of war, it will not always be sufficient to justify the extermination of the enemy state [status hostilis] and deposition of its legitimate native princes.' This suggests that by 'enemy' Vitoria means the enemy state, not the individuals.

[8] Vitoria, *IB*, q. 3 a. 4 n. 48 at p. 321.   [9] Vitoria, *IB*, q. 3 a. 4 n. 47 at pp. 320–1.

[10] Also in Vitoria, *In ST II-II*, q. 40 a. 1 n. 10 at p. 283. He gives one exception: that of Bayonne, which in 1523 successfully resisted a Spanish siege. Vitoria believes both that the siege was just and that the citizens of Bayonne resisted justly, 'as otherwise they would have been traitors'.

then proceed to reparation and punishment while avoiding inhumanity and cruelty'.[11] He then quotes Cicero, saying that one of the tasks of justice is to 'visit [those who injure us] with such retribution as justice and humanity will permit'.[12] And he quotes Sallust, saying that our forefathers 'from the vanquished they took naught save the power of doing harm'.[13] For Vitoria, this calculus does not yield the result that all culpable enemies can be killed, but rather only a portion of them. The passages from Cicero and Sallust make clear that going beyond that would not only be inhuman but also unjust.

Notice Vitoria's statist premise: the wrongs to be punished are wrongs of the enemy state. Killing individual enemy soldiers is not a way to punish them for their personal deeds but a way of punishing the enemy state.[14]

This statist stance is reaffirmed by Suárez when he tackles the same question. He subsumes the purposes of war singled out by Vitoria under the more general category of satisfaction.[15] Complete satisfaction should include (1) restoration of all unjustly withheld land and property by the enemy, (2) reimbursement for all expenses due to injuries inflicted by the enemy, (3) penalties for the injury inflicted ('for in war, regard must be had not only for commutative justice but also for vindicative justice'[16]), and (4) taking measures to preserve and guard peace in the future 'since the chief end of war is to establish that future peace'.[17] He then argues that in order to calculate the satisfaction and punishment owed after victory we need to compute as part of the satisfaction already exacted all the material losses endured by the enemy in the course of the war. He also believes that non-material harm already inflicted to the enemy in the course of war can be retrospectively treated as punishment under the principle that says that we should not unnecessarily multiply harms. So we can double-count harms, putting down the same harm simultaneously under different headings so as

---

[11] Vitoria, *IB*, q. 3 a. 4 n. 47 at pp. 320–1.
[12] Cicero, *On duties (De officiis)*, Walter Miller trans. (London: Heinemann, New York: Putnam and Sons, Loeb Classical Library, 1913) 2.5.18 at p. 187.
[13] Sallust, 'The War Against Catiline' in *Sallust*, J. C. Rolfe trans. (London: Heinemann, New York: Putnam's Sons, Loeb Classical Library, 1921) 12.4–5 at pp. 22–3; Vitoria, *IB*, q. 3 a. 4 n. 47 at pp. 320–1.
[14] Vitoria, *IB*, q. 3 a. 4 n. 47 at pp. 320–1.
[15] Suárez, *De fide, spe et charitate*, q. 13 sect. 7 n. 5 at p. 753.
[16] 'Vindicative justice' in this context is punitive justice directed towards non-subjects. It should not be understood either as an exercise of vengeance or as associated to the Roman Law action of *vindicatio*, namely the assertion of rights vulnerated. For a good explanation of the concept as used by the late scholastics and its connection to Aristotelian types of justice, see Haggenmacher, *Grotius*, pp. 399–441.
[17] Suárez, *De fide, spe et charitate*, q. 13 sect. 7 n. 5 at p. 753.

to reduce the amount of the enemy's exactable satisfaction. But even if after this double-counting the punishment already endured by the enemy state is insufficient to match the gravity of its wrongs, then we may permissibly kill some among the culpable enemies.[18] So, for instance, if a state wages a just, short and successful war against a genocidal regime that crumbles at the first shot, then there would be ample room for killing many of the culpable enemies. Killing all of them, however, is only permissible if there is 'urgent cause' or if there is a need 'to terrorize others', by which Suárez seems to have in mind future security concerns.[19]

For Suárez, as for Vitoria, the calculus of punishment must match the gravity not of individual crimes but of the wrongs committed by the enemy state. The punitive killing of enemy combatants does not punish them but rather their state *through* them. However, Suárez agrees with Vitoria that it is the enemies' personal deeds – that is, the personal culpability incurred by bearing arms without a valid excuse, such as ignorance or due obedience – that makes them conduits for punishing the state of which they are subjects.

Although Molina held a different view from Vitoria's, he did not draw attention to this discrepancy. Molina starts by saying that it is licit to kill all those enemy combatants whose culpability, in the judgment of prudent men, makes them deserving of capital punishment, just as domestic judges can pass judgment on common criminals. If there are many combatants in this category, it would only be licit to kill all of them if it were necessary for future peace and tranquillity or for the wellbeing of the Church. This is in line with Vitoria and Suárez.[20] When these considerations do not apply, Molina believes it is not licit to kill a multitude 'only for the purpose of vindicating the cause' (*solius vindictae causa crucidare*), especially if they are Christians.'[21] However, he adds, such killing would not provide grounds for restitution to the victims and their families, for it is not against justice but, rather, it is against charity.

So while Vitoria and Suárez think that killing all culpable enemy combatants, barring considerations of future security, is in all likelihood unjust because it is disproportionate to the wrongs of their state, Molina thinks killing each of them would be entirely just since each of them is culpable. The only considerations that intervene against the unlimited killing are those of charity, not of justice.[22] For Molina, the prince who metes out punishment to enemy combatants is punishing each of them for what they personally did; he is not using them as conduits for the

---

[18] Ibid. [19] Ibid. [20] Molina, *II*, lib. 1 tract. 2. d. 122 n. 4 at p. 257. [21] Ibid. [22] Ibid.

punishment of the wrongs of their state. He writes: 'it will also be licit to mete just vengeance to the enemies, according to the gravity of the crimes, sentencing to death, if necessary, those who are the most responsible for being the cause [of these crimes] and imposing other penalties such as proportionate tributes and similar punishments'.[23]

Unfortunately, Suárez did not discuss this or any other of Molina's views on war. Suárez had likely written his posthumously published work on war as lectures for the 1583–1584 academic year in Rome, before the 1597 publication of Molina's volume of *Iustitia et Iure* where he discusses war (probably based on his 1574–75 lectures).[24]

Later authors such as Oviedo, Diana, the Carmelites of Salamanca and Castro Palao follow Molina's line.[25] It would not be unjust to kill all of the culpable '*secundum merita*', as Diana says, but other considerations intervene in moderating the rigour of justice. Since these enemies have already been defeated and humiliated, it suffices to kill some of the leaders and spare the rest. Moreover, killing all may be detrimental to the republic, because it has the potential to depopulate cities (which harms the economy), cause scandal, or cause accidental harm to innocents. Castro Palao adds that it may also harm religion (one assumes, by making Christian polities more vulnerable in the event of infidel attacks) and would be an act of cruelty.[26]

9.3.2 Killing for Future Security

Vitoria says, 'A prince may do anything necessary in a just war to secure peace and security from attack'.[27] According to him, as discussed in the previous section, one can legitimately kill all the culpable among the enemy for the purposes of security. However, enemy *innocents* cannot be killed after victory for the sake of security. For example, it is forbidden to kill infants even when they can be assumed to eventually join their parents

---

[23] Molina, *II*, lib. 1 tract. 2 d. 117 n. 2 at p. 249. 'Item fas est sumere de hostibus [Fraga Iribarne provides the plural: 'enemigos'] iustam vindictam pro delictorum quantitate, capite, si ita fuerit opus, plectendo eos, qui delicta patrarunt, eorumve fuerunt causa, iustasque alias poenas impetendo, ut tributa pro quantitate culpae, vel alias similes poenas'.

[24] Scorraille, *François Suárez*, vol 1. p. 174; Fraga Iribarne, *Luis de Molina y el Derecho de la Guerra*, p. 25.

[25] Oviedo, *De virtutibus fide, spe et charitate*, contr. 12, punct. 7. num. 88 at p. 433. del Santísimo Sacramento and de la Concepción, *Quaestionum moralium*, tract. 8 d. 4 q. 3 at p. 248. Also Castro Palao, *Operis moralis*, tract. 6. d. 5 punct. 4 n. 5 at p. 465; Diana, *Resolutionum moralium*, pars 6 tract. 4 res. 22 at p. 11.

[26] Castro Palao, *Operis moralis*, tract. 6. d. 5 punct. 4 n. 5 at 465.

[27] Vitoria, *IB*, q. 1 a. 4 n. 18 at p. 305.

in their unjust war. The reason is not so much uncertainty about how these children will in fact turn out but the principle that one cannot be punished for a sin that might be committed but has not yet been committed (*neque fas est punire pro peccato, quod patrandum timetur, neque adhuc est commissum*).[28] Moreover, says Vitoria, there are many other ways of preventing future sin than killing enemies' children.[29]

So future security can only license the killing of the culpable, not innocent enemies. Lorca helpfully explains why future security justifies their killing thus: 'Security is not a sufficient cause to inflict death, but it is sufficient to not to remit the death penalty'.[30] The idea is that by culpably joining the unjust war you become liable to be killed. The need for future security is a sufficient reason not so much to kill you, since you already merit death, as not to save you. So security needs justify not remitting the penalty of those culpable enemy combatants that merit capital punishment.

Vitoria and Suárez cannot use Lorca's argument. They believe that killing all culpable enemy combatants would be disproportionate to the crime of their republic and, as such, would be unjust. But if it would be unjust to kill a particular enemy combatant because it would be one enemy combatant too many, then that combatant is not in principle liable to be killed and so does not stand in need of having his due punishment remitted. In other words, in his case, there is nothing to be remitted.

This points to a serious problem in Vitoria's and Suárez's position: if it would be unjust to kill a particular culpable enemy soldier (because it would be one killing too many), then how could it make it just to kill him only for the sake of security? Their position seems to allow departures from justice to ensure future security.

9.4 Plundering

9.4.1 The Rights of Captors

Is it morally permissible to plunder enemy innocents to meet the goals of the just war? In addressing this question the late scholastics had first to deal with a law of war understood to be part of the *ius gentium* that seems to make this question largely irrelevant. According to the *ius gentium* as

---

[28] Vitoria, *IB*, q. 3 a. 1 n. 38 at p. 316. The phrase features in Molina, *II*, lib. 1 tract. 2 d. 119 n. 4 at p. 254.
[29] Vitoria, *IB*, q. 3 a. 1 n. 38 at p. 316.
[30] Lorca, *In ST II-II*, sect. 3 d. 53 membr. 2. num. 8 at p. 982.

codified in Roman civil laws and taken to be supported by some biblical passages, all the enemy's possessions, movable and unmovable (without distinction here between enemy *nocentes* and innocents), pass to the victor.[31]

Vitoria takes this law to apply only to movable goods ('money, clothes or gold'), which includes captured persons who may then be enslaved. He agrees with Sylvester Prierias' view holding, in Vitoria's words, that this right 'should extend only so far as is consonant with an equitable satisfaction of the damage and injury sustained'.[32] 'We are not to suppose that if the French lay waste to a single village or some paltry town in Spain, the Spaniards thereby have the right to plunder the whole of France, even if they were able to do so. They must do so only in proportion to the extent of their own losses.'[33] Molina explicitly rejects such limits: all the captured movables belong to the victor even if their amount exceeds the satisfaction due.[34]

Suárez denies any independent force to this *ius gentium* law in the morality of war. What matters in order to determine the extent of plundering is that the punishment of the enemy state matches its fault and that the requirements imposed by future peace are kept in mind. In other words, one should not exploit this *ius gentium* provision to go beyond just satisfaction.[35]

When analysing the complex case of captured movable goods that are not legitimately owned by the enemy, Suárez tells us why it is that the Romans classed this law as part of the *ius gentium* and included it in their civil laws.[36] The reason is that they thought their wars to be just on both sides, 'and in fact they preferred to fight as if upon the tacit and mutual understanding that the conqueror should become absolute master'.[37] What Suárez does is to interpret this *ius gentium* law in a way that intentionally detaches it from its, in his view, questionable Roman rationale and subordinates it to the goals of just war. The only allowance made by Suárez beyond what is permitted as a matter of due satisfaction concerns movables

---

[31] *Digesta*, book 49, 15. 12 at p. 833 in *Corpus Iuris Civilis*, vol. 1, Paul Krueger and Theodor Mommsen (eds.) (Berlin: Weidmann, 1889) vol. 1.
[32] Sylvestro Mazzolino da Prierio, *Summa Sylvestrina* (Venice: Fabius & Augustinus Zopinos, 1586) 'bellum', 1. 10 at p. 69.
[33] Vitoria, *IB*, q. 3 a. 7 n. 51 at p. 322–3.   [34] Molina, *II*, lib. 1 tract. 2 d. 121 n. 4 at p. 256.
[35] Suárez, *De fide, spe et charitate*, q. 13 sect. 7 n. 7 at p. 753–4.   [36] Ibid., p. 754.
[37] In an interesting text, Molina (*II*, lib. 1 tract. 2 d. 118 n. 9) seems to suggest that the Romans were correct in considering their enemies no less just than themselves and this is the reason why they gave equal rights in war with respect to booty. Such equal rights do not apply in the case of Christians because they must diligently inquire into the justice of their cause before recurring to war.

actually seized by soldiers during the war; in his estimation they can keep some of these.[38]

9.4.2 Plundering Innocents for the Wrongs of Their Compatriots

Late scholastic discussion on the permissibility of plundering enemy subjects occupied itself with two different sorts of cases. One is when, in the midst of war, you seize property from enemy innocents to help your war effort or to thwart the enemy's war effort. The other is when you use force against some enemy subjects to exact satisfaction for the deeds perpetrated by other enemy subjects, as done in reprisals.

Reprisals seem not to fall into the post-victory category. Nevertheless, reprisals share an important common feature with post-victory actions. They were usually made against helpless, unarmed enemy subjects who did not pose a threat (typically merchant ships). Like post-victory actions, reprisals are not about the overcoming of resistance but rather about the exaction of a debt.

Vitoria's view is that one may plunder enemy innocents for restitution purposes only if the enemy state refuses to restore the owed property. So if the French king refuses to restore unjustly taken property, duly authorized Spanish combatants may plunder French merchants or farmers 'however innocent they may be'.[39] The French king's negligence in restoring property unjustly taken by some of its subjects makes some other subjects liable to have their property seized by the victim state.[40]

Reprisals at the time were mainly conducted by privateers who received licences or 'letters of marque' (*patentes de corso*) from the sovereign. Thus, the moral justification of reprisals, as Vitoria noted, could be dangerously abused because, although privateering can be just, reckless sovereigns could give letters of marque to unscrupulous privateers thereby state-sponsoring piracy.[41]

Molina regards reprisals as an instance of the just despoiling of innocent enemy subjects. 'The whole state is considered an enemy and therefore it is permissible to punish it in any of its members insofar as they are its parts with respect to external goods and the goods of fortune.'[42] The taking of such property is treated in the same way as the imposition of post-war

---

[38] Suárez, *De fide, spe et charitate*, q. 13 sect. 7 n. 7: This is a *ius gentium* provision, the rationale for which is that 'since the soldiers' lives are exposed to dangers so numerous and so grave, they should be allowed something'.
[39] Vitoria, *IB*, q. 3 a. 2 n. 41 at p. 318. [40] Ibid., pp. 318–9. [41] Ibid.
[42] Molina, *II*, lib. 1 tract. 2 d. 121 n. 4 at p. 256.

punitive tributes on the population of the defeated state.[43] He adds that the ruler of the enemy state, who is culpable for there being occasion for a reprisal, must compensate his despoiled innocent subjects for the seized property.[44]

Molina therefore gives a two-step defence of the vicarious liability of enemy subjects. A state is liable for its subjects' wrongs to foreigners if it fails to punish and compel them to provide satisfaction. If the state fails to do this, other subjects of the state become liable to punitive and restitutive measures. The result is that innocent subjects of a state may sometimes be liable for the wrongs of other culpable subjects of the same state. This liability is contracted by the mere fact of being a member in the political association.

Suárez's analysis is more extensive and sophisticated. The taking of property for the purpose of restitution and satisfaction needs to follow a lexical order. First you take the property of the enemy *nocentes*. If this is sufficient for reparation, you stop there. However, if it is insufficient, you may go on to take the property of the enemy innocents to the extent permitted by justice. As he writes, 'If such a course of action is essential to complete satisfaction, it is permissible to deprive the innocent of their goods, even of their liberty. The reason is that the innocent form a portion of one whole and unjust state; and on account of the crime [*delictum*] of the whole, this part may be punished even though they themselves did not take part in the crime.'[45] For Suárez, the vicarious liability of innocents is remedial: one becomes vicariously liable only if full satisfaction cannot be exacted from the subjects who actually committed the wrong.

In asserting this Suárez confronts (as did Vitoria and Molina) the view of Sylvester Prierias that after victory is attained the property of the enemy innocents should be restored to them.[46] Suárez retorts that there are some occasions in which a son may be punished on account of the sins of the father (a thesis defended elsewhere) and invokes the Canon Law principle, 'Punish no one except for a just cause *or* because of his fault' (*neminem puniri nisi vel ob causam justam, vel ob culpam*).[47] The principle must be

---

[43] Molina, *II*, lib. 1 tract. 2 d. 117 n. 2 at p. 249 with Vitoria, *IB* q. 3 a. 8 n. 57 at p. 325. In *II* lib. 1 tract. 2 d. 120 n. 1, Molina reiterates that the whole enemy republic can be punished through each of its parts as to the goods of fortune.

[44] Molina, *II*, lib. 1 tract. 2 d. 121 n. 5 at p. 255. Vitoria in *In ST II-II*, q. 40 n. 15 at p. 285 argues that the *nocentes* must compensate their innocent compatriots for the loss.

[45] Suárez, *De fide, spe et charitate*, q. 13 sect. 7 n. 12.

[46] *Summa Sylvestrina*, 'bellum', 1. q. 10 n. 12 'tertia ...' at p. 69.

[47] *Corpus juris canonici*, liber sextus, lib. 5 tit. 12, 'de regulis iuris' at col. 806. Rule 23 reads : 'sine culpa, nisi subsit causa, non est aliquis puniendus'.

disjunctively understood as stating that just cause alone without *culpa* is an appropriate ground for punishment.

How can the agreed upon view that plundering innocents is permissible be compatible with the no less agreed upon view that innocents cannot be intentionally killed before or after war? Suárez explains that there is a difference between life and other possessions. Property falls under human *dominium*: the republic possesses a 'greater right' over its subjects' property (perhaps he is alluding here to some form of eminent domain).[48] So, since in some way the property of the innocent subjects of the enemy state belongs to their state, when we plunder them we exact satisfaction from the state itself. This would make sense if we think about property rights as a form of protected stewardship over the state's goods, a view that seems derivable from Suárez view on the greater right of the republic. However, this is not the case as concerns life, over which the republic has no greater right.

In Suárez's account, the greater right that the state purportedly has over its subjects' private possessions performs two functions. First, it explains why being a subject of a state makes it the case that by depriving the subject of his goods one deprives the state of some of its goods. Second, it limits the type of goods which enemy subjects can be justifiably deprived of as a matter of vicarious liability. In other words, subjects are vicariously liable only to the loss of those goods over which the state has a superior right.

9.4.3 Lorca on Reprisals

The vast majority of authors – Diana lists eighteen – agreed with Vitoria, Molina and Suárez that reprisals to dispossess innocent enemies are permissible under some conditions.[49] There is, however, the almost solitary critical voice of Pedro de Lorca, who writes, 'I cannot but wonder at the fact that so many authors with so much confidence and consensus have regarded reprisals to be licit'.[50] After referring to many juridical sources questioning the legality of reprisals, Lorca notes that this practice is also against natural law insofar as a person is being punished for somebody else's sin, which 'cannot be done any more as regards [harm to] external goods than as to life itself'.[51] Lorca attacks as inconsistent the then-

---

[48] Suárez, *De fide, spe et charitate*, q. 13 sect. 7 n. 15.
[49] Diana, *Resolutionum moralium, pars quarta* (Venice: Apud Iuntas & Baba, 1647) tract. 4 miscellaneous res. 72 at p. 629.
[50] Lorca, *In ST II-II*, dubium appendix, a. 4 sect. 3 d. 52 n. 15 at p. 971.   [51] Ibid.

established view that denied vicarious liability as to life but allowed it as to property and liberty.

One of Lorca's main arguments is not based on a principled rejection of vicarious liability as such. Rather the argument is that the offences redressed by reprisals are not of the required magnitude to make some of the subjects of a state liable for the deeds of other subjects. In just wars, he concedes only for the sake of argument, the whole republic is an enemy and so may be punished in any of its parts. It was just war, rather than just reprisal, that St Augustine had in mind in the text that most authors interpreted as defending the permissibility of reprisals.[52] But a just war presupposes offences that are much more serious and extensive than the offences that reprisal seeks to address. These offences are serious enough to make punishment so imperative that punishing one subject for the deed of another becomes permissible. However, the sort of offences redressed by reprisal do not rise to the level necessary for making an innocent subject liable for the deeds of a non-innocent one. The wrongs redressed by reprisal do not provide an imperative reason for punishing such that every part of the republic becomes liable to be punished for the deeds of some of the subjects.[53]

Gaspar Hurtado (1575–1646) takes a more radical line. The state reprising against innocent enemy subjects cannot have a greater right against them than the right their own state has. But since the enemy state cannot deprive one innocent subject of his property to pay for another subject's debt, neither can the reprising state.[54] Hurtado, however, closes in a concessive tone saying that the opposite opinion is also probable and can be followed in good conscience.[55]

Giles de Coninck (1571–1633) took it upon himself to defend the basics of the mainstream view against Lorca.[56] Coninck says that even if a more serious wrong is necessary for a just war than for a just reprisal, the capacity of the political body to diffuse liability to its members does not depend on the sort of wrong that it or its subjects perpetrate: the republic is one body. Coninck explains this by saying that everyone agrees, and it is accepted in law, that when a state owes money to a foreign individual, if some of the

---

[52] St Augustine, *Quaestiones in Heptateuchum* 6.10 in CCSL (Turnhout: Brepols, 1958) vol. 33 at pp. 318–9.
[53] Lorca, *In ST II-II*, dubium appendix, sect. 3 d. 52 n. 15 at p. 971.
[54] Gaspar Hurtado, *De fide, spe et charitate* (Madrid: Francisco Ocampo, 1632) disp. 9 diff. 15 at pp. 504–5.
[55] Ibid., p. 506.
[56] Giles de Coninck, *De moralitate et effectibus actuus supernaturalibus* (Paris: Edmundus Martinus, 1624) d. 31 dub. 8 n. 131 at pp. 584–5.

members fail to pay, other members are liable and can be compelled to pay without any *culpa* being attributed to them. This is said to be a matter of contract and not to depend on the consent or awareness of the subjects to the debt (one infers that the thought is that for Coninck, there is some form of implicit contract between citizens making them remedially liable for each other's debts as you would have in a commercial partnership). Coninck concludes that if no *culpa* is necessary for forceful debt collection to be permissible, then no *culpa* is necessary in the case of plundering either.[57] So while Coninck concedes to Lorca that a state cannot *punish* a subject without *culpa*, it can compel him to satisfy his debt.[58]

Notice the interesting shift: the rationale for the plundering of enemy innocents' property is now presented as purely restitutive rather than as punitive. Remember that for Molina and Suárez, plundering had a punitive aspect to it. It seems somewhat less implausible to argue that a member of a political association can be liable for the association's debt (contracted because of its negligence to compel a different member to pay) than to say that a member of an association is punitively liable for the wrongs of another.

9.5 Enslaving and the Problem of the Moriscos

While in the matter of the plundering of innocents Lorca was more or less on his own in his opposition to Vitoria, Molina and Suárez, when it came to the enslavement of innocents he managed a somewhat greater following, which included the two Hurtados, Pedro and Gaspar.[59] The contribution of Pedro is of particular interest.

What brought Hurtado de Mendoza's treatment of just war into the spotlight in his time was his censure of the French joining forces with Protestant Dutch rebels against Spain during the Thirty Years War. Hurtado's censure provoked the ire of French Jesuits and the intervention of the Jesuit General Muzio Vitelleschi, who assured them that he would recall the book and have all copies burned. However, Hurtado de Mendoza's treatment contains other original elements worth our attention.[60]

---

[57] Coninck, *De moralitate*, d. 31 dub. 8 n. 135 at pp. 584–5.
[58] Coninck, *De moralitate*, dub. 8 n. 116 at p. 582.
[59] G. Hurtado, *De fide, spe et charitate*, disp. 9 diff. 15 at p. 506.
[60] On which, see Robert Bireley, *The Jesuits and the Thirty Year* War, pp. 169–70. The politically sensitive view of Hurtado de Mendoza can be found in *de tribus virtutis theologicis*, d. 169 sect. 9 n. 82–6 at pp. 1421–2.

Vitoria, Molina, Suárez and others believed that individual liberty belongs in the category of 'goods of fortune', just as other property does. This means that the state has a 'greater right' over the subject's liberty and is morally allowed in some circumstances to take it away. Therefore, the just victor acquires this right, which originally belonged to the defeated state, and can use it when the enslavement of the enemy innocent is necessary for the purposes of accomplishing full satisfaction. This means that enemy women and children could be enslaved.[61]

All the authors argued that the binding custom among Christian adversaries was not to enslave either enemy *nocentes* or *innocentes*. It was also more or less agreed that while Christian captives could not be reduced to legal slavery (*mancipium*) they could permissibly be held and put up for ransom.[62]

The view that *unbaptized* enemy innocents could be enslaved as a way of punishing the enemy state could not, however, do all the work that these authors wanted it to do. Covarrubias, following Pope Innocent III (*cap. olim in I restit. Spoliat*), noted that the principle could not justify the enslavement of *domestic* rebels (as opposed to subjects of an enemy state) since the quashing of a rebellion is not a war but rather an exercise of jurisdiction.[63]

Molina and Suárez sought to overcome this limitation.[64] The issue came up in connection with the Moriscos. These were Spanish subjects of Muslim descent who converted, generally forcibly, to Christianity and whom the king would decide to expel from Spain in 1609. The Moriscos of Suárez's native Kingdom of Granada conducted an insurrectionary war between 1568 and 1571, not much before both Suárez and Molina came to write on the topic of war (but after Covarrubias). The uprising, known as the War of the Alpujarras, was largely a reaction to laws prohibiting speaking Arabic andalusi dialect, wearing traditional clothing and, more generally, laws forcing cultural, not only religious, integration.[65] After the

---

[61] Vitoria *IB*, q. 3 a. 3 n. 42 at p. 318; Molina, *II*, lib. 1 tract. 2 d. 120 n. 1 at p. 255. Suárez, *De fide, spe et charitate*, q. 13 sect. 7 n. 12.
[62] Vitoria *IB*, q. 3 a. 3 n. 42 at p. 318; Suárez, *De fide, spe et charitate*, q. 13 sect. 7 n. 12.
[63] Covarrubias, *Regulae peccatum*, part. 9 n. 4 at p. 221. On this important jurist, see Inmaculada Pérez Martín and Margarita Becedas González (eds.), *Diego de Covarrubias y Leyva: el humanista y sus libros* (Salamanca: Universidad de Salamanca, 2012).
[64] Suárez, *De fide, spe et charitate*, q. 13 sect. 7 n. 12; Molina, *II*, lib. 1 tract. 2 d. 33 n. 6–13 pp. 173–5.
[65] On this, see Aurelia Martín Casares, *La esclavitud en Granada en el siglo XVI* (Granada: Editorial Universidad de Granada, Campus Universitario de Cartuja: Diputación Provincial de Granada, 2000). On the position of the church concerning the enslavement of the Moriscos, see pp. 82–6. Also Rafael Benítez Sancho-Blanco, 'El cautiverio de los Moriscos', *Manuscrits*, 28(2010)19–43; and

Justice After Victory

bloody suppression of the uprising, great numbers of Morisco women and children were enslaved to become personal slaves of their captors or to be sold.

In 1572, Felipe II made a law exempting Morisco children (girls under nine and a half years and boys under ten and a half) from slavery.[66] Molina posed the question of whether this law was a condoning of the punishment due to the Moriscos or an assertion of their natural rights. The problem with the Moriscos was double: not only were they baptized and so, as Christians, exempt from enslavement but they were also subjects of the Spanish king.

The first obstacle to their enslavement could be surmounted by pointing to the insincerity of their Christian faith so that, as baptized apostates, they could be excluded from the exemptions privileging Christians in war.

The second obstacle exposed the limitations of the doctrine of vicarious liability to punitive slavery that was defended by Molina and Suárez. Morisco children and the women who did not take part in the hostilities could not be punitively enslaved qua parts of an enemy state since they were not members of an enemy state but rather Spanish subjects.[67] The solution suggested by Molina was to say that, after rebelling, the Morisco population – including women and children – made themselves into a state with its own appointed leader or ruler (Hernando de Valor, who changed his name to Ibn Umayya or Aben Humeya).[68]

9.5.1 Lorca on Morisco Slavery

Lorca misleadingly asserted that the view that the innocent among the infidel enemy may be enslaved was a novelty. While it is true that Báñez, in a work published in 1586, had opposed the enslavement of Morisco children, one cannot find many other earlier opponents to infant slavery.[69]

William D. Phillips, Jr., *Slavery in Medieval and Early Modern Iberia* (Philadelphia: University of Pennsylvania Press, 2014) sp. pp. 37–9.

[66] Felipe II, King of Spain, *Pragmática y declaración sobre los Moriscos que fueron tomados por esclavos de edad de diez años y medio, y de las esclavas de nueve y medio, del Reyno de Granada* (Madrid: Alonso Gómez, 1572).

[67] Many Morisco women took part in the hostilities. See Aurelia Martín Casares, 'De pasivas a beligerantes: las mujeres en la guerra de las Alpujarras' in Mary Nash and Susana Tavera (eds.), *Las mujeres y las guerras: el papel de las mujeres en las guerras desde la Edad Antigua a la Contemporánea* (Barcelona: Icaria, 2003) pp. 132–45.

[68] Molina, *II*, lib. 1 tract. 2 d. 133 n. 9 at p. 272.

[69] Báñez, in ST II-II, q. 40 a. 1 d. 12 concl. 2 at p 531–2. Hurtado de Mendoza, *de tribus virtutis theologicis*, d. 169 sect. 11 n. 107 at p. 1424, notes that Báñez elsewhere contradicts his own view.

Lorca holds that the grounds offered by these authors to justify enslaving innocents are weak and false. He writes,

> A republic cannot be punished in its innocent members, nor a son for his father, nor in general one person for another. Nor does the moral conjunction that unites the parts of the republic suffice to that effect, nor is the republic like a natural body in which the parts are constituted as a unity per se, informed by one soul and ruled by one will, so that the liability to *culpa* [*reatus culparum*] redounds in all of the person and its parts. The moral unity of the republic is accidental [as opposed to *per se*]. Just as it does not eliminate the fact that one remains master of one's own acts, it does not suffice to make the *culpa* of one person redound in another person without his consent, so that one cannot justly inflict a punishment on one person in lieu of another.[70]

This passage (which Diana describes as 'mordacious') denies that the communal association fuses associates into one being such that innocent subjects are conduits of the punishment of the whole community. Hurtado de Mendoza seconded Lorca and argued, in the same vein, that the republic is a body only in a metaphorical sense. Different members of the political body have different wills. Only when you have a being with a unified will can one part be punished in lieu of another.[71] Anti-organicist arguments were standard among the late scholastics. As seen in the previous chapter this is precisely the sort of argument that was made against the purported right of the community to sacrifice Demosthenes to save Athens.

Lorca also attacked a different justification for slavery: that enslavement is a benign commutation of just capital punishment to which the enslaved is liable. He reasons that this does not apply to innocents since, as he established earlier, innocents cannot be justly punitively killed. Nor can custom justify the enslavement of the innocent since this custom, being unjust, cannot acquire the character of law.[72]

Lorca entertains an exception, however. When a just war against a people is prolonged and some harm could shorten the resistance of the enemy by diminishing and extenuating the number of those capable of fighting, enslavement may be a permissible option. Lorca supports this with the authority of a suggestive but somewhat cryptic biblical passage (Deut. 20:19), the meaning of which varies greatly across versions of the Bible. Here is the Douay-Rheims translation of this passage in the Vulgate:

---

[70] Lorca, *In ST II-II*, sect. 3 d. 55 membr. 2 num. 20 at p. 985.
[71] Hurtado de Mendoza, *de tribus virtutis theologicis*, d. 169 sect. 11 n. 109 at p. 1425.
[72] Lorca, *In ST II-II*, sect. 3 d. 55 membr. 2. num. 22 at p. 985.

When thou hast besieged a city a long time, and hath compassed it with bulwarks to take it, thou shalt not cut down the trees that may be eaten of, neither shalt thou spoil the country round about with axes: for it is a tree, and not a man, neither can it increase the number of them that fight against thee.[73]

The passage implies that you would be allowed to kill a member of the enemy ['cut down the fruit tree'] if he had the capacity to increase the numbers of the besieged. This, according to Lorca, could explain why, as his contemporaries agreed, it may be permissible to enslave 'Turkish and Saracen' women and children (here 'Saracen' includes the Moriscos). The reasoning is that if these women and children join the combatant body, it would make them liable to be killed. Thus their fate can be commuted to that of slavery.

9.5.2 Hurtado de Mendoza's Rejection of the Justifications for Morisco Slavery

Although Hurtado de Mendoza's criticism of the enslavement of innocents generally runs parallel to Lorca's, he differs from him in some important respects. In his remarkable text, he dismisses one by one the arguments offered by other theologians in support of the enslavement of innocent infidels.

His first argument, against the organicist justifications of the enslavement of enemy innocents advanced from Vitoria onwards, has already been mentioned. Let me recount some of his other arguments against other justifications for the enslavement of the Moriscos.

The second argument rejected by Hurtado de Mendoza comes from Giles de Coninck, who claims that, just as a republic has the right to deprive some of its innocent subjects of their property in case of necessity, so it can deprive them of their liberty. Therefore it can sell them as slaves to the enemy if this is the only way of achieving peace or of saving itself from destruction. This is not – says Coninck – unlike giving your own subjects as hostages to the enemy as a guarantee or collateral against breaches of peace agreements, which was in fact a customary feature of many peace treaties.[74] These hostages have the greater part of their liberty taken away from them, so they are in effect at least partial slaves.

---

[73] Edgar Swift (ed.), *The Vulgate Bible: The Douay-Rheims Translation* (Cambridge, Mass. and London: Harvard University Press, 2010) vol. 1 pp. 984–5.
[74] Coninck, *De moralitate*, d. 31, p. 538 n. 19. In the 1360 Treaty of Brétigny between France and England, the captured King Jean le Bon agreed to give to Edward III not only two of his sons and

Hurtado de Mendoza thought that the enemy republic may retain some right over its subjects' liberty, in that it can sell into slavery one of its citizens in the most urgent case – to save the republic from annihilation. But, he continues, the victorious republic's right to alienate the defeated republic's subjects' liberty cannot extend any further than the original right held by the defeated republic (namely that extreme necessity or urgency is required for alienating a subject's liberty). Hence, the victorious republic cannot deprive enemy innocents of their liberty in the case of 'Turks and Moriscos' since no such extreme necessity obtains.[75]

The third argument Hurtado de Mendoza rejects takes on the civil, ecclesiastical and military laws on war slavery. He argues that the laws about the enslavement of prisoners of just wars only apply to culpable (*nocentibus*) captives as opposed to innocent ones.[76]

The fourth argument Hurtado de Mendoza takes on – the only one that Lorca himself had accepted – was that Turks and Saracens may be enslaved if there are too many of them and a rebellion is feared, even if they are clearly innocent at the time of capture. He insists that no one can be punished for a sin he has not committed. So you cannot deprive 'innocent Turks of liberty as a punishment for future sins'. One should not inflict on others more harm than is necessary to prevent harm to oneself.[77]

Moreover, it is clear, he says, that the security of Christians (in Spain) can be preserved without depriving the Turks of their liberty. Their liberty is compatible with the introduction of severe laws preventing the Turks from fleeing or building an army. Therefore, the republic can be preserved merely by forcing the Turks to remain in the country, limiting their access to arms and other military resources. They should retain their rights to acquire property and enter into contracts, and they should retain their liberty.[78]

We should stop for a moment here to consider who are these 'Turks' referred to by Hurtado de Mendoza. By 'Turks' he may mean those infidels captured in the wars against the Ottoman Empire, whether Turk or not (including Ottoman slaves taken in battle).[79] This is supported by the fact

---

a number of princes and nobles but also four residents of Paris and two from each major French town as guarantee for the payment of his ransom. Under the 1526 Treaty of Madrid, Charles V took two of François I sons as hostages. For a thorough examination of the duties and rights of hostage takers and hostages, see Georg Braudlacht, *Pacificationum Austro-Hispanum-Gallicarum Historia* (Augsburg: Johannes Web, 1646) cons. 2 at pp. 16–27.

[75] Hurtado de Mendoza, *de tribus virtutis theologicis*, d. 169 sect. 11 n. 110 at p. 1425.
[76] Ibid., p. 1426.   [77] Ibid.   [78] Ibid.
[79] The category of traded 'Turkish slaves' imported from Constantinople included Russians, Abkhazians, Circassians and Mingrelians (from Georgia) and often people from the Balkans

that Hurtado de Mendoza wrote this text many years after the Moriscos were expelled from Spain in 1609. However, it is more likely that the reason why midway into the argument he switches to 'Turks' and ceases to refer to 'Turks and Saracens' is only a matter of brevity. After all, the arguments addressed by Hurtado de Mendoza were all arguments presented by their authors in support of the enslavement of innocent Moriscos. There were still many Morisco slaves in Hurtado de Mendoza's time (Morisco slaves were not expelled with the rest).[80] In addition, expelled Moriscos were clandestinely returning to Spain.[81] Moreover there were too few actual Turk slaves in Spain at the time to make one believe that they were what Hurtado de Mendoza had in mind when he discussed fears of internal insurrection.[82]

The fifth argument is that it is a common practice or custom (one assumes in Spain) to capture and enslave women and children of the Turks. Hurtado de Mendoza replies that this is essentially unlawful, but noted also that 'according to probable view this is licit incidentally' (*per accidens ex probabile sententia*).[83] Does Hurtado de Mendoza's answer to the fifth argument mean that in practical terms he does not differ from the advocates of Morisco infant slavery? This was the view, for example, of Antonio Escobar Mendoza, who says that Hurtado considers this slavery to be 'speculatively wrongful but practically permissible'.[84] Just one year after the publication of Pedro's book, Gaspar Hurtado, after sympathetically laying out Pedro's views, concludes (here using the label *maurorum*, that is, Moors): 'in fact, however, the unbaptized innocents can be reduced to

---

(particularly Bosnia) and East European regions under Ottoman rule. Most male 'Turks' were not traded as domestic slaves but rather were galley slaves. See Aurelia Martín Casares, 'Evolution of the Origin of Slaves Sold in Spain from the Late Middle Ages till the 18th Century' in Simonetta Cavaciocchi (ed.), *Schiavitù et servaggio nell'economia Europea: Secc. XI-XVIII* (Firenze: Firenze University Press, 2014) pp. 416–18; Onofre Vaquer Benàssar, *L'esclavitud a Mallorca 1448–1500* (Palma de Mallorca: Institut de Estudis Baleàrics, Consell Insular de Mallorca, 1997) p. 10.

[80] According to Aurelia Martín Casares (*La esclavitud*, p. 464), Morisco slavery disappeared by the second half of the seventeenth century.

[81] See Trevor J. Dadson, *Los moriscos de Villarrubia de los Ojos (Siglos XV-XVIII): Historia de una minoría asimilada, expulsada y reintegrada* (Madrid: Iberoamericana, 2007) pp. 655–66.

[82] For some incomplete numerical information on the precedence of slaves around Hurtado's time in Valencia, see Vicente Graullera Sanz, *La esclavitud en Valencia en los Siglos XVI y XVII* (Valencia: Instituto Valenciano de Estudios Históricos, Institución Alfonso el Magnánimo, Diputación Provincial de Valencia, Consejo Superior de Investigaciones Científicas, 1978) p. 135.

[83] Hurtado de Mendoza, *de tribus virtutis theologicis*, d. 169 sect. 11 n. 113 at p. 1426.

[84] Antonio Escobar Mendoza, *Liber Theologiae Moralis: Vingti-quatuor societatis iesu doctoribus referatus* (Brussels: Franciscus Vivienus, 1651) p. 219.

slavery in safe conscience because this is the common opinion and is most probable'.[85]

In context, Hurtado de Mendoza's acknowledgment of the probability of the opinion that he opposed is *not* a concessive move. Rather, this move is a way of dealing with the argument that capturing and enslaving 'Turk' women and children has become socially acceptable. If that observation carries any normative force at all, it must be because it implies something like 'well, if so many people do this all the time, it cannot be the case that it is wrongful to conduct oneself in this way; it must be permissible'. So Hurtado de Mendoza's response is to say that the practice is permissible only in an accidental or derivative sense, but it is not *really* permissible. What makes it permissible is this accidental feature of so many reputable people wrongly believing it to be permissible, not the intrinsic features of the action. In this way, Hurtado de Mendoza hoped to weaken the moral inference that could be made from what was then the general custom.

In assessing Hurtado de Mendoza's take on slavery one should note that he does allow for some cases of post-victory enslavement. He believed that non-innocent apostates (but not heretics) unjustly fighting against Christians (even against Christian heretics) may be enslaved, as could those who helped them. Moreover, one can enslave non-innocent Christian enemies if they fail to abide by the *ius gentium* agreement not to enslave other Christians (so Spain can enslave Dutch soldiers, given the fact that they sell Spanish captives to the Barbary state of Algiers).[86]

9.5.3 No One Cared about the Moriscos?

In her excellent study of Morisco slavery, Aurelia Martín Casares writes, 'There is no Vitoria or Bartolomé de las Casas to defend the Morisco population of the Kingdom of Granada. The status of the defeated Moriscos was perhaps lower than that of the Indians in the thinking of that period: they did not inspire the least feeling of humanity, nobody opposed their slavery.'[87]

In some sense this is true; the vast majority of late scholastics thought that enslavement of the defeated Moriscos was permissible.[88] Certainly one

---
[85] G. Hurtado, *De fide, spe et charitate*, disp. 9 diff. 15 at p. 506.
[86] Hurtado de Mendoza, *de tribus virtutis theologicis*, d. 169 sect. 11 n. 114 at p. 1426.
[87] See Martín Casares, *La esclavitud*, p. 179; also Pedro Parilla Ortíz, *La esclavitud en Cádiz durante el Siglo XVII* (Cádiz: Diputación de Cádiz, 2010) p. 52.
[88] Martín Casares (pp. 349–50) mentions Bartolomé Frías de Albornoz (1519–1573) as the only person who opposed the slavery of innocent women and children. She is referring, however, to a short

Justice After Victory 205

would have hoped for a more serious consideration on the part of the theologians of the obstacle presented by the Moriscos' baptism to their enslavement. However, it is worth noting that the case of the American natives and that of the Moriscos were entirely different. The fact that in both cases a considerable number of people suffered greatly at the hands of Spanish forces as such should not raise the expectation that Spanish theologians should have opposed Morisco slavery with the same zeal that many of them showed in their opposition to the arguments in favour of the subjection of the American natives. Note, crucially, that, unlike the Aztec and the Inca before the conquest, the Moriscos of Granada were rebels against the Spanish king.

Having said this, Lorca's criticisms and the remarkable text by Hurtado de Mendoza set them apart as theologians who went not just against general opinion but also headlong against the opinion of most of their contemporary theologians (unlike Vitoria and de las Casas, who operated within a largely supportive intellectual community).

Hurtado de Mendoza's views may reflect a possible shift among the Spanish elites' appraisal of past policies towards the Moriscos, including their expulsion. According to a number of historians, Felipe IV, who acceded the throne in 1622, and the Count-Duke of Olivares, who held the actual reins of power during much of the latter's reign, had a much more tolerant view of the Moriscos, including their resettlement.[89] Hurtado de Mendoza had significant contact – resented by his Jesuit General – with the political elites, given his considerable involvement in political business at the Court in Madrid.[90]

---

passage in which Albornoz makes no reference to the Moriscos or any other particular group nor confronts opposing arguments. Bartolomé de Albornoz, 'De la esclavitud', *Biblioteca de Autores Españoles*, vol. 65 (Atlas: Madrid, 1953) p. 232. Note also that there was significant opposition from religious quarters to the proposals to expel the Moriscos (finally carried out in 1609). One of the main opponents was the Jesuit Ignacio de las Casas (himself of Morisco descent).

[89] See Antonio Domínguez Ortíz, 'Felipe IV y los Moriscos', 55–66; John H. Elliott, *Imperial Spain 1469–1716* (Penguin: London, 1990), 308; Dadson, *Los moriscos de Villarrubia de los Ojos*, pp. 655–66; and, in a more critical note, Antonio Feros, 'Rhetorics of Expulsion', in Mercedes García-Arenal and Gerard Wiegers, (eds.), *The Expulsion of the Moriscos from Spain: A Mediterranean Diaspora* (Leyden and Boston: Brill, 2014) 86–101.

[90] Hurtado's involvement in the world of secular politics was a source of friction with the Jesuit General. In fact, Muzio Vitelleschi wrote to the King of Spain on the 20th of July 1626 asking him to remove Hurtado de Mendoza and another Jesuit, Hernando de Salazar, from political business. He writes about them: 'they are very good members of the religion [*religiosos*], excellent for the ministry of their religion. Yet, for those things that they deal with now such as political judgments [*arbitrios*] and temporal things, for that Sir, they are not [good] and when they deal in these things the harm is far greater than the benefit.' In Antonio Astrain, *Historia de la Compañía de Jesús en la asistencia de España*, vol. 5 (Madrid: Razón y Fe, 1916), 219.

9.6 Summary and Conclusions

The mainstream late scholastic view on the liability to punitive harm of members of the enemy who no longer pose a short-term threat can roughly be put thus:

1. Your punitive liability to lose your property and liberty requires only your being a member of the justly defeated state.
2. Your punitive liability to lose your life requires your having culpably participated in the war.

Both liabilities are subject to the constraints of punitive proportionality in such a way that punishment should not exceed the fault of the unjust enemy state (though Molina seems not to adhere to this). Within these boundaries, the actual infliction of punishment should take into account additional considerations, such as charity and humanity. However, future security trumps these considerations, so that the full extent of harm allowed by justice can be inflicted when it is required for future peace and tranquillity.

Security from future attacks is held not to allow the infliction of harm beyond what is allowed by justice. As concerns property dispossession, although all enemy subjects are conditionally liable to this, priority should be given to those among the enemy who are personally culpable.

The liability of innocent subjects of the defeated state is explained in three different ways. One way is to say that, by punishing the subject, the defeated republic gets punished. A second way is to say that the victorious state acquires the right that the defeated state had over its subjects' property and liberty and can therefore deprive its subjects of these for its own punitive purposes. A third way is to reframe punitive liability as debt liability: subjects of the enemy state incur a form of corporate debt such that each is a guarantor of the other in the case of non-payment.

The main historical case on which these views, particularly the views on innocents' liability to loss of freedom, were brought to bear was that of the innocent captives taken after the suppression of the Granada Morisco revolt.

It was Morisco slaves who opponents of the mainstream view, such as Lorca, Hurtado de Mendoza and to a lesser extent Gaspar Hurtado, had in mind. They advanced two principal lines of criticism. First, that membership in the political association as such does not make one subject vicariously liable for the wrongs of a different subject. Second, that the goals for which the defeated state could permissibly alienate their subjects' property and liberty do not include the punitive goals of the victorious state.

Hurtado de Mendoza went further than Lorca in denying that security requirements and the fear of future insurrection can justify the reduction of enemy innocents to slavery. In doing so, he was not only condemning the accepted practice in Spain at the time concerning the trading of non-Christian women and children captured from Muslim enemies but also the opinion that was held by virtually all of his colleagues that Morisco innocents could be enslaved. To advance this original point, Hurtado de Mendoza did not have to introduce novel ideas. He only had to press principles that were adhered to by all the moral theologians of his day, but which were not consistently applied to the case of innocent enemy subjects.

Concluding Remarks

The late historian Tony Judt, in his obituary piece on Leszek Kołakowski, retells the following anecdote from a talk that the Polish philosopher gave at Harvard. The lecture's title was 'The Devil in History'. As the talk progressed, the audience was engulfed in an increased sense of mystification. 'They could not decode the metaphor', recounts Judt. Eventually Timothy Garton Ash, seated next to Judt, whispered: 'I've got it, he really *is* talking about the Devil!'[1]

Many of the historical scholars interested in late scholastic moral theology have been driven by their interest in telling a larger story. In the case of Paolo Prodi, possibly the most influential modern historian who worked on Catholic moral theology, this was the story leading to the aspiration of the modern state to normatively regulate our moral lives.[2] By contrast, in this book I have been interested in the questions that the late scholastics themselves asked. Just as Kołakowski's talk on the devil was about the devil, when I examine, for example, the late scholastics on the permissibility of buying votes, I am actually discussing the permissibility of buying votes.

Since the various controversial questions examined here run, to a great extent, independent of each other, it would be contrived to offer in these concluding remarks a nutshell encapsulation of the political morality of the late scholastics. However, something should be said about these authors' general approach to political duty.

According to De Quincey, the moral theologians engaged in casuistry 'held aloft a torch for exploring guilty recesses of human life, which it is far better for us all to leave in their original darkness'.[3] While arguably (but just arguably), it may be salutary to leave some questions unasked as

---

[1] Tony Judt, 'Leszek Kołakowski (1927–2009)', *New York Review of Books*, 56(Sept. 2009) issue 14 pp. 6–8.
[2] Paolo Prodi, *Una storia della giustizia* (Bologna: Il Mulino, 2000).
[3] Thomas De Quincey, *Theological Essays and Other Papers* (Boston: Ticknor, Reed, and Fields, 1854), pp. 203–4

concern our private lives, this seems rather less salutary when political life is in question. Since abuse of power by rulers is rife and unjust laws and wars are not infrequent, asking questions about the moral limits of our duties to comply with the law and to obey orders can hardly be put down to the 'irritations of curiosity' and the 'lubricity of morals' which, according to standard critiques of casuistry from Pascal onwards, animated the work of the less sober among the casuists.[4]

'I am not writing a book of political casuistry', emphatically disclaimed Franz Lieber, better known for the Lieber Code of conduct in war, in his *Manual of Political Ethics*.[5] He went on to reiterate the standard criticism that 'in all probability' no works of casuistry, 'however ingenious and dialectic they may be, essentially contributed to guide consciences in the path of duty, while as we all know, not a few have, by their very ingenuity, blunted the moral edge, instead of sharpening it'.[6] Instead, Lieber wished to give 'moral vigor to political existence', to impress some with the 'sacredness of their political relations' and warm hearts 'with true patriotism'.[7]

It is true that late scholastic controversial literature cannot be said to have aimed at the moral edification of readers. But this is, I think, the nature of controversial literature in general. This is not to say, of course, that the late scholastics did not consider political duties to be grave and serious. The hard cases of conscience to which many of the discussions gravitated were treated as hard cases precisely because they involved a possible transgression of moral precepts held to be inviolable.

If the aim of the late scholastic controversies was not moral edification, what was the aim? The background assumption of these authors was that moral duty limits individual liberty and the individual pursuit of valuable non-spiritual goods. Toulmin and Jonsen perceptively noted that 'the Baroque era signals the definitive irruption into Christian culture of the secular as reality, and as value'.[8] The value that the baroque late scholastics attached to non-spiritual individual goods, foremost among them liberty, defined one of their main tasks as moral experts: to unmask merely apparent moral barriers and locate those moral barriers that are genuine with as much exactitude as possible. In the pursuit of this aim, the late scholastic authors had to examine philosophical problems such as 'What exactly counts as buying something?'; 'In what circumstances can custom

---

[4] Ibid. p. 203.
[5] Francis Lieber, *Manual of Political Ethics* (Boston: Charles C. Little and James Brown, 1839) part 2, p. 17.
[6] Ibid. [7] Ibid., p. 18. [8] Toulmin and Jonsen, *The Abuse of Casuistry*, p. 145.

acquire the force of law?'; 'What exactly is the difference between enabling and inducing another's act?'; 'Is my reputation my property?'; and 'Must one sacrifice justice for the sake of peace?' Ultimately, the late scholastics' identification of the basic problems that need to be examined in order to have a good answer to the practical questions that exercised them is not less valuable than the answers themselves.

Bibliography

Primary Sources

Adrian from Utrecht (Pope Adrian VI), *Quaestiones in quartum sententiarum praesertim circa sacramenta* (Leuven: Jocobus Dassoneville, 1516).
Adrian from Utrecht, (Pope Adrian VI), *Quaestiones quodlibeticae XII* (Paris: Nicolaus Savetirius, 1531).
Alberti, Alberto, *Paradoxia moralia de ornatu mulierum* (Milano: Montiae, 1650).
Albornoz, Bartolomé de, 'De la esclavitud', *Biblioteca de Autores Españoles* (Madrid: Atlas, 1953).
Alciatus, Andrea, *Emblematum Liber* (Ausburg: Heyrich Steyner, 1531).
Alfonso X, King of Spain, *Las Siete Partidas del Rey Don Alfonso el Sabio* (Madrid: Imprenta Real, 1807).
Ambrose of Milano, *De officiis*, Ivor J. Davidson (ed. and trans.) (Oxford: Oxford University Press, 2011).
Angles, Joseph, *Flores Theologicarum*, in *q. de restitutione* (Antwerpen: Pedro Beller, 1585).
Aquinas, Thomas, *Opera omnia iussu impensaque Leonis XIII P. M. edita: Secunda secundae Summae theologiae* (Rome: Typographia Polyglotta S. C. de Propaganda Fide, 1897–).
Aquinas, Thomas, *Scriptum Super Libros Sententiarum*, R. P. Mandonnet (ed.) (Paris: Lethielleux, 1929).
Aragón, Pedro de, *In Secundam secundae divi Thoma doctoris angelici commentaria* (Lyons: Petrus Landry, 1597).
Augustine of Hippo, *The City of God*, Marcus Dods trans. (New York: Hafner, 1948).
Augustine of Hippo, *S. Avreli Avgvstini Hipponiensis episcopi Epistvlae*, Alois Goldbacher (ed.) (Leipzig: G. Freytag; Vienna and Prague: F. Tempsky, 1898).
Augustine of Hippo, *Quaestiones in Heptateuchum* (Turnhout: Brepols, 1958) *Corpus Christianorum Series Latina*, vol. 33.
Azor, Juan, *Institutionum moralium in quibus universae questiones ad conscientiam recte, aut prave factorum pertinentes, breviter tractantur* (Cologne: Antonius Hierat, 1602).

Azpilcueta, Martín (Navarrus), *Capitulo veynte y ocho: de las addiciones del Manual de confessores* (Zaragoza: Widow of Bartholome de Nágera, 1570).
Azpilcueta, Martín (Navarrus), 'Commentarii de Lege Poenali', in *Martini ab Azpilcueta Doctoris Navarri, Iurisconsultum, ... Operum, tomus secundus* (Cologne: Ioannis Gymnici, 1626).
Azpilcueta, Martín (Navarrus), *Enchiridion sive Manuale confessariorum et poenitentium* (Rome: Victorinus Romanus, 1573).
Azpilcueta, Martín (Navarrus), *Manual de Confessores y penitentes* (Valladolid: Francisco Fernández de Córdoba, 1570).
Báñez, Domingo, *Decisiones de Iustitia et iure* (Venice: Minima Societas, 1545).
Barros, Tomás de, *Copia de vna carta qve escrivio el padre Tomas de Barros de la Compañia de Iesus en Iunio de 622. al Padre General, en que declara lo que los de la Compañia hizieron en el Imperio de Etiopia, en el dicto año de 622* at http://bdlb.bn.br/acervo/handle/123456789/47475.
Bassée, Eloy de la, *Flores totius theologiae practicae* (Lyon: Anisson, 1657).
Becanus, Martin, *De fide, spe et charitate* (Lyon: Nicolas Gay, 1644 c. 1614).
Beja Perestrello, Luiz de, *Responsionum casus conscientiae, secunda pars* (Venice: Ioannis Baptista and Ioannis Bernardus Sessam, 1597).
Benzoni, Rutilio, *Speculum Episcoporum & Curatorum* (Venice: Minima Societas, 1595).
Bernal Díaz de Luco, Juan, 'La "doctrina y amonestación charitativa" (1547) de Juan Bernal Diaz de Luco. Transcripción y aproximación a su contexto social' in Javier Laspalas (ed.), *Historia y Teoría de la Educación. Estudios en Honor del Profesor Emilio Redondo García* (Pamplona: EUNSA, 1999) pp. 311–28.
Bianchi, Paolo de, *Disceptationes de difficilioribus materiis casuus* (Venice: Evangelista Deuchinus, 1630).
Blas Navarro, Juan, *Disputatio de vectigalibus et eorum exactione in foro conscientiae* (Valencia: Pedro Patricio Mey, 1587).
Bodin, Jean, *The Six Books of a Common-Weale ... out of the French and Latin Copies*, Richard Knolles (ed.) (London: G. Bishop, 1606).
Bonacina, Martino, *Opera Omnia* (Lyon: Claudius Landry, 1629).
Boncompagno, Giacomo and Francesco-Luigi Barelli da Nizza, *Resolutionum practicarum pro confessariis monialum, in congregationibus mensualibus habitis* (Bologna: Fernandus Pisarri, 1719).
Borromeo, Carlo, *Instructionum fabricae et supellectis ecclesiasticae, libri II* reprinted with Italian trans. (Vatican: Libreria Editrice Vaticana, 2000).
Bosso, Giovanni, *Moralia varia* (Lyon: Phillip Borde and Laurence Arnaud, 1649).
Braganza, Francisco, *Copia de los pareceres y censuras de los revenderissimos padres y señores maestros catedráticos de las universidades de Salamanca y Alcalá, y de otras personas doctas sobre el abuso de las figuras* (Madrid: Viuda de Alonso Martín, 1632).
Braudlacht, Georg, *Pacificationum Austro-Hispanum-Gallicarum Historia* (Augsburg: Johannes Web, 1646).
Brezmes Diez de Prado, Martín, *Teatro Moral* (Salamanca: Gregorio Ortíz Gallardo y Aponte, 1685).

Cajetan (Tommaso de Vio), *Commentaria in Summa Theologiae*, in *Thomas Aquinas, Opera omnia iussu impensaque Leonis XIII P. M. edita: Secunda secundae Summae theologiae* (Rome: Typographia Polyglotta S. C. de Propaganda Fide, 1888–1906).

Cajetan, *Peccatorum Summula* (Douay: Balthazar Beller, 1627).

Cajetan, *Opuscula Omnia* (Lyon: Gulielmus Rovillius, 1588).

Caramuel y Lobkowitz, Juan, *In D. Benedicti Regulam Commentarius Historicus Scholasticus Moralis Iudicialis Politicus* (Bruges: Nreyghels, 1650).

Carletti di Chivasso, Angelo, *Summa Angelica de Casibus Conscientialibus* (Venice: Aegidius Regazola, 1578).

Carlevalius, Thomas, *Disputationum de iuris variarium, De foro competente et legitima iudicum potestate, tomus prio* (Madrid: Typographia Regia, 1656).

Castro, Alonso de, *De potestatis leges poenalis, libri duo* (Louvain: Antonius Maria Bergagne, 1557).

Castro Palao, Fernando de, *Operis moralis de virtutibus, et vitiis contrariis, pars prima* (Lyon: Guiglielmi Barbier, 1682).

Cellarius, Christianus, *Oratio contra mendicitatem pro nova pauperum subventione* (Antwerp: Henricus Petri Middelburgenis, 1531).

Cellarius, Christianus, *Oratio pro pauperibus, ut eis liceat mendicare* (Antwerp: Henricus Petri, 1530).

Cervantes de Saavedra, Miguel, *El ingenioso hidaldo Don Quijote de la Mancha* (Madrid: Espasa-Calpe, 1967).

Chrysostom, John, *Sermo de Eleemosyna*, Johannes Oecolampadius (trans.) (Mainz: Schöffer, 1522).

Chrysostom, John, *Sermon on Alms*, Margaret M. Sherwood (trans.) (New York: New York School of Philanthropy, 1917).

Cicero, Marcus Tullius, *On Duties*, Loeb Classical Library, Walter Miller trans. (London: Heinemann; New York: Putnam and Sons, 1913).

Cipolla, Bartolomeo, *Tractatus de servitutibus tam urbanorum, quam rusticorum praediorum* (Cologne: Franciscus Metternich, 1701).

Concepción, Manuel de la and Leandro del Santísimo Sacramento, *Quaestionum moralium theologicarum pars IV* (Avignon: Salmanticenses, 1692).

Coninck, Giles de, *De moralitate et effectibus actuus supernaturalibus* (Paris: Edmundus Martinus, 1624).

Contzen, Adam, *Politicorum Libri Decem* (Mainz: Ioannis Kinkius, 1621).

Córdoba, Antonio de, *Libellus de Detractione et famae restitutione: cum annotationibus eiusdem in tractatum de Secreto magistri Soto Ordinis Praedicatorum* (Alcalá de Henares: Juan de Brocar, 1553).

Córdoba, Antonio de, *Quaestionarium theologicum* (Venice: Ziletti; Toledo: Ayala, 1569–70).

Córdoba, Antonio de, *Tratado de casos de consciencia* (Toledo: Pedro López de Haro, 1584).

Corpus juris canonici emendatum et notis illustratum Gregorii XIII. pont. max. iussu editum (Rome: In aedibus Populi Romani, 1582).

Cotonne, Antonio, *Controversiae celebres* (Venice: Tomasinus and Hertz, 1661).

Covarrubias Orozco, Sebastian, *Tesoro de la Lengua castellana o Española* (Madrid: Luis Sánchez, 1611).
Covarrubias y Leyva, Diego, *Regulae peccatum. De regul iur. Lib. IV Relectio* (Lyon: Sebastian Honoratus, 1560).
D'Afflitto, Matteo, *Commentaria in feudorum usus et consuetudines absolutissima* (Frankfurt: Clemens Schelchius and Peter de Zetter, 1629).
Diana, Antonino, *Resolutionum moralium, pars quinta* (Lyon: Laurentii Durand, 1639).
Diana, Antonino, *Resolutionum moralium, pars sexta* (Venice: Apud Iuntas & Baba, 1645).
Diana, Antonino, *Resolutionum moralium, pars quarta* (Venice: Apud Iuntas & Baba, 1647).
Diana, Antonino, *Resolutionum moralium, pars undecima* (Lyon: Borde, Arnauld and Rigaud, 1655).
Dominican Order, *Regula Sancti Augustini et Constitutionum Ordinis Praedicatorum* (Rome: Niccolò Angelo Tinassi, 1690).
Drexel, Jeremias, *Gazophylacium Christi eleemosyna* (Monaco: Widow of Ioannes Cnobbarus, 1651).
Escobar Mendoza, Antonio, *Liber Theologiae Moralis: Vingti-quatuor societatis iesu doctoribus referatus* (Brussels: Franciscus Vivienus, 1651)
Examen Theologal que el Catholico Rey Don Felipe mando hacer para seguridad de su consciencia, antes de apprehender la possession de los Reynos y señorios de la Corona de Portugal (Archivo General de Simancas, PTR, LEG 51, DOC.2.).
Felipe II, King of Spain, *Pragmática y declaración sobre los Moriscos que fueron tomados por esclavos de edad de diez años y medio, y de las esclavas de nueve y medio, del Reyno de Granada* (Madrid: Alonso Gómez, 1572).
Ferrari, Lucio, *Prompta bibliotheca canonica, juridica, moralis, theologica, nec non ascetica, polemica, rubricistica, historica* (Paris: J.-P Migne, 1861) vol. 3.
Ferrantino de Ancona, Girolamo, *Theoreticae ac practicae disputationes* (Roma: Inheritors of Corbelletti, 1653).
Filiarchi, Cosimo, *De officio sacerdotis, tomus primus* (Venice: Apud Iuntas, 1597).
Francés de Urrutigoyti, Tomás, *Consultationes in re morali* (Toulouse: Guillermus Ludovicus Colomerius and Hieronymus Possuet, 1682).
Giginta, Miguel de, *Tratado del remedio de los pobres*, Félix Santolaria Sierra (ed.) (Barcelona: Ariel, 2000).
Gonzáles de Salcedo, Pedro, *De lege politica* (Madrid: Jose Fernández del Buendía, 1678).
Gonzáles, Francisco Antonio (ed.), *Colección de cánones y de todos los concilios de la iglesia española* (Madrid: Antonio Santa Coloma, 1850).
Grotius, Hugo, *The Rights of Peace and War*, Richard Tuck (ed. and intro.) (Indianapolis: Liberty Fund, 2005).
Gutiérrez, Juan, *Tractatus de Gabellis* (Antwerp: Joannes and Peter Beller, 1618).
Henry of Ghent, *Quodlibeta magistri Henrici Goethals a Gandauo doctoris solemnis socii Sorbonici & archidiaconi Tornacensis* (Paris: Iodocus Badius, 1518).

Hopffer, Benedikt and Buckhard Bardili, *China inhospitalis, seu de mutua peregrinandi et commercandi libertate inter gentes, dissertatio historico-politica* (Tubingen: Reisius, 1678).
Hurtado de Mendoza, Pedro, *Scholasticae et morales disputationes de tribus virtutibus theologicis* (Salamanca: Jacinto Taberniel, 1631).
Hurtado, Gaspar, *De fide, spe et charitate* (Madrid: Francisco Ocampo, 1632).
Hurtado, Tomás, *Resolutiones Orthodoxo-morales* (Cologne: Cornelius de Egmond, 1655).
Hyperius, Andreas, *Forma subventionis pauperum* (Antwerpen: Martinus Cesar, 1531).
Jacobus de Voragine, *The Golden Legend: Readings on the Saints*, William Granger Ryan (trans.) (New Jersey: Princeton University Press, 2012).
Jesús María, José de, *Primera parte de las excelencias de la castidad* (Viuda de Juan Gracián, 1601).
Krueger, Paul and Theodor Mommsen eds., *Corpus Iuris Civilis* (Berlin: Weidmann, 1889).
Laínez, Diego, *Quaestiones theologicae de vectigalibus in Disputationes Tridentinae*, Hartmannus Grisar (ed.) (Innsbruck: Felicianus Rauch, 1886) vol. 2.
Lassarte y Molina, Ignacio, *De decimum venditiones & permutationis quae Alcavala nuncupatur* (Alcalá: Juan Gracián, 1589).
Laymann, Paul, *Theologia moralis* (Munich: Hendrik Niclaes, 1630).
Ledesma, Martín de, *Secunda quartae* (Coimbra: Juan Álvarez, 1560).
Ledesma, Pedro de, *Segunda parte de la Summa* (Zaragoza: Lucas Sánchez, 1611).
Leibniz, Gottfried Wilhelm, 'Letter to Nicolas-François Rémond de Montmort' in Marcelo Dascal (ed.), *The Art of Controversies* (Dordrecht: Springer, 2006).
Lessius, Leonardus, *De iustitia et iure* (Leuven: Ioannes Masus, 1605).
Lipsius, Justus, *Roma Illustrata* (Amsterdam: Elzeciriana, 1657).
López, Luis, *Instructorii conscientiae* (Lyon: Petrus Landry, 1591).
Lorca, Pedro de, *Commentaria et disputationes in secunda secundae divi Thomae* (Madrid: Luis Sánchez, 1614).
Lugo, Juan de, *Disputationum de iustitia et iure, tomus secundus* (Lyon: Philippe Borde, Laurent Arnaud and Claude Rigaud, 1652).
Lugo, Juan de, *Disputationum de iustitia et iure, tomus primus* (Lyon: Inheritors of Petrus Prost, Phillippus Borde and Laurentius Arnaud, 1646).
Machado de Cháves, Juan, *Perfeto confessor i cura de almas* (Barcelona: Pedro Lacavallería, 1641).
Madre de Dios, Andrés de la, *Cursus theologiae moralis* (Venice: Nicola Pezzana, 1750).
Mazzolino da Prierio, Sylvestro, *Summa Sylvestrina* (Venice: Fabius & Augustinus Zopini, 1586).
Medina, Bartolomé de, *Breve instrucción de como se ha de administrar el sacramento de la penitencia* (Huesca: Juan Pérez de Valdivieso, 1581).
Medina, Bartolomé de, *Expositio in prima secundae angelici doctoris D. Thomae Aquinatis* (Salamanca: Mateo Gasti, 1582).

Medina, Juan de, *Codex de eleemosyna* (Alcalá de Henares: Athanasio Salzedo, 1544).
Medina, Juan de, *Codex de restitutione* (Alcalá: Juan de Brocar, 1546).
Molanus, Johannes (Jan Vermeulen), *De historia ss. Imaginum et picturarum, libri IV* (Leuven: Ioannes Bogardus, 1594).
Molina, Luis de, *De iustitia et iure* (Cologny: Marci-Michaelis Bousquet, 1733), 5 vols.
Molina, Luis de, *Luis de Molina y el Derecho de Guerra*, Fraga Iribarne (trans. and ed.) (Madrid: CSIC, 1947).
Montesinos, Luis de, *Commentaria in Primam Secundae Divi Thomae Aquinatis* (Complutense: Widow of Juan Gracián de Antisco, 1621).
Naldi, Antonio, *Summa seu Resolutiones practicae* (Cologne: Peter Henning, 1625).
Navarra, Pedro de, *De ablatorum restitutione in foro conscientiae* (Lyon: Iuntae, 1593).
Nieva, Bernardo de la, *Sumario Manual de Información de la Christiana Consciencia* (Medina del Campo: Francisco del Canto, 1556).
Núñez Avendaño, Pedro, *Dictionarium Hispanum vocum antiquarum in Quadraginta responsa quibus quamplurimas leges regias explicantur* (Salamanca: Inheritors of Juan de Cánova, 1576).
Osuna, Francisco de, *Quinta parte del abecedario espiritual* (Burgos: Juan de la Junta, 1542).
Ottonelli, Giovanni Domenico and Pietro da Cortona, *Trattato della pittura e scultura, uso et abuso loro composto da un theologo, e da un pittore* (Firenze: Bonardi, 1652).
Oviedo, Francisco de, *Tractatus Theologici, Scholastici & Morales De virtutibus fide, spe et charitate* (Lyon: Philippus Borde, Laurentius Arnauld and Claudius Rigaud, 1651).
Paleotti, Gabriele, *Discourse on Sacred and Profane Images*, William McCuaig (trans.) (Los Angeles: Getty Research Institute, 2012).
Pascal, Blaise, *The Provincial Letters of Pascal* (Cambridge: Deighton, Bell and Co.; London: George Bell and Sons, 1880).
Pasqualigo, Alvise, *Lettere Amorose* (Venice: Niccolo Moretti, 1587).
Pasqualigo, Zaccaria, *Decisiones Morales* (Verona: Bartholomeus Merlua, 1641).
Passerini, Pietro Maria, *Tractatus de electione canonica* (Roma: Felix Caefarettus, 1693).
Peltanus, Theodor, *De tertia et postrema satisfactionis parte* (Ingolstadt: Weinffenhorn, 1572).
Peltanus, Theodor, *De tribus bonorum operum generibus* (Ingolstadt: Weiffenhorn, 1580).
Pérez de Herrera, Cristobal, *Amparo de los pobres*, Michel Cavillac (ed.) (Madrid: Espasa-Calpe, 1975).
Philip Schaff, (ed.), *Nicene and Post-Nicene Fathers*, First Series (Buffalo, NY: Christian Literature Publishing Co., 1887).
Pignatelli, Jacopo, *Consultationes canonicae* (Lyon: Gabriel and Samuel de Tournes, 1700).

Pizarro, Fernando, *Varones ilustres del nuevo mundo* (Madrid: Diego Díaz de las Carreras, 1639).
Plutarch, *Plutarch's Lives*, Loeb's Classical Library, trans. Bernardotte Perrin (Cambridge, Mass.: Harvard University Press; London: William Heinemann).
Ponce de León, Basilio, *De sacramento matrimonii tractatus* (Venice: Combi, 1645).
Quaderno de las alcavalas (Salamanca: Juan de la Junta: 1547).
Quevedo, Francisco de, *Obras completas en verso*, Luis Astrana Marín (ed.) (Madrid: Aguilar, 1952).
Raggi, Giacomo Francesco (Girago), *Dubiorum centuria de regimine regularium* (Lyon: Inheritors of Petrus Prost, Philippus Borde and Laurentius Arnauld, 1646).
Raynaud, Théophile, *De virtutibus et vitiis* (Lyon: Horatius Boissat and Georgius Remeus, 1665).
Rosales, Bernabé de, *Relectio fratris Barnabae a Rosalibus ordinis divi Hieronymi de tribus poenitentiae partibus atque opinionum varietate, quae videlicet tenenda sit* (Valencia: Juan Mey, 1540).
Salas, Juan de, *Disputationum Ioannis de Salas Castellani in Primam Secundae Divi Thomae* (Barcelona: Gabriel Graells and Giraldo Dotil, 1607).
Salas, Juan de, *In Primam Secundae Divi Thomae, tomi primi, secunda pars* (Barcelona: Gabriel Graells and Gerardo Dotil, 1607).
Sallust, 'The War Against Catiline' in *Sallust*, Loeb Classical Library, J. C. Rolfe trans. (London: Heinemann; New York: Putnam's Sons, 1921).
Salón, Miguel Bartolomé, *Controversiae de iustitiae et iure, tomus secundus* (Venice: Baretius Baretius, 1608).
Samuelli, Francesco Maria, *Disputationum controversiae de canonica electione* (Venice: Turrinus, 1644).
San Joaquín, Sebastián de (Salmanticensis), *Cursus theologiae moralis, tomus quintus* (Venice: Niccolo Pezzana, 1715).
Sánchez, Juan, *Selectae illaeque practicae disputationes* (Venice: Bertanos, 1639).
Sánchez, Tomás, *Consiliorum Moralium in Consilia seu Opuscula Moralia* (Lyon: Laurentius Arnaud, Petrus Borde, Joannes & Petrus Arnaud, 1681).
Sánchez, Tomás, *Opus morale in praecepta decalogi* (Madrid: Luis Sánchez and Juan Hasrey, 1613).
Santísimo Sacramento, Leandro del and Manuel de la Concepción, *Quaestionum moralium* (Avignon: the Authors, 1692).
São Tomás, João de (Poinsot), *Cursus theologici in primam secundae Thomae pars prima* (Cologne: Wilhelm Metternich, 1711).
São Tomás, João de (Poinsot), *Cursus theologici in secundam secundae Divi Thomae* (Cologne: Wilhelm Metternich, 1711).
Sayer, Gregory, *Clavis Regia Sacerdotum* (Venice: Baretius Baretius, 1605).
Schiara, Antonio Tomasso, *Theologia bellica* (Rome: Ioannes Francisci de Buagnis, 1702).
Simmler, Josias, *Bibliotheca instituta et collecta primum a Conrado Gesnero* (Zurich: Christophorus Froschoverus, 1579).

Soto, Domingo de, *Relecciones y Opúsculos*, Antonio Osuna (ed.) (Salamanca: San Esteban, 2000) vol. II-1.
Soto, Domingo de, *Deliberación en la causa de los pobres* (Salamanca: Juan de la Junta, 1545).
Soto, Domingo, *De la justicia y el derecho* (Madrid: Instituto de Estudios Políticos, 1967) Spanish trans. by Marcelino Gonzáles Ordóñez, with fascimilar of *De iustitia et iure* (Salamanca: Portonariis, 1556).
Soto, Domingo, *Relecciones y opúsculos*, Sixto-Sánchez Lauro and Jaime Buffau Prats (eds.) (Salamanca: San Esteban, 2011) vol. II-2.
Suárez, Francisco, *De bonitate et malitia humanorum actus* in *Opera Omnia* M. André and C. Berton. (eds.) (Paris: Ludovicus Vivès, 1856) vol. 4.
Suárez, Francisco, *De fide, spe, et charitate* in *Opera Omnia*, C. Berton. (ed.) (Paris: Ludovicus Vivès, 1858) vol. 12.
Suárez, Francisco, *De incarnatione verbi* in *Opera Omnia*, C. Berton (ed.) (Paris: Vivès, 1860) vol. 17.
Suárez, Francisco, *De obligationibus religiosorum* in *Opera Omnia*, C. Berton (ed.) (Paris: Vivès, 1860) vol. 16.
Suárez, Francisco, *De virtute et statu religionis* in *Opera Omnia*, C. Berton (ed.) (Paris: Lodovicus Vivès, 1859) vol.13.
Suárez, Francisco, *Disputatio de iustitia* in *Opera Omnia*, M. André and C. Berton (eds.) (Paris: Vivès, 1886) vol. 11.
Suárez, Francisco, *Disputationes de censuris in communi* in *Opera Omnia*, C. Berton (ed.) (Paris: Vivès, 1861) vol. 23.
Suárez, Francisco, *Tractatus de legibus ac Deo legislatore*, C. Baciero, A. M. Barrero, J. M. García Añovero and J. M. Soto (eds.), (Madrid: CSIC, 2010).
Sylvius, Franciscus, *In totam Primam Partem* (Douay: Gerardus Patte, 1649).
Tamburini, Tomasso, *Explicationes in decalogum et alias opera moralia* (Lyon: Ioannis-Antonius and Marci-Antonius Ravaud, 1659).
Tancredi, Vicenzo, *Quaestiones morales* (Palermo: Josephus Bisagni, 1659).
Tanner, Adam, *Theologiae scholasticae* (Ingolstadt: Ioannis Bayr & People and Senate of the City, 1627).
Toledo, Francisco de, *De instructione sacerdotum libri septem cum bulla coena* (Lyon: Horatius Cardon, 1599).
Toro, Gabriel del, *Tesoro de la Misericordia Divina y Humana* (Valencia: Pedro de Huete, 1575).
Torquemada, Juan de, *In Gratiani decretorum primam doctissimi commentarii* (Venice: Hieronymus Scoti, 1578).
Torres, Luis, *Disputationum in secundam secundae D. Thomae* (Lyon: Iacobi Cardon and Petri Cavellat, 1621).
Torres, Luis, *Selectarum disputationes* (Lyon: Jacob Cardon, 1634).
Trullench, Juan Egidio, *Operis moralis, tomus primus* (Lyon: Laurentius Anisson, 1652).
Trullench, Juan Gil, *Operis moralis, tomus secundus* (Lyon: Laurentius Anisson, 1652)

Bibliography

Valencia, Gregorio de, *Commentariorum theologicorum* (Ingolstadt: David Sartorius, 1595).

Vázquez de Menchaca, Fernando, *Controversiarum illustrium* (Venice: Franciscus Rampazetus, 1564).

Vázquez, Gabriel, *Commentariorum ac disputationum in primam secundae S. Thomae, tomus secundus* (Alcalá de Henares: Justo Sánchez Crespo, 1605).

Vázquez, Gabriel, *Commentariorum ac disputationum in primam secundae S. Thomae, tomus primus* (Alcalá de Henares: Widow of Juan Gracián, 1614).

Vázquez, Gabriel, *Opuscula Moralia* (Alcalá: Juan Gracián, 1617).

Vázquez, Gabriel, *Opuscula Theologica Omnia* (Alcalá: Juan Gracián, 1617).

Vázquez, *Parecer sobre la Conquista de Portugal in Opera theologica*, Archivo Nacional de Madrid (ES.28079.AHN/1.2.2.1.9/Universidades, L. 1197).

Velasco de Govea, Francisco, *Perfidia de Alemania y de Castilla en la prisión, entrega, acusación y proceso del serenísimo infante de Portugal Don Duarte* (Lisbon: Craesbeek, 1652).

Venegas, Alexio, *Primera parte de las differencias de libros que hay en el universo* (Madrid: Alonso Gómez, 1569).

Villalobos, Enrique de, *Suma de la teología moral y canónica, segunda parte* (Barcelona: Sebastián de Cormellas, 1636).

Villalobos, Enrique de, *Summa de la theología moral y canónica, primera parte* (Barcelona: Sebastián de Cormellas, 1637).

Villavicencio, Lorenzo de, *Oeconomia Sacra circa pauperum curam* (Antwerp: Christophorus Plantini, 1564).

Vitoria, Francisco de, *Political Writings*, Anthony Pagden and Jeremy Lawrance (eds.) (Cambridge: Cambridge University Press, 1991).

Vitoria, Francisco de, *Comentarios a la Secunda secundae de Santo Tomás*, Vicente Beltrán Heredia (ed.) (Salamanca: Biblioteca de Teólogos Españoles, Apartado 17, 1932–52).

Vitoria, Francisco de, *On Homicide & Commentary on Summa theologiae IIa-IIae q. 64 (Thomas Aquinas)*, John P. Doyle (trans. intro. and notes) (Milwaukee: Marquette University Press, 1997).

Vitoria, Francisco de, *Relectio de Indiis, o libertad de los indios*, Vicente Pereña and José Manuél Pérez Prendes (eds. and trans.)(Madrid: CSIC, 1967).

Vitoria, Francisco de, *Relectio de iure belli, o paz dinámica: escuela española de la paz, primera generación 1526–156*, Luciano Pereña, Vidal Abril Castelló, Carlos Baciero, Antonio García and Francisco Maseda (eds.) (Madrid: CSIC, 1981).

Vives, Juan Luis, *Selected Works of J.L. Vives*, Constant Matheeussen and Charles Fantazzi (eds.) (Leiden and Boston: Brill, 2002) vol. 4.

Wiggers, Ioannes, *De iure et iustitia* (Leuven: Cyprianius Coenenstenius & Georgius Lipsius, 1661).

William of Auxerre, *Summa aurea in quattuor libros Sententiarum* (Paris: Philippus Pigouchet, 1500).

Wyts, Git, *De continendis et alendis domi pauperibus* (Antwerpen: Guilelmus Silvius, 1562).

Zavaleta, Juan, *Obras históricas, poliíticas, filosóficas y morales de Juan Zavaleta* (Barcelona: Ioseph Texido, 1704).
Ziegler, Kaspar, *In Hugonis Grotii de Jure Belli ac Pacis* (Frankfurt and Leipzig: Quensted & Schumacher, 1686).

Secondary Literature

Aliaga Girbés, José, *Los tributos e impuestos valencianos en el siglo XVI: Su justicia y moralidad según Fr. Miguel Bartolomé Salón, O.S.A. (1539?-1621)* (Rome: Instituto Español de Historia Eclesiástica: 1972).
Andolffato, David, 'A Theory of Inalienable Property', *Journal of Political Economy*, 110(2002)382–93.
Arigita y Lasa, Mariano, *El Doctor Navarro Don Martín de Azpilcueta y sus obras: Estudio histórico-crítico* (Pamplona: Imprenta Provincial, 1895).
Arneson, Richard, 'What is Wrongful Discrimination?', *San Diego Law Review*, 43 (2006)775–807.
Arras, John D., 'Getting Down to Cases: The Revival of Casuistry in Bioethics', *Journal of Medicine and Philosophy*, 16(1991)29–51.
Astrain, Antonio, *Historia de la Compañía de Jesús en la asistencia de España* (Madrid: Razón y Fe, 1916), vol. 5.
Battafarano, Italo Michele, 'Armenfürsorge bei Albertinus und Drexel. Ein sozialpolitisches Thema im erbaulichen Traktat zweier Schriftsteller des Münchner Hofes', *Zeitschrift für Bayerische Landesgeschichte*, 47(1984)141–80.
Bellamy, Alex J., *Just Wars: From Cicero to Iraq* (Cambridge: Polity, 2006).
Benítez Sancho-Blanco, Rafael, 'El cautiverio de los Moriscos', *Manuscrits*, 28 (2010)19–43.
Bireley, Robert, *Maximilian von Bayern, Adam Contzen S. J. und die Gegenreformation in Deutschland 1624–1635* (Göttingen: Vandenhoeck und Ruprecht, 1975).
Bireley, Robert, *The Jesuits and the Thirty Year War* (Cambridge: Cambridge University Press, 2003).
Bireley, Robert, *Ferdinand II: Counter-Reformation Emperor, 1578–1637* (New York: Cambridge University Press, 2014).
Blanck, Andreas, 'Domingo Soto on Justice for the Poor', *Intellectual History Review*, 25(2015)136–46.
Blic, Jaques de, 'Barthélémy Medina et les origines du probabilisme', *Ephemerides Theologiae Lovaniensis*, 7(1930)46–93, 264–91.
Blockmans, Wim P., 'La position du comté de Flandre dans le royaume à la fin du XVe siècle' in B. Chevalier and P. Contamine, (eds.), *La France de la fin du XVe siècle: Renouveau et apogée* (Paris: CNRS, 1985), pp. 71–89.
Bowman, Jeffrey A., 'Infamy and Proof in Medieval Spain' in Thelma Fenster and Daniel Lord Smail (eds.), *Fama: The Politics of Talk and Reputation in Medieval Europe* (Ithaca and London: Cornell University Press, 2003), pp. 95–117.

Brennan, Jason, *The Ethics of Voting* (New Jersey: Princeton University Press, 2012).
Brennan, Jason and Peter Jaworski, 'Markets without Symbolic Limits', *Ethics*, 125 (2015)1053–77.
Brett, Annabel, 'Scholastic Political Thought and the Concept of the State' in Annabel Brett and James Tully (eds.), *Rethinking the Foundations of Modern Political Thought* (Cambridge: Cambridge University Press, 2006).
Brett, Annabel, *Changes of State* (Princeton, NJ: Princeton University Press, 2011).
Cantera Montenegro, Enrique, 'El Compromiso de Caspe' in Vicente Ángel Álvarez Palenzuela (ed.), *Historia de España de la Edad Media* (Barcelona: Ariel, 2008) pp. 707–27.
Castro, Américo, Agustín Millares Carlo and Ángel José Battistessa, *Biblia medieval romanceada según los manuscritos escurialenses I-j-3, I-j-8 y I-j-6* (Buenos Aires: J. Peuser, 1927).
Chisholm, Rodrerick, 'The Structure of Intention,' *Journal of Philosophy*, 67(1970) 633–47.
Chisholm, Rodrerick, *Person and Object* (La Salle, IL: Open Court, 1976).
Cobben, Alan B.,'Medieval Student Power', *Past & Present*, 53(1971)28–66.
Colomer, Josep M. and Ian McClean, 'Electing Popes: Approval Balloting with Qualified Majority Rule', *Journal of Interdisciplinary History*, 29(1998)1–22.
Congar, Yves, 'Quod omnes tangit ab omnibus approbari debet' in Yves Congar, *Droit ancien et structures ecclésiales* (London: Variorum, 1982) pp. 210–59.
Cruz Cruz, Juan, 'El caso del juez árbitro en caso de guerra, según los Maestros de Siglo de Oro', at http://leynatural.es.
Dadson, Trevor J., *Los moriscos de Villarrubia de los Ojos (Siglos XV-XVIII): Historia de una minoría asimilada, expulsada y reintegrada* (Madrid: Iberoamericana, 2007).
Daniel, William, *Purely Penal Law Theory in the Spanish Theologians from Vitoria to Suárez* (Rome: Gregorian University Press, 1968).
Deman, Thomas, 'Probabilisme' in A. Vacant, E. Mangenot and E. Amann (eds.), *Dictionnaire de Théologie Catholique*, XIII (Paris: Letouzey et Ané, 1936), cols. 417–619.
Domínguez Ortíz, Antonio, 'Felipe IV y los Moriscos', *Miscelánea de Estudios Árabes y Hebraicos*, 8(1959)55–65.
Elliott, John E., *Imperial Spain 1469–1716* (Penguin: London, 1990).
Feros, Antonio, 'Rhetorics of Expulsion', in Mercedes García-Arenal and Gerard Wiegers, (eds.), *The Expulsion of the Moriscos from Spain: A Mediterranean Diaspora* (Leyden and Boston: Brill, 2014), pp. 86–101.
Ficarrotta, J. Carl, 'Review of Frances M. Kamm's *The Moral Target*', *Ethics*, 124 (2014)192–7.
Figuier, Louis, *Les merveilles de la science: ou Description populaire des inventions modernes* (Paris: Furne et Jouvet, 1869).
Filippini, Orietta, 'Aspetti della direzione della coscienza regale e dell' operato di un confessore regio durante le campagne militari. Juan de santo Tomás, O. P. e Filippo IV in Aragona nel 1643 e nel 1644' in Enrique García Hernán

and Davide Maffi (eds.), *Guerra y sociedad en la monarquía hispánica. Política, estrategia y cultura en la Europa moderna (1500–1700)* (Madrid: Mapfre, Laberinto and CSIC, 2006) vol. 2 pp. 743–64.

Finnis, John, *Natural Law and Natural Rights* (Oxford: Oxford University Press, 2011 second edn.).

Fiorelli, Piero, *La tortura giudiziaria nel diritto commune* (Varese: Giuffré, 1953).

Fleming, Julia, *Defending Probabilism: The Moral Theology of Juan Caramuel* (Washington, DC: Georgetown University Press, 2006).

Fraga Iribarne, Manuel, *Luis de Molina y el derecho de guerra* (Madrid, 1947).

Franklin, James, *The Science of Conjecture: Evidence and Probability before Pascal* (Baltimore: Johns Hopkins University Press, 2001).

García Vilar, José Antonio, 'El maquiavelismo en las relaciones internacionales. La anexión de Portugal a España en 1580', *Revista de Estudios Internacionales* 2(1981) 599–645.

García Vilar, José Antonio, 'Teoría de la guerra y arbitraje internacional en Gabriel Vázquez' in Manuel Medina, Roberto Mesa and Primitivo Mariño (eds.), *Pensamiento Jurídico y Sociedad Internacional: Estudios en honor del professor D. Antonio Truyol Serra* (Madrid: Centro de Estudios Constitucionales, 1986, 2 vols.) pp. 461–82.

García Villoslada, Ricardo, *La universidad de París durante los estudios de Francisco de Vitoria* (Rome: Gregorian University, 1939).

Gómez Álvarez, Ubaldo, *Revisión histórica de la presión fiscal castellana (siglos XVI-XVIII)* (Oviedo: Universidad de Oviedo, Servicio de Publicaciones, 1993).

Gordley, James, *Foundations of Private Law: Property, Tort, Contract, Unjust Enrichment* (Oxford: Oxford University Press, 2006).

Graullera Sanz, Vicente, *La esclavitud en Valencia en los Siglos XVI y XVII* (Valencia: Instituto Valenciano de Estudios Históricos, Institución Alfonso el Magnánimo, Diputación Provincial de Valencia, Consejo Superior de Investigaciones Científicas, 1978).

Grell, Ole Peter, Andrew Cunningham and Jon Arrizabalaga, *Health Care and Poor Relief in Counter-Reformation Europe* (London and New York: Routledge, 1999).

Gross, Charles, 'The Early History of the Ballot in England', *American Historical Review*, 3(1898)456–63.

Haggenmacher, Peter, *Grotius et la doctrine de la guerre juste* (Paris: Presses Universitaires de France, 1983).

Haggenmacher, Peter, 'Just War and Regular War in Sixteenth-Century Spanish Doctrine', *International Review of the Red Cross*, 290(1992)434–45.

Helmholz R. H., *The Spirit of Classical Canon Law* (Athens, GA: Georgia University Press, 2010).

Heredia, Beltran, *Domingo de Soto: Estudio biográfico documentado* (Salamanca: Biblioteca de Teólogos Españoles, 1960).

Holland, Alisha C., 'Forbearance', *American Political Science Review*, 110(2016) 232–46.

Ignacio Gutiérrez Nieto, Juan, 'El pensamiento económico, político y social de los arbitristas' in Ramon Menéndez Pidal and Jover Zamora (eds.), *El siglo de Don Quijote (1580–1680): Religión, filosofía, ciencia* (Barcelona: Espasa Calpe, 1993, *Historia de España*, vol. 26) pp. 331–465

Jago, Charles J., 'Taxation and Political Culture in Castile 1590-1640' in Richard L. Kagan and Geoffrey Parker (eds.), *Spain, Europe and the Atlantic World: Essays in Honour of John H. Elliott* (Cambridge: Cambridge University Press, 1995) pp. 48–72.

Jimenez Salas, María, *Historia de la Asistencia Social en España en la Edad Moderna* (Madrid: CSIC, 1958).

Jonsen, Albert R. and Stephen E. Toulmin, *The Abuse of Casuistry: A History of Moral Reasoning* (Berkeley and Los Angeles: University of California Press, 1988).

Judt, Tony, 'Leszek Kołakowski (1927–2009)', *New York Review of Books*, 56(sept. 2009)6–8.

Kagan, Shelly, *The Limits of Morality* (New York: Oxford University Press, 1989).

Kantola, Ilkka, *Probability and Moral Uncertainty in Late Medieval and Early Modern Times* (Helsinki: Luther-Agricola, 1994).

Kittsteiner, H. D., 'Kant and Casuistry' in Edmund Leites (ed.), *Conscience and Casuistry in Early Modern Europe* (Cambridge and Paris: Cambridge University Press and Maison des Sciences de l'Homme, 1989) pp. 185–213.

Lavenia, Vicenzo, 'Fraus et Cautela: Théologie morale et fiscalité au début des temps modernes' in Serge Boarini (ed.), *La casuistique classique: Genèse, forms, devenir* (Saint-Juste-de-la-Pendue: Publications de'Université de Saint-Étienne, 2009) pp. 43–57.

Lazar, Seth, 'Method in the Morality of War', in Seth Lazar and Helen Frowe (eds.), *The Oxford Handbook of Ethics of War* (Oxford: Oxford University Press, 2018) pp. 21–40.

Leinsle, Ulrich G., *Introduction to Scholastic Theology*, Michael J. Miller (trans.) (Washington, DC: Catholic University of America Press, 2010).

Lieber, Francis, *Manual of Political Ethics* (Boston: Charles C. Little and James Brown, 1839).

Livingston, John Morgan, *Infamia in the Decretists from Rufinus to Johannes Teutonicus* (University of Wisconsin, Doctoral dissertation, 1961).

Lottin, Odon, 'Le tutiorisme du trèizieme siècle', *Recherches de théologie ancienne et médiévale*, 5(1933)292–301.

Lottin, Odon, *Psychologie et morale aux XIIe et XIIIe siècles* (Leuven: Abadie du Mont César; Gembloux: J. Duculot, 1948, vol. 2).

Manin, Bernard, *The Principles of Representative Government* (Cambridge: Cambridge University Press, 1991).

Martín Casares, Aurelia, *La esclavitud en Granada en el siglo XVI* (Granada: Editorial Universidad de Granada, Campus Universitario de Cartuja: Diputación Provincial de Granada, 2000).

Martín Casares, Aurelia, 'De pasivas a beligerantes: las mujeres en la guerra de las Alpujarras' in Mary Nash and Susana Tavera (eds.), *Las mujeres y las guerras: el papel de las mujeres en las guerras desde la Edad Antigua a la Contemporánea* (Barcelona: Icaria, 2003) pp. 132–45.

Martín Casares, Aurelia, 'Evolution of the Origin of Slaves Sold in Spain from the Late Middle Ages till the 18th Century' in Simonetta Cavaciocchi (ed.), *Schiavitù et servaggio nell'economia Europea: Secc. XI-XVIII* (Firenze: Firenze University Press, 2014) pp. 409–30.

Martz, Linda, *Poverty and Welfare in Habsburg Spain* (Cambridge: Cambridge University Press, 1983).

Maryks, Robert Aleksander, *Saint Cicero and the Jesuits: The Influence of the Liberal Arts on the Adoption of Moral Probabilism* (Aldershot: Ashgate, 2008).

Mazón, Cándido, *Las leyes de los religiosos: su obligación y naturaleza jurídica* (Rome: Gregorian University, 1940).

McLean, Ian and Haidee Lorrey, *Voting in Medieval Universities and Orders*, Conference Paper (UCLA, 2001), at www.researchgate.net/publication/228419265_Voting_in_medieval_universities_and_religious_orders.

McLean, Ian, Haidee Lorrey and Josep Colomer, 'Voting in the Medieval Papacy and Religious Orders' in Vincenç Torra, Yasuo Narukawa and Yuji Yoshida (eds.), *Modeling Decisions for Artificial Intelligence* (Springer: Dordrecht, 2007), pp. 30–44.

McMahan, Jeff, *Killing in War* (Oxford: Oxford University Press, 2009).

Méndez Pidal, Ramón, 'El Compromiso de Caspe: Autodeterminación de un Pueblo' in *Historia de España* (Barcelona, 1965) vol. XV pp. IX-CLXIV.

Michaud- Quentin, Pierre, *Sommes de casuistique et manuels de confesseurs au moyen âge (XIIe-XVe S.)* (Louvain, Lille and Montreal: Nawelaerts, Giard and Librairie Dominicaine, 1962).

Migliorino, Francesco, *Fama e infamia: problemi della società medievale nel pensiero giuridico nei secoli XII e XIII* (Catania: Gianotta, 1985).

Mohanan, Arthur P., *Consent, Coercion and Limit: The Medieval Origins of Parliamentary Democracy* (Montreal: McGill-Queen University Press, 1987).

Moulin, Léo, 'Policy-Making in the Religious Orders', *Government and Opposition*, 1(1965)25–54.

Moulin, Léo, 'Les origines religieuses des techniques électorales et délibératives modernes', *Politix*, 11(1998)117–62.

Murphy, James B., *The Philosophy of Customary Law* (Oxford: Oxford University Press, 2014).

Najemy, John M., *Corporatism and Consensus in Florentine Electoral Politics, 1280–1400* (Chapel Hill: University of North Carolina Press, 1982).

Neff, Stephen C., *Just War and the Law of Nations: A General History* (Cambridge: Cambridge University Press, 2005).

Novotný, Daniel D., 'In Defense of Baroque Scholasticism', *Studia Neo-Aristotelica*, 6(2009)209–31.

O'Reilly, Francisco, *Duda y Opinión: La conciencia moral en Soto y Medina* (Pamplona: Publicaciones de la Universidad de Navarra, 2006).

Ohlin, Jens David, 'Justice After War' in Seth Lazar and Helen Frowe (eds.), *The Oxford Handbook of the Ethics of War* (Oxford: Oxford University Press, 2018) 519–37.

Parilla Ortíz, Pedro, *La esclavitud en Cádiz durante el Siglo XVII* (Cádiz: Diputación de Cádiz, 2010).

Parsons, Graham, 'Public War and the Moral Equality of Combatants', *Journal of Military Ethics*, 11(2012)299–317.

Parsons, Graham, 'What is the Classical Theory of Just Cause? A Response to Reichberg', *Journal of Military Ethics*, 12(2013)357–69.

Pereña Vicente, Luciano, 'Importantes documentos inéditos de Gabriel Vázquez', *Revista Española de Teología*, 16(1956)193–213.

Pereña Vicente, Luciano, *Teoría de la guerra en Francisco Suárez* (Madrid: CSIC, 1954) vol. I.

Pérez Martín, Inmaculada and Margarita Becedas González (eds.), *Diego de Covarrubias y Leyva: el humanista y sus libros* (Salamanca: Universidad de Salamanca, 2012).

Phillips, William D. Jr., *Slavery in Medieval and Early Modern Iberia* (Philadelphia: University of Pennsylvania Press, 2014).

Pinckaers, Servais, *The Sources of Christian Ethics*, Sr. Mary Thomas Noble (trans.) (Washington DC: Catholic University of America Press, 1995).

Portús Pérez, Javier, 'Indecencia, mortificación y modos de ver la pintura en el Siglo de Oro', *Espacio, tiempo y forma*, Serie VII, 8(1995)55–88.

Post, Gaines, 'A Romano-Canonical Maxim: *Quod Omnes Tangit* in Bracton and in Early Parliaments', in Gaines Post (eds.), *Studies in Medieval Legal Thought: Public Law and the State, 1100–1322* (Princeton, NJ: Princeton University Press, 1964) pp. 163–240.

Potts, Timothy, 'Conscience', in N. Kretzmann, A. Kenny and J. Pinborg (eds.), *The Cambridge History of Later Medieval Philosophy* (Cambridge: Cambridge University Press, 1980) pp. 687–704.

Prodi, Paolo, *Una storia della giustizia* (Bologna: Il Mulino, 2000).

Quincey, Thomas de, 'The Casuistry of Duelling' in James Hogg (ed.), *Uncollected Writings of Thomas De Quincey* (London: Swan Sonnenschein, 1890) vol. II.

Quincey, Thomas De, *Theological Essays and Other Papers* (Boston: Ticknor, Reed and Fields, 1854).

Quinn, Warren, 'Actions, Intentions, and Consequences: The Doctrine of Double Effect', *Philosophy and Public Affairs*, 18(1989)334–51.

Regout, Robert Willem Hubert, *La doctrine de la guerre juste, de Saint Augustin a nous jours* (Paris: Pedone, 1935).

Reichberg, Gregory M., 'The Moral Equality of Combatants – A doctrine in Classical Just War Theory? A Response to Graham Parsons', *Journal of Military Ethics*, 12(2013)181–94.

Reichberg, Gregory M., Henrik Syse and Endre Begby (eds.), *The Ethics of War: Classic and Contemporary Readings* (Oxford: Blackwell, 2006).

Reinhardt, Nicole, *Voices of Conscience: Royal Confessors and Political Counsel in Seventeenth-Century Spain and France* (Oxford: Oxford University Press, 2016).

Ripstein, Arthur, 'Distinction of Power and the Power of Distinctions: A Response to Professor Koskenniemi', *University of Toronto Law Journal*, 619 (2011)37–43.

Rodríguez Molinero, Marcelino, *Origen español de la ciencia del derecho penal: Alfonso de Castro y su sistema penal* (Madrid: Editorial Cisneros, 1959).

Rodríguez San Pedro Bezares, Luis Enrique and Juan Luis Polo Rodríguez, 'Cátedras y catédraticos: grupos de poder y promoción, siglos XVI-XVIII' in Luis Enrique Rodríguez San Pedro Bezares (ed.), *Historia de la Universidad de Salamanca* (Salamanca: Editorial Universidad de Salamanca, 2004) vol. II.

Sánchez González, Dolores Mar, *El deber de Consejo en el Estado Moderno. Las Juntas 'Ad hoc' en España (1471–1665)* (Madrid: Polifemo, 1993).

Sandel, Michael, *What Money Can't Buy* (New York: Farrar, Straus, and Giroux, 2012).

Santolaria Sierra, Félix, 'Estudio Introductorio' in *El gran debate sobre los pobres en el siglo XVI: Domingo de Soto y Juan de Robles 1545* (Barcelona: Ariel, 2003) pp. 11–46.

Schepers, Elisabeth, *Als der Bettel in Bayern abgeschafft werden sollte* (Regensburg: Friedrich Pustet, 2000).

Schüßler, Rudolf, 'On the Anatomy of Probabilism' in Jill Kraye and Risto Saarinen (eds.), *Moral Philosophy on the Threshold of Modernity* (Dordrecht: Springer, 2005) pp. 91–114.

Schüßler, Rudolf, '*Moral Self-Ownership and Ius Possessionis in Scholastics*' in Virpi Mäkinen and Petter Korkman (eds.), *Transformations in Medieval and Early-Modern Rights Discourse* (Dordrecht: Springer, 2006) pp. 160–4.

Schwartz, Daniel, 'Suárez on Distributive Justice' in Daniel Schwartz (ed.), *Interpreting Suárez: Critical Essays* (Cambridge: Cambridge University Press, 2011) pp. 163–84.

Schwartz, Daniel, 'Probabilism, Just War and Sovereign Supremacy in the Work of Gabriel Vázquez', *History of Political Thought*, 34(2013)177–94.

Schwartz, Daniel, 'Probabilism Reconsidered: Deference to Experts, Types of Uncertainty, and Medicines', *Journal of the History of Ideas*, 75(2014)373–93.

Schwartz, Daniel, 'Scandal and Moral Demandingness in the Late Scholastics', *British Journal of the History of Philosophy*, 23(2015)256–76.

Schwartz, Daniel, 'Late-Scholastic Just War Theory' in Seth Lazar and Helen Frowe (eds.), *Oxford Handbook of Just War Theory* (Oxford: Oxford University Press, 2018), pp. 122–44.

Scorraille, Raoul de, *François Suárez de la Compagnie de Jésus* (Paris: Lethielléux, 1914).

Stahn, Carsten, Jennifer S. Easterday and Jens Iverson (eds.), *Jus Post Bellum: Mapping the Normative Foundations* (Oxord: Oxford University Press, 2014).

Story, Joseph, *Commentaries on the Conflict of Laws Foreign and Domestic* (London: A. Maxwell; Dublin: A. Milliken; Edinburgh: T. Clark, 1841).

Sweet, Alfred H., 'The Control of English Episcopal Elections in the Thirteenth Century', *Catholic Historical Review*, 12(1927)573–82.

Swift, Edgar (ed.), *The Vulgate Bible: The Douay-Rheims Translation* (Cambridge, MA and London: Harvard University Press, 2010).
Taylor, Scott K., *Honor and Violence in Golden Age Spain* (New Haven and London: Yale University Press, 2008).
Théry, Julien, 'Fama : l'opinion publique comme preuve judiciaire. Aperçu sur la révolution médiévale de l'inquisitoire (xiie-xive)' in Bruno Lemesle (ed.), *La prevue en justice: de l'Antiquité à nos jours* (Rennes: Presses Universitaires de Rennes, 2003) pp. 119–47.
Vanderpol, Alfred, *La doctrine de la guerre juste* (Paris: A. Pedone, 1919)
Vaquer Benàssar, Onofre, *L'esclavitud a Mallorca 1448–1500* (Palma de Mallorca: Institut de Estudis Balèarics, Consell Insular de Mallorca, 1997).
Vicente y Caravantes, José de, *Tratado critico filosófico, histórico de los procedimientos judiciales en material civil* (Madrid: Gaspar y Roig, 1856).
Walzer, Michael, *Spheres of Justice* (New York: Basic Books, 1983).
Walzer, Michael, *Just and Unjust Wars* (New York: Basic Books, 2000).
Weinstein, Donald, *The Captain's Concubine: Love, Honor and Violence in Renaissance Tuscany* (Baltimore and London: Johns Hopkins University Press, 2000).
Wendell Holmes, Oliver, 'The Path of Law', *Harvard Law Review*, 10(1897) 457–78.
Zohar, Noam J., 'Collective War and Individualistic Ethics: Against the Conscription of "Self-Defense"', *Political Theory*, 21(1993)606–22.

Index

actor sequitur forum rei, 175
acts
  goals of (as opposed to the agent's goal), 157
  indifferent and non-indifferent, 108–10, 115, 152
Adrian from Utrecht (Pope Adrian VI), 121, 125, 126, 133, 142
  and tutiorism, 127
  on good faith and doubt, 164
  on obedience, 123–5
Afghanistan, 183
Alberti, Alberto, 113
Albornoz, Bartolomé Frías de, 204
alcabala, 34, 35, 39, 43, 44, 45, 46, 47, 48, 49
Alcalá
  theologians, 104, 173
Alciatus, Andrea
  Book of Moral Emblems, 72
Alexander the Great, 144
Algiers, 204
Alpujarras, War, 198
Ambrose of Milano, 69, 86, 187
Angles, Joseph, 46, 48, 53
applied philosophy, 6–8
Aquinas, Thomas, 18, 22, 75, 78, 82, 84
  finis operis/finis operantis, 157
  on just laws, 34
  on occasioning and inducing sins, 110
  on scandal, 101
Aragón, Kingdom of, 156, 176, 177
Aragón, Pedro de, 23, 85, 89, 98
  on making inquiries upon selling, 109
  on reputation, 88–90
  on secrets, 78
arbitration
  arbiters
    as peace makers, 169
  distinction between arbiter and judge-arbiter, 169
  duty of, 166–9
arbitristas, 33, 34

Aristotle, 19, 81, 85, 86
assent
  and fear, 135
  grounds for, 136
  opinative, 141, 180
Augustine of Hippo, St., 87, 110, 117, 196
  scandal and overdemandingness, 108
Azor, Juan, 111, 113
  on authorities, 136
  on types of conscience, 132
Azpilcueta, Martín. *see* Navarrus
Aztecs, 205

Bach, Johann Sebastian, 6
bad-man theory of law, 41
Báñez, Domingo de
  on Demosthenes, 149
  on Morisco slavery, 199
  on taxes, 45, 46, 48, 49
Barelli da Nizza, Francesco-Luigi, 107
Barros, Tomás, 145
Bassée, Eloy de la, 63, 68
Bavaria, 63, 69, 70, 77
Becanus, Martin de, 67, 69, 70
beggars, 6, 58, 59, 66, 72
  foreign, 11, 59, 64, 70, 74
  and disease, 66
  and heresy, 66
Beja Perestrello, Luiz de, 40
Bernal Díaz de Luco, Juan, 61
Bianchi, Paolo de, 154
Blank, Andreas, 59
Bodin, Jean, 66
body metaphor, 71–4
Bonacina, Martino de, 113
Boncompagno, Giacomo, 107
Borromeo, Carlo, 103
Bosso, Giovanni, 152
Brabant, 69
Bragança, Duarte de, 145
Braganza, Enrique, 104

Index

Brennan, Jason, 19
Brett, Annabel, 64, 73
Brezmes Diez de Prado, Martín, 102
Bruges, 60
Buckhard, Bardili, 66
Burgo de Osma, Spain, 173

Caesar, Julius, 129
Caiaphas, 154
Cajetan (Thomas de Vio), 16, 78, 92, 95, 96, 98, 99
   and judicial model of just war, 163
   doubt
      speculative and practical, distinction between, 125
   obligatoriness of human law, 39
   on reputation, 84–6
   on self-defamation, 85, 87
   selling and presumptions, 109
Cambrai, Treaty of, 174
Cano, Melchor, 61
Caramuel y Lobkowitz, Juan, 9
Carletti di Chivasso, Angelo, 40
Carlevalius, Thomas, 176
Carlos V, King of Spain, 164
Casas, Bartolomé de las, 204
Casas, Ignacio de las, 204
Caspe, Spain (Compromise of), 176
Castile, 46, 48, 56, 173, 176, 177
   pretensions over Portugal, 173
Castro Palao, Fernando, 30, 31, 142, 162, 164, 190
   on arbitration, 168
   on disobedience, 138, 139
   on portraits, 112, 114
Castro, Alfonso de, 4, 31, 36, 38, 40, 41, 43, 45, 75, 76,
   on taxes, 56
   on the poor, 67
casuistry, 6–7
casuists, 6, 6
Catalonia
   uprising, 156
causality, artificial, 146
Cellarius, Christianus, 62
China, 64
   isolationist policies, 66
Chisholm, Rodrerick, 156
Christian prisoners
   cooperation with Ottoman captors, 153
Chrysostom, John, 73
Cicero, Marcus Tulius, 188
   on foreigners, 66
Cipolla, Bartolomeo, 65

city as body, 146
Concepción, Manuel de la, 113
Coninck, Giles de, 201
   on reprisals, 196
conscience, 121
   types of, 132
controversies, 9
Contzen, Adam, 66, 70
cooperation with sin
   and proximity, 105
Córdoba, Antonio de, 133
   on obedience, 133, 134
   on secrets, 78
   on taxes, 48
   on types of conscience, 132
   tutiorism, 134
Cornejo, Francisco, 106
Cortes of Toledo, 60
Cortona, Pietro da, 109
Cotonne, Antonio, 64
Counter-Reformation, 103
Covarrubias y Leyva, Diego de, 47, 171, 198
   on taxes, 42, 46, 48
   on war enslavement, 198
custom
   and law, 51
   and voluntarism, 51

D'Afflitto, Matteo, 65
Daniel, prophet, 73
Daniel, William, 37, 38, 49, 54
de Quincey, Thomas, 6
decisory mechanisms, 167
deferring to your peers, 17
delectatio morosa, 115
Demosthenes, 144, 145, 147, 149
detraction, 82
Diana, Antonino, 7, 63, 68, 190, 200
   on portraits, 113
   on reprisals, 195
   on selling, 116
disobedience
   civil, 143
Dominican Order, 36
   constitutions, 36
Don Quixote, 59
Double Effect, Doctrine of, 155
   and proximity of effects, 155
doubts
   and good faith, 125–6
   legal and factual, 179
   speculative and practical, 125
Drexel, Jeremias, 70
duty to defend compatriots, 152

elections, 17, 19, 22, 32
  by compromise, 20
  by inspiration, 20
  by scrutiny, 20
  ecclesiastical, 15
  in Spanish colonies, 15
  in universities, 7, 15, 16, 22
  justifications for, 20
  pandering, 17
  rationales for, 21
  simoniac, 17
electoral promises, 17
electoral reciprocity, 17
electoral vexations, 21–3
  and animosity, 25
eminent domain, 93, 195
epieikeia, 46, 50
Escobar Mendoza, Antonio, 203
Ethiopia, 145

Felipe II, King of Spain, 172, 173, 177, 199
Felipe IV, King of Spain, 205
Ferrantino de Ancona, Girolamo, 115
  on portraits, 112
Ferrara, Huguccio de, 130
Ficarrotta, Carl J., 6
Filiarchi, Cosimo, 96, 97, 98
  on possession of portraits, 111
Finnis, John M., 37
Flanders, County, 174
foreign poor
  heresy, 69
foreigners
  and Roman decadence, 69
foro conscientiae, 22, 24
forum shopping, 175
France, 174, 192
Francés de Urrutigoyti, Tomás, 116
  on portraits, 113–17
fraternal correction, 96, 98
Fulgosius, Raphaël, 129

García Vilar, José Antonio, 172
Giginta, Miguel de, 61
Gómez Álvarez, Ubaldo, 33
Gonzáles de Salcedo, Pedro, 69
good faith, 35, 124, 125, 126, 151, 164
  and doubt, 125–6
Gordley, James, 81
Granada, Kingdom of, 198, 204
Grotius, Hugo, 145
  and Vázquez de Menchaca, 151
  follows Salón on Demosthenes' case, 150
Gutiérrez, Juan, 46, 47
Guzmán, Gaspar, Count-Duke of Olivares, 205

Henrique I, King of Portugal, 177
Henry of Ghent, 36
Hobbes, Thomas, 151
Holland, Alisha, 48
Holmes, Oliver Wendell, 41
Hopffer, Benedikt, 66
Horace (Quintus Horatius Flaccus), 105, 158
Hormisdas, Pope, 18
hospitality, 67
hostages, 201
human law
  obligatoriness of, 39
Hurtado de Mendoza, Pedro, 30, 197, 203, 206, 207
  body metaphor, 200
  involvement in politics, 205
  on French alliance with Dutch rebels, 197
  on killing fleeing soldiers, 186
Hurtado, Gaspar, 196, 203
Hurtado, Tomás, 95, 96, 98
  on reputation, 92–4
  and citizenship, 94–5
  on secrets, 78
Hyperius, Andreas, 62

ignorance
  invincible, 131, 171
  and war just on both sides, 161
imagination, 105
In Coena Domini, 152
Incas, 205
infamia, 43
  as legal condition, 85
Ingolstadt, 63, 68, 70
innocents
  in war, 185
Iraq, 183
Irish Scholastics, 12
ius acquirendum, 27
ius acquisitum, 27
ius gentium, 64, 65, 66, 69, 191, 192, 204
  on plundering, 192
ius possidentis, 164–5, 179
ius proprium, 26

Jago, Charles, 55
Jaworski, Peter, 19
Jesuits, 70, 197
Jesus Christ, 155
Jesús María, José de, 104
João III, King of Portugal, 164
Jonah, Prophet, 158
Jonsen, Albert, 6
juntas (consultative ad-hoc bodies), 55
jurisdiction

Index

by reason of territory, 174
choice-of-law rules, 178
grounds for
  loci contractus, 176
  ratione delicti, 176
  ratione domicilii, 175
  rei sitae, 178
just war
  and certainty, 161
  and enslavement, 198
  and killing
    for future security, 190
  and terror, 189
  goals of, 185
  ius ad bellum, 184
  ius in bello, 184
  ius post-bellum, 183
    as post-victory justice, 185
  judicial model, 161, 163
  just causes of, 161
  on both sides, 161, 165, 170, 171
  and Juán Sánchez, 179–81
  plundering, 191–5
  punitive killing, 186–90
  statist approach, 188
  victory, 184
justice
  commutative, 81
  distributive, 2, 4, 19, 21, 26, 28, 47, 48, 81
  and free movement, 75
  legal, 1
  vindicative, 188

Kagan, Shelly, 159
Kamm, Frances M., 8
Kant, Immanuel, 6
Krestos, Sela, 145

Laínez, Diego, 43
  on taxes, 34, 38, 56
Langton, Stephen, 127
late scholastics, 5–7, 79, 133, 191
  on patriotism, 1
Lavenia, Vicenzo, 40
law
  customary, 51
  promulgation of, 179
Laymann, Paul, 68
Ledesma, Martín de, 67, 75, 76
Ledesma, Pedro de, 49
Leibniz, Gottfried Wilhelm, 12
Lessius, Leonardus, 16, 97
  on Demosthenes, 149
  on secrets, 78
  on the enforceability of patriotic duty, 148

Lex Papia de peregrinos, 69
Libya, 183
Lipsius, Justus, 69
López, Luis, 149
Lorca, Pedro de, 68, 196, 201, 206, 207
  criticism of reprisals, 195
  on killing for future security, 191
  on Morisco slavery, 199–201
Lugo, Juan de, 16, 28, 93, 96, 98
  on reputation, 90–2
  on secrets, 78

Machado de Chaves, Juan
  on arbitration, 169
Madre Dios, Andrés de la, 157
Martial (Marcus Valerius Martialis), 105
Martín Casares, Aurelia, 204
Mazón, Candido, 36
McMahan, Jeff, 4
Medina, Bartolomé, 47
  and probabilism, 135
Medina, Juan de, 62, 64, 67, 76
  on prescription and good faith, 126
  on the poor, 62–4, 67
Michaud-Quentin, Pierre, 8
Molanus (Jan Vermeulen), 103
Molina, Luis de, 4, 7, 97, 149, 158, 159, 162, 165, 171, 172, 181, 206
  and captive rowers, 152
  criticism of Salón on Demosthenes, 151
  on arbitration, 169
  on artificial causuality, 147
  on enslavement of Morisco children, 199
  on indifferent acts, 109
  on open borders, 66
  on plundering, 192
  on post-victory punitive killing, 186, 189
  on reprisals, 193
  on secrets, 78
  on self-defamation, 87, 88
  on taxes, 47
  on the duty to defend compatriots, 152
  on the enforceability of patriotic duty, 148
  on the Moluccas, 164
Moluccas, 164
Montesinos, Luis de, 162
moral equality of combatants, 129
moral responsibility, 154
moral theology, 2, 6, 10
  confessional orientation, 2
morality of beliefs, 31
Moriscos, 198
  children, 199
  expulsion from Spain, 198
  resettlement in Spain, 205

Moriscos (cont.)
  women, 199
Moulin, Leo, 16
Murphy, James B., 52
mystical body, 72

Naldi, Antonio, 111
Native Americans, 204
natural law, 8, 39, 44, 64, 67, 72, 135, 178, 195
Navarra
  anti Castilian sentiment, 40
Navarra, Pedro, 149
Navarro, Blas, 47
Navarrus (Martín de Azpilcueta), 16, 38, 42, 44, 97, 162, 166, 181
  on scandal
    on renouncing to rights, 114
  on secrets, 78
  on taxes, 56
Núñez Avendaño, Pedro, 46
Nuremberg, 58

obedience, 122
  and probabilism, 132–138
  and tutiorism, 128
obscenity and memory, 114
Osiander, Johann Adam, 145
Ottoman captives, 152
Ottoman Navy, 152
Ottonelli, Giovanni Domenico, 113
  on moral duties of portraitists, 109
Ovid (Publius Ovidius Naso), 105
Oviedo, Francisco de, 190
  on killing fleeing soldiers, 186

paintings
  and nudity, 103, 104, 105, 106, 111
  justifications for, 106
  and pagan mythology, 103
Paleotti, Gabriele, 103
  on the morality of portraits, 111
pareceres on Portugal, 172
Parsons, Graham, 130, 132
Pascal, Blaise, 6, 7
Pasqualigo, Alvise, 107, 112
patriotic duty, 148
Paul, St, 72, 123, 149
Peltanus, Theodor, 63, 68, 69, 71
Pérez de Herrera, Cristóbal, 61
Pignatelli, Jacopo, 68
Pilate, Pontius, 155
Pinckaers, Servais
  criticism of late scholastic moral theology, 8
Pistoia, 107
Pizarro, Fernando, 69

plundering, 191–5
Plutarch, 144
Pompey, Gnaeus, 129
Ponce de León, Basilio, 30
poor laws
  Bavaria, 70
  reforms, 59
portazgo, 39, 65
portraits
  and courtship, 107
Portugal, 164, 173, 174, 176, 177
post-war satisfaction, 188
pre-election compacts, 17
preemptive killing in war, 191
privateers, 193
Probabiliorism, 122
Probabilism, 3, 122, 181
  and obedience, 132–138
  and war, 161
probability
  instrinsic and extrinsic, 137
  sources of
    intrinsic and extrinsic principles, 134, 136
proportionality as war requirement, 187
Punch, John, 12
purely penal laws, 35–8, 39, 40, 44, 51, 54, 55, 56, 57

Quevedo, Francisco de, 33
Quinn, Warren, 156
quod omnes tangit, 20

Raynaud, Théophile, 67
Reichberg, Gregory M., 130, 132
Reinhardt, Nicole, 55
reprisals, 193–7
  objections to, 195
reputation, 81
  and honour, difference, 81
  as property, 88
  inalienability, 97
  moral role of, 81
  unmerited, 89
res publica christiana, 171
right of succession, 177
right to be voted for, 17, 19, 21
rights
  acquired, 22
  unacquired, 22
Ripstein, Arthur, 5
Robles, Juan/Medina, Juan de, 61, 62
Rodríguez Molinero, Marcelino, 38
Rome
  exclusivist policies, 69
Rosales, Bernabé de, 133

Index

saints, female, 103
Salamanca, 60, 78, 190
   theologians, 104
Salas, Juan de, 162
Salazar, Hernando de, 205
Sallust (Gaius Sallustius Crispus), 188
Salmanticenses (Carmelites of Salamanca), 113, 157, 167
Salón, Miguel Bartolomé de, 47, 147, 150, 151, 158
   on cooperating with evil, 147, 149
   on taxes, 47
San Joaquín, Sebastián de, 167
Sánchez, Juan, 141, 142, 162, 182
   on disobedience, 138–141
   on domestic war, 141
   on war just on both sides, 179–81
Sánchez, Tomás, 16, 19, 46, 50, 51, 138
   on portraits, 112
   reponse to attacks, 9
Sancho Panza, 59
Sandel, Michael, 18, 32
Santísimo Sacramento, Leandro del, 113
São Tomás, João (Poinsot), 146, 149, 151, 158, 159,
   on Classical literature, 105
   on the Demosthenes case, 156–8
   on the effects of paintings, 104
   war experience, 156
Sayer, Gregory
   on types of conscience, 132
scandal, 101–3
   acceptum, 101
   active, 101
   cases examined by moral theologians, 102
   datum, 101
   passive, 101
Schiara, Antonio Tommaso, 145
Scotists, 12
Sebastião I, King of Portugal, 172
self-defamation, 83
   and charity, 86
semiotic objection to the market, 19
Senlis, Treaty of, 174
sieges, 186
Simon Magus, 18
simony, 18–19, 21, 22, 23, 24, 30
   and sacraments, 26
sins
   occasioning and inducing, distinction between, 110, 116
slavery in Spain
   procedence of slaves, 203
social contract theory, 151

Soto, Domingo de, 4, 16, 22, 23, 46, 47, 62, 63, 76, 77, 80, 81, 97, 98, 142, 149, 150, 158
   and tutiorism, 126
   Deliberación en la causa de los pobres, 64–7
   differences between Latin and Spanish versions, 72
   on cooperating with evil, 147
   on Demosthenes and Alexander, 144
   on doubt and good faith, 126
   on reputation, 86–7
   on secrets, 78
   on self-defamation, 85
   on taxes, 45
   on the enforceability of patriotic duty, 148
   on the poor, 58
   lack of engagement with his views, 76
secrets
   social need for, 81
Spain, 164, 174, 175, 192
Sparta, 69
strategic voting, 17
Suárez, Francisco de, 4, 7, 16, 18, 23, 28, 29, 30, 37, 45, 51, 52, 75, 133, 141, 144, 162, 165, 166, 171, 172, 181
   and voluntarism, 37
   on components of post-war satisfaction, 188
   on contractual rights of candidates, 27–8
   on arbitration, 166–9
   on captive rowers, 153
   on electoral vexations, 24–5
   on indifferent and non-indifferent acts, 108
   on ius possidentis, 165
   on legal justice, 1
   on plundering, 192
   on post-victory killing, 186
   on reprisals, 194
   on restitution of property after war, 194
   on Roman laws of war, 192
   on scandal, 101
   on scandal and renouncing to rights, 114
   on taxes, 42, 44, 49, 50, 51–5
   on the distinction between indifferents and non-indifferents, 116
   on tutiorism and obedience, 128
   reasons against the permissibility of giving money to electors, 26–7
   statism, 188
   on suzerain states, 174
Sylvester Prierias (Mazzolino da Prierio), 192, 194
Sylvius, Franciscus, 63, 68

Tancredi, Vincenzo, 113
Tanner, Adam, 63, 65, 68, 70, 77
   on the poor, 58
Tavera, Juan Pablo, Cardinal, 60, 62

tax
    and customary law, 46–8
    and forebearance, 48
    and penalties for non-payment, 53
    evasion, 40
        toleration of, 43, 56
    harshness of, 46
    in Castile, 33
    in Valencia, 47
    justice of, 34
    moderation, 46
    payment on demand, 45
    revolts, 55
    sovereign consent to deferred payment, 50–1
    spontaneous payment, 50
    tolls, 46
    types of, 44
Theodosius I, Emperor, 187
theology
    speculative, 7
Thessalonica, Massacre of, 187
Toledo, Francisco de, 153
Toledo, Spain, 75
Tordesillas, Treaty of, 164
Toro, Gabriel del, 61, 73
Torquemada, Juan de, 20
Torres, Luis, 106, 150
Tostado, Alonso (Abulensis), 171
Toulmin, Stephen, 6
Trullench, Juan Egidio, 68, 113
Tutiorism, 121, 137
    and obedience, 128

vacant thrones, 176
Valencia, Gregorio de, 16, 68, 70, 93, 97, 155
    on electoral vexations, 24
    on the moral role of reputation, 81
    on the poor, 58, 68
Valencia, Kingdom of, 34, 48, 203
Valladolid, 60
Valor, Hernando de/Ibn Umayya/Aben Humeya, 199
Vázquez de Menchaca, Fernando, 145, 151
Vázquez, Gabriel, 7, 16, 30, 50, 142, 162, 171, 172, 175, 176, 179, 181, 182
    on Navarrus on arbitration, 170
    on Suárez on arbitration, 167
    on the poor, 67, 68
    probabilist defence of obedience, 132–138
    on taxes, 42, 43
vexations
    removal, 23
via publica, 65
Vicent Ferrer, St., 177
Villalobos, Enrique de, 28, 31, 175

Villavicencio, Lorenzo de, 62
Vilna Ghetto, 145
Vitelleschi, Muzio
    criticism of Hurtado de Mendoza, 205
Vitoria, Francisco de, 4, 7, 36, 46, 142, 150, 162, 165, 166, 171, 178, 181, 184, 192, 201
    and excused fighting, 130
    and justified fighting, 131
    and the duty to fight, 131
    and the moral equality of combatants, 129
    and just war
        doubtful, 163
    on certainty and just war, 161
    on doubt and good faith, 125–6
    on *ius possidentis*, 164
    on killing and proportionality, 187
    on killing for future security, 190
    on killing innocents, 144
    on plundering innnocents, 193
    on post-victory killing, 186
    on privateering, 193
    on taxes, 45
    on the right to travel, 64
    on tutiorism and obedience, 127
    on vacant thrones, 176
    on victory, 184
    statism, 188
Vives, Juan Luis, 60, 73
voluntarism, 37, 51, 52

Wadding, Luke, 12
Walzer, Michael, 4, 18, 32
war
    domestic, 141
    prisoners, 186
war slavery
    of apostates, 204
    of Christians, 204
    of heretics, 204
Wiggers, Jan, 154, 155
William of Auxerre, 127
Wittenberg, 145
worthiest candidate
    attributes, 20, 24, 31
    moral duty to vote for, 17
Wyts, Git, 62

Ypres, 58

Zamora, 60, 75
Zaragoza, 58
Zaragoza, Treaty of, 164
Zavaleta, Juan, 107
Ziegler, Kaspar, 145, 152